CHRONOLOGICALLY
GIFTED

Aging with Gusto

A PRACTICAL GUIDE FOR HEALTHY LIVING TO AGE 123

ERICA MILLER, PH.D.

Published by Best Seller Publishing®, Pasadena, CA
Best Seller Publishing® is a registered trademark
Printed in the United States of America.
ISBN 978-1-946978-26-4

This publication is designed to provide accurate and authoritative information with regard to the subject matter covered. It is sold with the understanding that the publisher is not engaged in rendering legal, accounting, or other professional advice. If legal advice or other expert assistance is required, the services of a competent professional should be sought. The opinions expressed by the author in this book are not endorsed by Best Seller Publishing® and are the sole responsibility of the author rendering the opinion.

Most Best Seller Publishing® titles are available at special quantity discounts for bulk purchases for sales promotions, premiums, fundraising, and educational use. Special versions or book excerpts can also be created to fit specific needs.

For more information, please write:
Best Seller Publishing®
1346 Walnut Street, #205
Pasadena, CA 91106
or call 1(626) 765 9750
Toll Free: 1(844) 850-3500

Visit us online at: www.BestSellerPublishing.org

DEDICATION

I dedicate this book to people of all ages, from all walks of life who choose to join me on this wonderful adventure called "life." Here's to a long, healthy, purposeful journey until the ripe age of 123! You Can Do It!

ACKNOWLEDGEMENTS

I want to acknowledge my editors, Gerri Knilans and Debbie Beavers-Moss from Trade Press Services. I realize it took a great deal of effort during the editing process to maintain my intent and authentic voice, and I appreciate their dedication and perseverance.

Table of Contents

Chronologically Gifted: Aging with Gusto -
A Practical Guide for Healthy Living to Age 123

FOREWORD

By Dr. Peter H. Grossman M.D.

In his classic novel *Illusions*, Richard Bach writes: " Argue for your limitations, and sure enough, they are yours". If we look at chronological age as purely a number, it is the inevitable advancement of time. However, the physical, cognitive and emotional decline associated with aging, may not be so inevitable.

Today, advancements in computer technology have given mankind the ability to solve problems exponentially faster than ever before. It is not a matter of if, but when, we will see substantial human age extension.

In her book, *Chronologically Gifted: Aging with Gusto - A Practical Guide for Healthy Living to Age 123*, Dr. Erica Miller takes the reader through the research of human life extension and more importantly, teaches us how to make that life extension more purposeful, rewarding and fun. Dr. Miller explains that age, simply for the sake of longevity, is a goal that may be fraught with health, economic, and social problems. On the other hand, longevity as a byproduct of good health and attitude, where we live biologically in a more youthful state than our chronological age, is not only a desirable goal, but something that is quite achievable.

Presently, many of the tools for substantial life extension exist only in the hands of scientists and government regulation. However, Dr. Miller details the power that we already have within ourselves right now, to age better. Dr. Miller's own life exemplifies her teaching. Exuberant, and positive, she takes control of her destiny.

Dr. Miller explains that beyond science, we possess these tools that will allow us to live happier, healthier, more substantive and subsequently longer lives. _Chronologically Gifted_ shows us all how to get started today, on the road to happier, healthier and longer lives. In the words of Dr. Miller, "I can do it, and so can you!"

Peter Grossman M.D.
Grossman Burn Center
www.grossmanmed.com

– 1 –
What Does "Old" Really Mean?

Ask a handful of people to describe what comes to mind when they hear the word "old," and you might be surprised at the answers you receive. "Old" is one of those words that has both positive and negative connotations, depending on the context in which it appears. Unfortunately, when we apply the word to people, many of those connotations are largely negative. Words like "obsolete" or "weak," for instance, or phrases like "past their prime" and the always popular "over the hill" may come to mind. These expressions indicate how readily our culture relegates the latter years of life to a period of lamentable decline—not only in physiological health, but also in social prominence, personal originality, and cultural relevance.

"Does the worth of human life diminish with age?" asks Dr. Andrew Weil. "I'm afraid that in the judgment of many in our

3

society, it does."[1] No matter where we are in life right now, if we're not careful, we'll find that we instinctively default to this generally negative attitude toward the aging process. Moreover, we'll react to the prospect of aging in a patently unhelpful way—with denial, dread, or even despair. Instead of gearing up for this vital season in life, we'll find ourselves subconsciously giving up even before we reach those milestones. And that's a bigger deal than you might think.

According to studies performed by Becca Levy at Yale University's School for Public Health, a pervasive (even subconscious) negative stereotype regarding aging has a demonstrable effect on long-term health outcomes. In one study, participants were separated into two groups. One group was exposed to subliminal, positive messages about aging, while the other group was not. The results were incredible: participants in the second group—people who were otherwise equal on health, educational, and socioeconomic factors—showed greater declines in a variety of areas than their peers who were in the first group.

There were physiological symptoms, like shakier hands and poorer memory retention, higher rates of cardiac disease, and more difficulty recovering from disability. But there were also behavioral symptoms like a greater propensity to eat in an unhealthy way, a more sedentary lifestyle, and an unwillingness to follow dosage instructions for age-related prescription medications. The net result? A median difference in survival rate of 7.5 years.[2] That's staggering! People could live about seven years longer if they would simply refuse to "buy in" to the stereotypical rubbish that tells us that getting older has to mean life is over.

So here's the good news. We can do that!

Once we tune out this pervasively negative cultural message, we find that there are plenty of other words— considerably more positive ones—that people associate with the word "old." Words like "wise" and "mature," "seasoned" and "experienced." Think about it: usually we revere our elders for their accumulation of knowledge and experience, and we naturally gravitate to them for instruction and advice. Even those who haven't accomplished much of special merit exhibit a time-tested combination of cultivated skills and experiential wisdom. It's one that rightly inspires humility in younger people who do well to capitalize on their insights.

So, almost by default, age demands a modicum of respect. "Growing old should increase, not decrease, the value of human life," Weil affirms. "Just as with bourbon, it has the potential to smooth out roughness, add agreeable qualities, and improve character."[3] If we're smart, we'll embrace that message rather than the cultural mantra of irrelevance and obsolescence.

We can start taking steps right now to help us approach the later years of our lives with optimism and determination. It will help us recognize that we never have to lose our cultural edge unless we let someone else define "old" for us in an unhelpful way. That's why I decided it was time to write this book—to inform and to inspire people about how to do just that. This is a new venture for me; but here I am: a spry eighty-something dynamo, actively and passionately engaged in this mysterious journey we call "life"—compelled to invite others along for the ride. I've made it my personal mission to spread this contagious exuberance for life. I'm convinced it's what will make it possible for me to die healthy at age 123. After all, people are living longer, healthier lives every day, all over the world. So why not me?

More importantly: WHY NOT YOU?

I decided to write this book because I'm convinced that I can do it. And in the pages that follow, I'll show you how.

I talk to a lot of people on both ends of the age spectrum. Those who are approaching the later years of life are often sadly complacent about the impending limitations of their age, being the first to admit they're a burden and a waste of space. Or they're in such denial about their age that they angrily lash out at anyone who dares classify them as "elderly" or a "senior citizen." Meanwhile, too many of the young people I meet behave as though the decisions they make today have little or no impact on whether they'll live a longer, healthier life. To so many of them, the prospect of getting older seems distantly unreal, like something that happens to others but will never happen to them.

All of these perspectives are unhealthy. They reflect the paradoxical truth of a National Public Radio feature on this very issue. "Everyone wants to live a long time, but no one wants to actually *be* old."[4] Everyone wants to live well past 100, but no one wants to imagine there will come a time when it means having a less significant life than they do now because they failed to take the steps necessary to prepare for it. But that's why I'm inviting you to hear what I have to say right now. I'm convinced that a huge part of why aging seems to come upon us so suddenly and so overwhelmingly is because we don't take steps now to give ourselves the best possible chance of living long, healthy, and meaningful lives. We wouldn't need to live in denial over the reality of aging if we had a healthier, more balanced perspective on this beautiful life process to begin with.

I've known many people—and I consider myself one of them—who have chosen not to age this way. I've learned that it's entirely possible to face the aging process with a healthy mixture of acceptance and enthusiasm, and this leads people to live happier (and often longer) lives. I like to call these people the *chronologically gifted*. They regard their age as a gift, the seal of a lifelong journey for which they are profoundly grateful. It's a journey that began at birth and one that they hope to continue through a personal legacy that immortalizes them in the memories of others.

Facing their own mortality, the chronologically gifted are determined to live with significance, passion, and purpose in the here and now. Even as they seize control over their attitude about aging, they surrender the illusion of control over the reality of aging. Somewhere in the mix, they lose their concern over whether they live to see five more years, thirty more years, or fifty. Yet as a group, they still tend to live longer and more rewarding lives than those who constantly preoccupy themselves with thoughts of getting older.

If you choose to, you can be chronologically gifted, too. *YOU CAN DO IT!*

It begins with a decision. If you're ready to make that choice, then now's the time—the earlier, the better. But no matter how old (or young) you are or consider yourself at the present, your follow-through from this point on is what matters the most. In this book, we're going to talk about how, through a combination of determination and discipline, we can condition ourselves right now to face our final season of life—whenever it ultimately comes—with honesty, gratitude, and enthusiasm.

Before we delve into the "how," let's first explore the "why."

Why do we age?

This is a surprisingly difficult question to answer. Biologists, psychologists, philosophers and theologians have wrestled for centuries with the problem of senescence. The process of senescence includes the gradual, functional deterioration that most living creatures undergo as they approach the end of their lifespans. However, not everyone agrees that aging is necessarily a bad process. In fact, the emerging consensus among those who study senescence seems to be that it is to our evolutionary advantage that we age and die.

In this section, we're going to spend a little time talking about some of the major theories of aging. Like most scholars who major in this field of research, however, we won't be trying to understand senescence in order to figure out how to beat it. Instead, we'll be trying to better appreciate the wonder of nature that results in aging and, eventually, makes room for a subsequent generation to thrive in our place. The chronologically gifted embrace senescence and welcome it, not as a specter of fear, but as a benign intervention of nature that contributes to the flourishing of life. Our goal here is to begin our quest toward a longer and more fulfilling life by fearlessly confronting and unashamedly marveling at nature's wisdom.

There are a number of factors that scientists think might contribute to the aging process. For instance, many talk about the gradual accumulation of cellular damage by unstable oxygen molecules in the body ("free radicals"), which may cause certain cells to stop functioning over time. Others talk about how hormonal changes and gene expressions are regulated by a sort of "biological clock." That measurement becomes active at some point in our lives and accelerates the pace of aging in a manner similar to the way we grow and develop rapidly during childhood, before slowing down in maturity. (Remember, aging is a form of growth.) This could explain the relatively sudden decommissioning of certain physiological processes we associate with senescence. Declining immune system function, in particular, leaves us more vulnerable to infectious disease and autoimmune disorders as we get older.

But whatever the root cause of aging—and no one has the answer to that question yet—scientists generally agree that senescence is a complex process we're only beginning to understand. "No single theory or phenomenon can completely explain why aging occurs," says Mayo Clinic physician Edward Creagan. "Researchers generally view aging as many processes that interact and influence each other."[5] Some of those processes we have a measure of control over. (We'll talk about those later on.) Others are completely out of our hands, and it's important for us to recognize the difference.

Not long ago, scientists thought that biological cells were inherently immortal. That is, given the right combination of nutrients and favorable circumstances, a normally functioning population of cells would never have an intrinsic reason to deteriorate and die. Old cells would simply be replaced by new ones, indefinitely. In 1961, however, the American anatomist, Leonard Hayflick, refuted this hypothesis by demonstrating that, even within a favorable growth environment, a culture of human fetal cells would only divide between 40 and 60 times before entering a senescence phase, when cells would slow their rate of division and eventually stop dividing altogether.

Hayflick's experiments, which have been replicated by many others since, demonstrated that genetically cell division seems to be programmed to stop after a certain number of divisions. This number has been termed the "Hayflick limit," and it varies from one species to another. To give you an idea of how it relates to lifespan, consider that a relatively short-lived laboratory mouse (approximately three years old) has a Hayflick limit of 15, while the long-lived Galapagos tortoise (approaching 200 years old) has a Hayflick limit of 110.[6] That puts humans right about in the middle of the spectrum. Though we're not the longest-living creatures, we do have the longest average lifespan of any mammal.

Hayflick's observations have been corroborated by geneticists, who explain that damage to our DNA occurs after a certain number of cell divisions due to gradual telomere shortening. To avoid getting too technical, let's just describe telomeres as a sort of protective cap at the end of chromosomes that help preserve DNA—the biological coding for life contained in every cell. Each time a chromosome divides, a portion of its telomere is truncated, until eventually the DNA on the chromosome is exposed to damage, and cells can no longer divide properly. Once cell division halts, old cells can no longer be replaced by new cells. This circumstance helps explain much of the anatomical deterioration we experience as normal biological aging. Also, it clarifies why muscles lose their ability to support our skeletal structures in old age, and why people become more fragile and susceptible to bones breaking over time. It helps us make sense of the way our skin becomes less elastic and why our hair eventually loses color. It also illuminates our understanding of cognitive decline, since deterioration of brain tissue contributes to dementia and Alzheimer's disease.

Some speculate that there are very good reasons why cells have this programmed limit. Senescence provides a natural guard against the development of cancerous growths that result from the unregulated division of cells.[7] Imagine a world where it was both normal and expected that after a certain number of years everyone would die as a result of developing multiple forms of cancer. It's not a pretty thought. If death is inevitable, it's possible that the relatively slow decay of senescence is nature's wise selection against the more abrupt and painful decline we associate with aggressive cancer.

I certainly don't want to minimize the fact that cancer remains the second leading cause of death in the United States. Many of us will struggle with it as we get older. Nevertheless, I find encouragement in the thought that the same cellular process that is causing me to display the wear and tear of my age may also be nature's way of providing me time to begin coping with the end of life—to process what's going on and to make good decisions about how to tap into my remaining resources.

And then there are the social considerations, of which there are also many intertwining tributaries of thought.[8] It's possible, for instance, that senescence is an evolutionary trait that promotes the flourishing of a species by causing one generation to "get out of the way" and make room for the next. As we're already beginning to see, medical technology is helping members of the Baby Boomer generation live longer. The combination of high birth rates and high longevity rates is a perfect storm of demand for precious life-supporting resources. If everyone were to live forever—or even if we were all to live to 100—our earth simply couldn't sustain us all. We would revert to animal-like competition and war (even more than we already do) over the scarce resources of this beautiful planet.

Interestingly, many of the educated societies of the world have substantially lower fertility rates than the world's average. As of 2017, the global average is 2.33 children per woman. Compare that with an average of 1.4 children per woman in Japan and Italy. Without discounting the complexity of sociological factors that play into such figures, it shouldn't be lost on us that these are also nations with some of the world's highest life expectancies (83.10 years in Japan, 82.94 years in Italy).

Here's another intriguing social possibility for why we age. Some believe that our biological programming is tied in some mysterious way to child rearing. Perhaps there's some hormonal cue that's triggered once our days of direct child rearing are over. Something signals our bodies that the demands of propagating the species have passed to our children, and the useful period of our own generation is coming to an end. (Incidentally, this may help explain why grandparents who play a primary role in the care of grandchildren seem to thrive into old age where others decline. Perhaps there are biological cues that retard senescence in those who are still tasked with child rearing.)

Whatever the case may be, it's abundantly clear that aging is a complex natural process that involves a grand design that has more to do with *LIFE* than we usually imagine. Just think about that for a moment. What would it look like for us to age as if we were *LIVING* rather than dying? For those with eyes to see it the way the chronologically gifted do, aging is a way of joyfully connecting with something bigger than ourselves. We can't be in denial about these realities.

We have to face aging with gusto, refusing to become enmeshed in our own personal experiences as though our own lives are the most important aspect in the big picture. Our aging has to do with more than just us, and people who "get" that tend to live longer. Why? Because they don't feel like their years belong to them; they're on loan to them for the sake of a larger purpose. Theirs is not to decide how long to live as much as how to live for as long as they have. So they start putting those years to good use—right here and right now.

If you're ready, let's get started. *YOU CAN DO IT!*

Might age reversal be possible someday?

We live in an age of unprecedented scientific and technological advancement. Many diseases that used to ravage society are now all but eradicated in the developed West. Many health conditions that once spelled sudden, early death—conditions like meningitis and heart disease—can now be prevented through vaccines and early detection screenings. Even those chronic diseases for which we lack cures—AIDS and cancer, for instance—can be surprisingly well-managed with modern therapies that prolong patients' meaningful lives for years, sometimes decades. And it's only a matter of time before we discover cures for those diseases, too.

As a result of these and other achievements, citizens of developed countries are enjoying longer lifespans than ever before in human history. Today's average life expectancy is 80 years for men and slightly longer for women. Statistically, very few people live to age 100—only about two in ten thousand[9]—and the majority are women. Jeanne Calment of France was the oldest known human being when she died in 1997 at the record age of 122. Nevertheless, while the math suggests that living past 100 is still relatively rare, it's also a scientific fact that people are living longer every day, and the population density of individuals living past 80 will only increase with each passing year.[10] Some call this the "silver tsunami," fearing that our healthcare and social structures aren't adequately poised to respond to this relatively sudden influx of geriatric citizens.

They may be right, but there are places in the world— the Blue Zones[11]—where indigenous populations have far greater concentrations of centenarians than most places in the United States. Several of those populations have thrived under conditions that seem considerably less advanced than our modern medical infrastructures. They rely instead upon traditional family care models passed down through the centuries.

Many believe that as we continue to live longer, increasingly we're going to look to the wisdom of people in the world's Blue Zones to figure out how to adjust our societal structures accordingly. This wisdom may gradually change our cultural understanding of what constitutes "old". It is particularly true as social structures emerge to support younger family members caring for older family members and in communal living arrangements and neighborhoods where complimentary interactions between young and elderly people become the norm rather than the exception to the rule.

Still, the question at hand concerns age reversal, and that's where an important distinction comes into play. *Lifespan* has been increasing steadily, but *health span* has not kept pace. That is, while we're living longer, we're not necessarily enjoying our longer lives. "The period of disease and disability at the end of life, the dreaded decline of old age, has actually been getting longer," writes gerontologist Bill Gifford. "The only thing that changes, as we live longer and longer, is that we fall victim to different ailments."[12]

Chronologically gifted individuals don't settle for long life at the expense of their health. They're not interested in living forever if that means a prolonged state of disability and more opportunity for cognitive decline. Frankly, they would rather live functionally meaningful lives until 80 and then drop dead quietly, in their sleep.[13] So the real question when it comes to longevity is how to extend the health span of our lives, not simply how to live a few more years. Fortunately, researchers are going public with some promising discoveries on that front.

Only very recently has the U.S. Food and Drug Administration (FDA) been willing to give the green light to a study examining the potential anti-aging properties of a drug therapy. The reason for this is simple: aging hasn't been considered a disease, and so drugs targeting the natural process of aging were considered unnecessary and perhaps even inappropriate. Personally, I think the FDA's philosophy on this matter is spot-on. Aging is not a disease in itself, and it's not helpful for us to think of it as such. Understandably, this has had a serious cooling effect on the market for age reversal studies. Even if a researcher was to discover a veritable "fountain of youth" drug, there would be no viable route for taking it to market and thus no profit motive to fund the research in the first place. That may be changing, though.

In 2015, the agency approved a clinical trial of the anti-diabetic medication, Metformin, in order to assess its anti-aging properties. Metformin is an inexpensive drug of first recourse in treating diabetes. Also, it's such a common prescription that the World Health Organization even lists it as an "essential" medication. Somewhat serendipitously, because so many people are already taking the drug, certain interesting patterns came to researchers' attention through epidemiological studies—epidemiology being the scientific study of the patterns, causes and effects of health and disease conditions within defined populations. The patterns revealed a lower incidence of cancer and other health problems among patients on Metformin.

In particular, the 2014 analysis of British patient data demonstrated an intriguing correlation between Metformin and longevity: those who were taking the drug were actually living 18 percent longer than diabetics who were taking a different class of medications. This showed that it was Metformin itself, and not merely the control of diabetes, that was responsible for the elongated survival. Nir Barzilai, director of the Institute for Aging Research at the Albert Einstein College of Medicine (Yeshiva University), believes Metformin may alter our metabolism to make it look more like that of a centenarian. "It looks like a super-drug ... involved in many things related to aging."[14] Should the clinical trials yield promising results, many believe the FDA may open the gates for additional anti-aging drug therapy research. Funding organizations like Age Reversal Therapeutics, Inc.[15], are standing by to help accelerate the push for bona fide age reversal therapies to become mainstream reality within the foreseeable future.

We're also beginning to learn about some of the more complex anti-aging properties of naturally-occurring substances. These include tocotrienols (members of the vitamin E family) and quercetin (a flavonol found in high concentrations in many fruits and vegetables). When used in combination, these substances may offer scientists the ability to selectively target malignant cells to stimulate senescence (causing apoptosis, or cell death, and reversing tumor growth). Simultaneously these substances are promoting longevity in healthy cells by slowing senescence and removing accumulated "senile" cells from the body and staving off the dump of inflammatory chemicals that come with them. It very well might represent a new approach to fighting cancer and promoting longevity in the form of dietary supplements.[16]

Meanwhile, even more exciting discoveries in the field of genetics may offer the key to engineering longer-lived societies. One of the most talked-about (and most controversial) applications of the human genome map in recent years pertains to an enzyme technology known as CRISPER-Cas9. Without getting too technical, let's just say that CRISPR research is real-life "gene hacking" that allows technicians to "edit" a flawed strand of DNA to promote normal function. The potential applications, as you might imagine, are beyond incredible:

> The technology has already transformed cancer research by making it easier to engineer tumor cells in the laboratory, and then test various drugs to see which can stop them from growing. Soon doctors may be able to use CRISPR to treat some diseases directly. Stem cells taken from people with hemophilia, for example, could be edited outside of the body to correct the genetic flaw that causes the disease, and then the normal cells could be inserted to repopulate a patient's bloodstream.
>
> In the next two years we may see an even more dramatic medical advance. ... For years, scientists have searched for a way to use animal organs to ease the donor shortage [for transplant patients who would otherwise die before a donor was located]. Pigs have long been considered the mammal of choice ... but a pig's genome is riddled with viruses called PERVs (porcine endogenous retroviruses), which are similar to the virus that causes AIDS and have been shown to be capable of infecting human cells. ... Until recently,

nobody has been able to rid the pig of its retroviruses. Now, by using CRISPR to edit the genome in pig organs, researchers seem well on their way to solving that problem.[17]

These advances sound like science fiction. As a result, it raises all kinds of ethical questions, but the technology to engineer longer life is already within reach of today's scientific community. We're on the cusp of being able to literally "edit out" genetic diseases and to treat many of the conditions that would otherwise lead to premature death. Meanwhile, CRISPR may offer hope for revising our DNA to more closely resemble that of centenarians in the world's Blue Zones. The result will enable us to become more genetically predisposed to live longer, enjoy better lives and remove much of the apparent luck associated with living to 100 (and beyond).

So, is age reversal possible? Possibly, but only time will tell. But whether that's even desirable will depend on whether our health spans can keep pace with the longer lifespans these technologies might enable. (Fortunately, the strategies described in this book will give you the best shot at that.)

Should the chronologically gifted person hinge his or her life on this hope that science fiction medicine will soon become therapeutic reality? ABSOLUTELY NOT.

I hate to burst that bubble, but if you're holding out for miracles, then you're on the road to disappointment. The first step to becoming chronologically gifted is shedding the illusion. Make no mistake: I love reading about this stuff. I subscribe to health and wellness magazines. I read up on popular science and life extension literature, and I frequently talk about these topics with friends. But you won't find me staking my future on it.

It's encouraging that scientists are better understanding the biology of senescence. It's wonderful that researchers and funding organizations are taking greater interest in viable age reversal therapies. Also, it's inspiring to imagine what new options might be available to 80-year-old people in the next ten or twenty years to make living a long and healthy life as a centenarian more the rule than the exception. I unashamedly hope and trust that I'll live to see those advances in technology.

Nevertheless, the chronologically gifted perspective on life has little or nothing to do with the science of age reversal per se. It garners certain immediately practical insights from the latest research—especially regarding nutrition and exercise— but beyond that, being chronologically gifted is more about an attitude adjustment that leads to meaningful lifestyle change. It's not about riding the technological wave with the hope of being first in line for some innovative rejuvenation therapy.

More to the point, the chronologically gifted don't have time to wait around for science to solve the "problem" of aging— because they don't regard aging as a problem in the first place. They are living their best years now, whether science keeps up or not. They know the facts: genes are responsible for no more than 20 percent of our longevity; the remaining 80 percent is up to us. Genetics are important, but we are not our genes. Even with the biological odds stacked against us, we can successfully overcome the maladies that might otherwise cut our lives short through energetic, healthy lifestyles and personalized, proactive medical care. We can determine at any age to reverse our functional deterioration and live our best years now—with or without our genes' cooperation.

It all begins with attitude.

So now we understand some of the biology—enough, I hope, that we're in agreement that there's not (yet) a magical way to halt or reverse the aging process. We're making tremendous strides, but anyone who thinks they can avoid it entirely is grievously mistaken. "The denial of aging and the attempt to fight it are counterproductive," counsels Dr. Weil, "a failure to understand and accept an important aspect of our experience."[18] So step one in my program for becoming chronologically gifted is simple: *admit that you're getting older.*

Stop fighting it.

Embrace it.

Own it.

Love it.

You might wonder how it's possible to love the aging process, but really it all begins with attitude. I'm not asking you to love the limitations that aging might bring. My younger readers don't yet know this, but it's not fun having to stop for a breather while other, younger peers run on ahead of you. It's not fun having to make more frequent trips to the bathroom.

But my older readers can take heart because there's good news: being chronologically gifted doesn't mean you have to pretend to be young! Isn't that a relief? Aren't you glad to hear that it's *okay* to be old—to act your age? And for my younger readers, there's good news, too. Being chronologically gifted means it's *okay* to get older. You don't have to cling to your youth as though there's nothing left to look forward to once the gray hairs outnumber the colored ones. In fact, on that day, you'll actually have more to enjoy about life than you can possibly imagine from where you are right now.

Now don't misunderstand me. I'm not saying that older people can just aggressively tell the world, "I'm old...deal with it!" The world is going to move forward with or without us as we age. If we want to continue having a meaningful opportunity to participate in life, then we're going to need a healthy mind and a healthy body. We won't always be young, but we'll always be growing. So let's focus less on the number our age represents, and more on the fact that we're continuously evolving— all the way to our last breath. This need for meaningful development is something that 20-year-olds and 80-year-olds have in common. In their own, age-appropriate ways, both groups are on their way to becoming a better version tomorrow of who they are today.

That's right. No matter what our age is, we only thrive inasmuch as we continue growing into better, more well-rounded people. I use that word "better" in its basic qualitative sense. Each time we acquire a piece of knowledge or improve upon a skill that helps us deepen relationships, appreciate our experiences, and leave a more robust legacy, we've made ourselves better people than we were before. It doesn't matter how small the change is as long as it's a true change. Period. And that's the goal we have to keep before us if we hope to live the way the chronologically gifted do. We have to get up each morning asking ourselves what we can think, say, and do that will help us go to bed that night feeling good about ourselves. And when we lay down for rest at the end of one day, we should do so excitedly looking forward to our next day's journey, confident in our personal relevance, engagement, and sense of life purpose.

The day we decide to stop growing is really the day we begin to die. For some people, that happens way too early in life, even while they're still relatively young and still involved in their careers. For other people, it never happens. Up until the end, they're on the road toward a vision of their better selves.

In a sense, those people never really die. They just stop breathing one day. And that's how I plan to go, too—content and healthy (at age 123).

Let's get to work!

We've barely scratched the surface of topics we're going to explore in this book, but it's not too early to start thinking about practical ways we can put what we're learning to good use. Before we begin delving into the insights we can glean from others' work in the field, it might be a good idea to spend a little time—perhaps a week or more—reflecting on your own reasons for wanting to live to 100 (and beyond). Getting a handle on the thoughts that are driving you to become chronologically gifted will help us do so with focus and momentum. At the end of the book, you'll have a chance to check in with yourself and see whether and how some of thoughts, ideas and perspectives have changed.

Suggestion #1: Think hard about why you want to live longer.

Everyone is hardwired with a survival instinct. It's the evolutionary feature that makes human beings—and all animals—reluctant to take unnecessary risks, to flee from danger, and to take steps to protect themselves when they feel threatened. Also, it's partly responsible for the resistance to the effects of senescence. For those of you who are not careful, it can lead to a stubborn denial of the reality that you're facing some limitations as you get older. If you experience severe depression and become suicidal, you are suffering from, among other illnesses, a malfunction of this basic facet of your humanity.

Yet, chances are, the mere fact that you are taking the time to read this book, suggest that you're not ready to die yet. You might be struggling to articulate a good reason for continuing to live. If that describes you, by all means continue reading. Equally important, I hope you will get in touch with a professional counselor. Depression is a serious matter, and aging can make it worse. There's no shame in admitting that you need help. One of the characteristics of the chronologically gifted is their ability to assess when they need help and to get it—without getting hung up on whether they "do" or "don't" need help.

There are two basic reasons why people want to live longer. Either they have something to live for, or they're simply afraid to die. One of these attitudes is helpful, and the other is not.

Everyone fears death to some degree. Even those who claim not to be afraid of death usually have some doubts that make them uneasy, and this is both natural and healthy. But the difference between the chronologically gifted and everyone else in the world is the way they're so busy living for something that they spend very little time worrying about when they're going to die.

So the first exercise we'll do together is a really simple one. Ask yourself, *"Why do I want to live to a ripe old age?"* The question may sound obvious. But as you're probably discovering, it's a haunting question that's hard to articulate an answer to—even for those who just know they have a lot to live for.

Language is a very powerful tool, which is why this exercise is so important. Identifying your motivations will help clarify them, which will help you capitalize on opportunities for improving them over the course of our time together. If you find that you're answering the question in terms of seeking a purpose for your remaining years, then you're already well on your way to becoming chronologicaliy gifted. If, however, you find that fear is dominating your thoughts, then you're not alone. It's time to face that fear for what it is. Put it out there, and name the elephant in the room. Don't be ashamed, but do realize that by the time you're done, you'll probably find that fear of death is no longer the most compelling reason you hope to live the longest life possible.

Suggestion #2: Make a list of things you think you're getting too old to do.

Be honest here. This is extremely important because when you reach the end of this book, I'm going to ask you to revisit this question to see what, if anything, has changed about your self-awareness. This exercise is equally important for younger readers. If that's you, please don't skip over this section. While you may struggle to think of anything you're getting too old to do, it would be a mistake to assume there aren't activities you've already consigned to the years behind you. And this is precisely the point of doing this exercise: to reveal how arbitrary many of those decisions are—especially the ones we've made without quite realizing it!

The simple fact is that there are many activities that older people are not especially suited for, at least not in the manner they might have been in their younger years. There is nothing inherently unhealthy about admitting that you're too old to do something that you used to enjoy doing. Nor is there anything wrong with deciding for yourself that there are certain age-appropriate activities that are reserved for younger bodies. But there is one question I'd challenge you to answer as honestly as you can:

does your present perception of your limitations line up with biological reality, or is it essentially the product of insidious social conditioning? Are you really *too old* to sign up for ballet classes at 30? To go back to school at 50? Or to start your own business at 65?

Social conditioning applies to younger folks more than you may think. There's a tremendous amount of pressure to grow up as quickly as possible and never look back. For example, I'd like to suggest that adults can still have good-humored pillow fights and costume parties (with or without children). Adults can still shamelessly enjoy rides on the merry-go-round or spin in circles staring up at the stars before falling onto the soft grass—just to feel the world turn.

Children may not have the maturity that comes with adulthood, but neither are they burdened with the world's cares the way most people are. Let's not be too quick to dismiss the fact that even by age 30, there are many behaviors society tell us we're *too old* for that have nothing to do with biological reality—and could actually help us live longer.

Now, there are real limits to what we can and should do as we age, so spend some time honestly listing out a few concerns that are most important to you. It probably won't be hard for you to think of at least two or three, but don't feel badly if you immediately think of five or ten. (Keep in mind younger readers, these don't necessarily have to be activities you're already *too old* for. Your list could include things you worry that someday you will be *too old* for.) It's healthy to purge these thoughts and get them out there where you can face them honestly. The goal is simply for you to list clearly what your perceived limitations are (or someday might be), so that you can ask yourself: are they real or merely self-imposed?

Write out your list, but don't dwell on the items right now. Put your list away somewhere, confident that some of what you have written will probably change by the time you understand better what it means to be chronologically gifted. But make no mistake—some of it won't change, and that's okay, too. Why? Because even if you're spot-on about what you're too old for now (or will be someday), in the future, you will have a much healthier, more optimistic attitude about those limitations—and what you can do right now to delay their onset and reduce their impact.

Suggestion #3: Make a list of activities you're not willing to give up at any age, no matter what.

This exercise is for the younger readers too. It might be helpful for you to frame this question in terms of, "What am I determined not to give up on, no matter how old I get?" Okay, this is a much more enjoyable exercise than the last one—and I hope that this list will be at least three times as long as your previous list. This suggestion is different because it invites you to think past the possibility of limitations and look for ways to embrace what really matters out of life at any age.

Make this a two-part endeavor. First, list everything that comes to mind when you think of what makes your life worth living. Be specific, too. Don't just write: "my career," "community," or "travel." Instead, write ideas like: "feeling a sense of personal fulfillment in my career," "being involved in something important in my community," or "making it a point to have at least one new adventure every year."

If you find that you could go on and on, that's rewarding! But don't. Stop after about 15-20 minutes of reflection. Then go back over the list you've just written, and circle your top three. That's going to be tough, of course, because it will feel like you're limiting yourself. But don't think of it that way. Instead, think of it as a way of focusing on three items—a manageable number—that at this time give your life its greatest joy.

Now for the hard part. I want you to spend the next week thinking about the three items on your list. By the end of the week, see if you can come up with one way that you're already short-changing your enjoyment of those activities. For instance, to continue with the career example, perhaps upon further reflection you would find that fear of failure is keeping you from applying for a major promotion that would unlock new opportunities for you. Maybe you've become so comfortable in your routine that you're afraid to leave your dead-end job and change careers. Or perhaps you've been contemplating an innovative start-up idea, but you haven't given yourself permission to follow your dreams.

The goal of this exercise is to begin focusing on the facets that make your life meaningful and start thinking creatively about ways that you can amplify your enjoyment of them and launch new adventures—at any age. Even the happiest people in the world have opportunities to enjoy more of their lives than they do right now. YOU CAN DO IT!

Suggestion #4: Be Gifted. Spend some time in front of the mirror. Fall in love with yourself all over again.

It may sound like I'm encouraging you to be narcissistic here, but I promise that's not the point of this exercise. I'm simply calling our collective bluff. It's no secret that as we get older we become more and more reluctant to honor the faces and bodies we see in the mirror. We become more camera-shy, and we prefer lovemaking in the dark (especially us girls).

Younger readers who may notice relatively few of the signs of aging on their bodies would do well to spend this time reminding themselves that the body they see now will one day look different. That's okay, because the person residing within that body will be more well-rounded than the person looking in the mirror today.

Chronologically gifted individuals have a healthy sense of self-love. It's a kind of love that makes them feel confident in their own skin—wrinkles and all. It's a kind of love that invites others to look on them without fear of offending them with comments that give away their age. After all, age is just a number, and it's one of the realities they love about themselves! (Just imagine living in such a way that younger friends felt no need to dance around the topic of age. How refreshing would that be for you?)

This week, stop and stare at yourself in the mirror a few times each day. As you notice the signs of aging, come up with a reminder. Tell yourself, "I'm not just getting older. I'm learning to live better." Let the features that reveal your age be the ones that remind you of the wisdom and maturity that you prize as a result of your life experiences. Fall in love with the person looking back at you in the mirror because that's the person who has a lot to offer the world.

The bottom line

Aging is not optional, but growth is. I'm convinced that we have far more power over how we age than society conditions us to believe. And that's what this book is all about. "Most of what we call aging, and most of what we dread about getting older," observe experts Chris Crowley and Dr. Henry Lodge, "is actually decay. [...] You will get older, no matter what. But you do not have to *act* old or *feel* old. That's what counts. We haven't figured out a way to last forever, but aging can be a slow, minimal, and surprisingly graceful process."[19]

If you're with me this far, then congratulations! You've already taken the first step toward becoming chronologically gifted. You've decided you don't just want to live longer, but you want to live better. That means focusing on each day you're blessed to have left, beginning right here, right now. You may not be sure about what you need to do next, and perhaps you're even feeling a little overwhelmed. That's perfectly all right. It means you're starting to get the picture of what you've been missing out on in life before now. But don't worry! You're already living your life more fully simply by bringing it into your consciousness. You've already taken one life-giving step away from the dull, mindless existence into which our culture so seductively lures us. You may die tomorrow or you might die sixty years from now (or more), but you can be confident of this much: you'll leave this world more complete now than you would have if you had expired even a few hours earlier.

Take comfort in knowing that everything you do from this point on takes you one step closer to living the kind of mindful, joyful, seize-the-day life you decide to live. Let each topic we discuss in this book become a springboard for deeper engagement with the life inside of you—the timeless part of you that is desperate to express itself, despite the best efforts of an age-fearing culture to suppress it.

Are you ready?

Okay, then. Let's dance.

Personal Journal Pages

Steps I need to and *will* take to promote my healthy journey to age 123:

_____

_____

_____

_____

_____

_____

_____

_____

_____

_____

_____

_____

_____

_____

_____

_____

_____

_____

_____

_____

_____

_____

_____

_____

_____

_____

_____

_____

_____

_____

_____

_____

_____

_____

– 2 –

A Reason to Get Up in the Morning

Here's a statement you might not expect to find in a book about aging with gusto:

Living longer isn't necessarily a good thing.

That's right. I said it. It needs to be said at the beginning of this book because it's a sobering mantra that the chronologically gifted live by. On its own, mere survival is a pathetic goal to set. We don't merely want to live longer; we want to live well. That's what really matters.

Be honest with yourself. If you knew for a fact that you would be unable to enjoy any of life's joys that truly make you happy after age 85, would you really want to hang on until your late 90s? I suspect not. After all, what good would it do for you or for anyone else?

It's just common sense. Living without meaningful purpose is nothing more than a stubborn refusal to die. It's not really living in the fullest sense of the word, and that's what we're going to talk about in this chapter.

The chronologically gifted understand that there's an important trade-off in progress when we talk about longevity. "Living an extra two years on life support may not necessarily be your goal," remarks Dr. Robert Kane of the Minnesota Geriatric Education Center. "The question is: can you delay or prevent the onset of disability?' Good years' is a very important concept. ... Things that give you a sense of fulfillment, a good life, the sense of being valued, the sense of being cared for, and the sense that you are liked—these are all very positive."[20]

Before we delve into any essential topics in this book, we need to get a handle on what Dr. Kane and others mean by the phrase "good years." It's a cliché we hear all the time, which is precisely why we have to think harder about it than some of the other topics we'll consider later. We have to recognize up front that what constitutes "good years" for one person might not constitute "good years" for another. Frankly, some of us have higher personal expectations than others. If we have to lower those expectations in order to be happy living a longer life, we've missed the point of becoming chronologically gifted in the first place. We should never have to lower our expectations. We need only modify them to suit a changing reality.

More to the point. We're going to explore whether we still have a reason for getting up in the morning after we reach the ripe old age of 90 and beyond or whether we're just doggedly holding on because we're too afraid to let go. There's a very important reason why I like to talk about this topic first whenever I'm explaining the way the chronologically gifted live. It's the engine that drives the whole enterprise. If you don't get this part right, then none of the other topics we talk about in this book will have a lasting effect. Sure, you might see some short-term results, and you'll feel great—for a while. But then all your strides may start to feel more and more like a tiresome list of chores. In the moment, it will become harder to remember what makes all the work worth it in the first place. Eventually, you might give up because you're only human. And that's what humans have a tendency to do.

Not even the best-maintained car will go very far down the road without a powerful, reliable, and well-tuned engine under the hood—and plenty of fuel to keep the engine running. For the chronologically gifted, that engine is a keenly defined sense of personal worth, fueled by activities and relationships that continually reinforce it. It's a sense of worth that doesn't come from outward social affirmation, either. On the contrary, it's rooted in passions that reach deep into the very core of our being. It's what drives the chronologically gifted to do whatever it takes to preserve their ability to be real players in the world and not merely passive spectators on their way out of it. It's an audacity, if you will, that renders them deaf to the voices of decay and obsolescence that pepper so much of the popular rhetoric about getting older. When you have a reason to get up in the morning, it's so much easier to resist the lure of staying in bed.

Not surprisingly, in the Blue Zones where people routinely live longer lives, there is usually a distinct cultural emphasis on discovering one's individual life purpose. In Japan, it's called *Ikigai*. In Costa Rica, it's called *plan de vida*. In western psychology, we call it "self-actualization." Whatever the term, it refers to the ephemeral concept of deep inward fulfillment or whatever it is that makes us want to keep ticking for one more day. As we'll discuss in a later chapter, this is also the more holistic (and less religious) definition of spirituality. People with spiritual balance live with integrated world views that connect them to something larger than themselves.

You may think you have a good sense of what that is in your life right now. That's why you're trying to learn more about how to prolong your years, so that you can keep doing that which gives your life purpose. If so, great! But read this chapter anyway. Aging can bring challenges that may force you to reexamine your sense of purpose from time to time, and it's helpful to think through these scenarios in advance of those challenges. That way, you can adapt gracefully and find new ways to discover and express your inner passions instead of giving up on them altogether late in life (which is what far too many of us do).

For those who don't yet have a clearly defined sense of life purpose, don't worry. You're in good company. A lot of people, young and old, go through life with only a hazy idea of what it is they're really living for. Older people simply don't have the luxury of taking a lot of time to passively figure it out. It's my hope that this chapter will give you the skills you need to begin mindfully living in the moment at any age. If you can connect with previously dormant inward passions, they will inspire you to make the most of life's opportunities. You owe it to yourself so you can join the chronologically gifted, who have learned the art of exploiting everything the world throws at them for their gain. They go to bed without regrets and wake up each morning eager to do it all again.

It's there in the research

In 1921, psychologist Lewis Terman initiated what is now the oldest and longest-running longitudinal study in the world. It's based on an observational research method that tracks data from the same subjects over a long period of time. This study has followed the lives and achievements of over 1,500 "gifted" young people into adulthood.[21] One of the benefits of the study to those interested in longevity is the way it offers key insights about the life paths of those in the Terman study, including those who died relatively young as compared with those who died much later. (And not all of them are dead yet.)

Within the study, there was a demonstrated connection between conscientiousness and longevity. Conscientiousness is a personality trait that describes people who are organized, dutiful, and self-disciplined. They are the types who tend to think about the long-range consequences of their behavior, and so they act less impulsively than others. They are the kind who set and keep long-term goals. They pay attention to details without losing sight of the big picture. They take obligations seriously—for themselves and for others around them. And, perhaps most importantly, they're task- rather than time-oriented. And that's a very important distinction. They spend less time waiting for a chronological milestone to signal that they're done and instead push through until the task at hand is complete. These are the people who reach the end of their shifts at work and say, "You know what? I'm not quite at a good stopping place yet. I'm going to stay an extra hour or two and knock this out before calling it quits."

It's not hard to understand the link between conscientiousness and longevity when you think about it in those terms. When life is one long workday, one big project to be completed, those who are task-oriented are more likely to signal to their bodies that they're not quite ready to call it quits than those who are time-oriented and more susceptible to cultural messaging that suggests it's time for them to move aside and die.[22]

Also, conscientious people are far less likely to engage in risk-taking behaviors—a leading cause of premature death—and they resist engaging in self-destructive behaviors like excessive drinking or binge eating as a way of coping with major life losses. Instead of succumbing to depression and suicidal thoughts, they're more likely to strategize a way forward for themselves, leaning on relationships and meaningful activities to overcome obstacles. Conscientious people seek the fulfillment of accomplishment through hard work. They take pride in what they do and are internally motivated to succeed in whatever it is they have set their minds to accomplish. Those in the Terman study who were most disappointed with their achievements tended to die the youngest.[23]

As I said before, conscientiousness is a personality trait. That means some people are more inclined to be mindful, dependable and reliable than others. I'm not writing about this trait in order to discourage those who are less conscientious.

I'm writing about it because chances are if you're reading this book, you're already motivated by a strong goal to live longer, even if you're having trouble getting a grasp on why you want to live longer. In other words, by taking the time to investigate longevity and self-improvement, you're already exhibiting the kind of conscientiousness that will help you live longer than your more lackadaisical peers. They are more inclined to retire at age 65 because they believe they've earned it. They will take it easy and assume that most of their major contributions to society are now behind them and it's time for them to be served by others.

You don't need to be a disciplined perfectionist who never takes risks to get to age 100. In fact, quite the opposite. Hyper-conscientiousness leads to an unhealthy level of perfectionism. This creates extraordinary stress, especially in old age. That is when unavoidable physical impairment begins, reducing the level and quality of work that individuals used to be able to perform. Such stress can lead to depression or to premature death as a result of cardiovascular disease. That's why long-lived individuals are conscientious without being obsessive. You just need to be the kind of person who stops to think about the future without forgetting to enjoy the present. You need to be the kind of person who not only wants to live longer, but who wants to live a fuller, more meaningful life—beginning right now.

So even if you've never thought of yourself as conscientious before now, it's time to start cultivating that aspect of your personality. Clearly you have traces of it already. It's important for you to begin your journey to becoming chronologically gifted with some serious, thoughtful consideration of what the purpose is (or will be) for the rest of your life's journey. A strong sense of purpose catalyzes conscientiousness by giving you a reason to hold out against the odds and work through challenges with sound thinking and deliberate action. It protects you against setbacks and frustrations, and it encourages you to delight in the achievement of small goals on the way to bigger goals in life.

And here's where ironically it gets easier for my older readers than for my younger readers. The younger you are, the more opportunities you'll likely encounter for cultural messaging and other life demands to steer you off-course and derail your attempts to realize your most cherished, deeply-seated personal goals.

It may be helpful to consider the way marathoners prepare to run 26.2 miles. Psychologist (and runner) Glenn Geher talks about how these athletes belong to a peculiar culture all their own. They train themselves to be able to hold out against the odds by surrounding themselves with like-minded runners who "get" their ambitions. They keep the goal of finishing well in front of them, no matter what happens during their training, content with whatever place they finish as long as it represents their best effort. And most noteworthy, they're just getting started after their first marathon. Or the second. Or the third. Something in marathoners' spirits compels them to keep signing up and training for one more race![24] If you apply that insight to the way you view your remaining years, or if you treated life like a chain of marathons that you're determined to run just for the joy of finishing, most runners would be surprised to discover just how many races they have left.

But you have to know in which direction to run, right?

One funny word. One powerful concept: *ikigai* (Pronounced "ee-kih-GUY.")

Psychologists Howard Friedman and Leslie Martin have followed Terman's study subjects with particular interest in profiling the personality qualities that characterize the longest-lived among them. They note:

> *The qualities and lifestyles cultivated ... reflect an active pursuit of goals, a deep satisfaction with life, and a strong sense of accomplishment. That's not to say these people possessed a giddy sense of happiness.... But having a large social network, engaging in physical activities that naturally draw you in, giving back to your community, enjoying and thriving in your career, and nurturing a healthy marriage or close friendships can do more than add many years to your life. Together, they represent the living with purpose that comes from working hard, reaching out to others, and bouncing back from difficult times.*[25]

In later chapters, we'll cover more personality qualities of the chronologically gifted in greater detail, including the need for meaningful relationships and physical activity that naturally draw you in. At this point, the key observation is how all of this represents the behavior of people who are living with a strong sense of purpose. They reflect a drive to achieve particular goals that will inspire them to set new ones. After achieving those goals, they establish a new set. This cycle continues until eventually death overtakes them, usually much later than the world would have expected.

These individuals—the chronologically gifted—live with a healthy sense of restless discontent that prevents them from ever truly retiring from life. Drs. Friedman and Martin's research on the Terman study participants strongly suggests that, regardless of the health-related factors that contribute to one's cause of death, the likelihood of living a longer, more meaningful life derives from what we'll refer to as the Okinawan term, *Ikigai*. Remember, Okinawa is one of the Blue Zones.

In Japan, traditional cultural pressures dictate that individuals discover their *reason for getting up in the morning* early in life. This is what they mean by *Ikigai*, and the very fact that there exists such a specific term in their vocabulary is telling. It takes two or more English words to express the same idea, and even then it only captures one facet of the Japanese concept. These people take life's purpose very seriously. You're considered unhealthy if you get up in the morning and don't have a clear sense of the reason for which you got out of bed. This reason is usually connected to something far bigger than yourself. And you're not alone. Part of reason Sardinians live up to six years longer than average is the way their culture embraces the elderly and reveres their wisdom. It assigns their grandparents and great-grandparents important roles in the nurturing of young parents and raising grandchildren.[26]

In many parts of the world, retirement introduces great confusion about a person's life purpose, but not in Sardinia.

You'll recall that Sardinia, Italy, is also one of the Blue Zones. For people living in this part of the world, retirement is just transitioning from one vital role to another in the community. I believe that's an amazing perspective. I often talk with people about how invigorating it has been for me to become "bubbe" (Yiddish for "grandmother") to my own grandchildren. It has given my years since their birth a rather acute focus. In Jewish culture, grandparents have very specific roles to play in the lives of their grandchildren.[27]

If you want to live longer and better lives, you need to find creative ways to tap into this idea of an evolving and ongoing sense of life's purpose. This represents a conviction that we have something to get out of bed for at every stage in life, even if it's something different from one season to the next. Research shows that absence of *ikigai* has a measurable effect on mortality. One Japanese expert discusses how you see this especially with teachers and policemen in Japan. "Police and teachers have very clear senses of purpose and relatively high status. Once they retire, they lose both of those qualities and they tend to decline rapidly."[28]

Renowned gerontologist Robert Butler and his collaborators undertook a major longitudinal study in the 1960s. It was funded by the National Institutes of Health and followed the lives of highly functioning people between the ages of 65 and 92, over a period of 11 years. Among their discoveries was the recognition that "people who had some purpose, some reason to get up in the morning lived longer and better."[29] More recently, a 2008 cohort study in Japan found that those who did not find a sense of *ikigai* were "significantly associated with an increased risk of all-cause mortality."[30]

It's not hard to imagine how this plays out. People who have a clear sense of life purpose engineer their lives around the goal of fulfilling that resolve. Lack of it is a big obstacle, and the chronologically gifted recognize that they need to keep their bodies and minds in shape. For them, it's not just about physical or mental fitness, though. It's about personal identity and the role they plan in their communities.

Part of what makes the concept of *Ikigai* so powerful is the way it leaves ample room for personal fulfillment of one's life purpose to take different forms at different life stages. In youth, for instance, a person longing to protect and serve the vulnerable might enroll in the police academy and work a regular police beat. By middle age, he or she might be a supervising officer who does relatively little beat work, but who assists in the training of new cadets and applies his or her investigative expertise to coordinating other officers in the field. After retiring from the force, he or she might work with nonprofit organizations that intervene to keep at-risk youth off the streets and out of prisons.

Of course, many of us begin our careers and live much of our lives with little or no clear sense of our *Ikigai*. Often when you hear people talk about their mid-life crises, what they're really describing is a poor alignment of their present life trajectory with the *Ikigai* they're only vaguely coming to appreciate within themselves. The chronologically gifted recognize and get excited about the fact that, as their life circumstances change, their *Ikigai* also may change. Life purpose is not a stagnant concept. Discovering it should be a joyful process at any age.

A REASON TO GET UP IN

So, what makes YOU want to get up in the morning?

The upshot of the scientific explanation is so simple and so profoundly intuitive that most of us are in danger of minimizing or ignoring it altogether. What you must always remember is: A clear sense of life purpose adds good years to your life. Write that down, and put it where you'll see it daily. It's that important. That's why we're spending an entire chapter on this topic.

Notice that I didn't say a clear sense of life purpose will necessarily make you live a long time. It will certainly help, but that's not the point. We'd all like to live to age 100 and beyond, and then suddenly die in our sleep having had the time of our lives right up until the end. But that's just not the biological reality for all of us. What is, however, is pursuing the goal we talked about in the previous chapter—to avoid or delay the onset of disability as long as possible so you can enjoy the pursuit of meaningful activities well into your last years, dying healthy and content. You don't hear this a lot in our culture, but old age doesn't automatically mean disability, and dying healthy is actually a very reasonable and highly achievable personal goal. For the chronologically gifted, death is just another part of life, and whether it comes at 65 or at 123 (my personal goal) is irrelevant. What matters is that every single year of life before that point is a "good" year. Only those with a clear sense of their ikigai know what represents a "good" year.

So it's time for a heart check. Do you know what your sense of life purpose is? Are you like the Okinawans or Sardinians? Are you able to answer that question even without thinking about it? Or does it make you scratch your head in bewilderment?

If it does, don't worry. You're not alone. Many of us give far too little consideration to life purpose. We operate on automatic. We just get up, go to work, pay the bills, eat meals and enjoy entertainment along the way. Then, we go to bed at night and do it all again the next day. Our culture doesn't train us (or resource us) to think critically about what we're hardwired to do best in our communities. It just expects us to figure it out and go to work. To do this successfully, let's talk about four key questions you can ask yourself in order to discover your own personal *Ikigai.*

1. *What are you good at doing?*

    Think hard about this. What comes more easily to you than others you know? Are you better at working with your hands or with your mind? Perhaps, you're naturally gifted at working with people, or you have an intuitive ability to lead and inspire others. Maybe you're good with numbers, organized to a fault, and tend to recognize errors more immediately than others. These insights help reveal your *Ikigai.*

    These are important questions because what we do well is not always what we enjoy doing—at least not yet. If you don't believe me, just ask some of the most passionate athletes. Many will tell you that they never thought they'd be so interested in cycling or running. Once they discovered they were good at those activities, it tapped into a new well of interest and enjoyment.

Likewise, many of us become stuck in dead-end careers that may seem outwardly enjoyable. They may even come with the financial rewards and benefits that sustain our idea of what constitutes an enjoyable life. But, they don't engage the parts of our personalities that thrive on doing what we do best. A brilliant scientist might make an excellent accountant, but that doesn't necessarily mean that his abilities are being put to the best use. This likely means diminished enjoyment of the work he does for a living—even if he goes to work every day completely unaware that something else would make him happier.

And that brings us to our next question.

2. *What can you be paid to do?*

Let's face it. We have bills to pay. Life isn't cheap, so we have to be engaged in activities that are remunerative for the better part of our lives. Even after our most productive years are behind us, many of us will still need to find part-time jobs to supplement our reduced income. But in asking this question, there's a more important factor than paying the bills. By determining what we could be paid for, we're also discovering which of our skills and which aspects of our personality the world values most.

Answering this question means considering everything you've done up to this point in life. What jobs have you held in the past? What transferable skills did you acquire as a result? How could those skills be leveraged in other fields that might be more exciting than those you've worked in before? What new employable skills do you think you could acquire reasonably if you worked at a different job, began a start-up company, or engaged in some other type of business adventure?

Even if you're no longer in the workforce, it's helpful to ask questions like these regarding your daily activities—even if they're not for pay. Could you help save charitable organizations money, for instance, by volunteering your services in some tangible form? Could you mentor a young professional in a particular career trajectory? Again, it's not about whether you actually make money from such endeavors. It's about what value you have to offer the community. Knowing your value to others is a vital component of life purpose.

3. *What does the world need from you?*

When you look around, do you see opportunities where your skills might make life a little easier for others? Do you see places where you could naturally "plug in" and contribute to something larger than yourself? Are there unmet needs in your community over which you would like to take ownership? What about the next generation? Are you doing your part to develop young lives and prepare them for the realities of life? Such questions invite us to look beyond our own interests and to see ourselves as citizens of a larger community with a role to play in lives other than our own.

Considering what the world needs from us is not supposed to be an occasion for feeling undue obligation to perform. It's not so much about "pulling your weight" as "greasing the wheels." I'm not asking you to think about these ideas because you need to be working on something for the benefit of others. I'm asking you to think about them because people who move forward every day with a clear sense of how and why the world needs them, stay active longer, draw more enjoyment from the work they do, feel more valued by others around them, and (you guessed it) live longer and more fulfilled lives as a result.

4. *What do you love to do or what would you love to do?*

This is where the rubber meets the road for longevity. Feeling a sense of personal fulfillment as we engage in the activities where we spend the majority of our time is as close to a "fountain of youth" as we're likely to find in this world. A great sage among my Jewish ancestors once observed, "There is nothing better, than that a man should rejoice in his works; for that is his portion."[31] In other words, for better or worse, the span of time we're given is ours to enjoy. Let's do what brings us enjoyment, not what makes us go home feeling unrewarded, unappreciated, and tired of getting up in the morning to repeat it all.

This question is important for people who are already working. That's because many get comfortable in their daily routines without even realizing that a subtle kind of discontent has settled into the background. People might ask us if we're happy, and we'd probably say yes. But if we were a little more penetrating in our introspection, we'd have to admit that there are other pursuits we would prefer working toward. We'd have to realize the work we do may come easily for us now that we've been doing it awhile, but it doesn't really bring us a lot of satisfaction. It's like running laps on the track: great exercise, but it's not really getting you anyplace you want to go. However, if you enjoy walking or running with friends at the local track, think of it as an excellent source of exercise and social connection!

Once you've considered these questions thoughtfully, you're prepared to begin assessing how well your current lifestyle aligns with what you may have been born to do. Here are four concepts that can help you digest your answers:

- *Professional* describes the intersection of what you're good at doing and what you can get paid to do. Basically, it's what makes a job interview go well for you. You have certain skills, and the marketplace sees enough value in them to offer you a job. That's why we say someone is a professional when they get paid for something they do. It means they not only do it well, they do it well enough that others are willing to express value for their work in concrete terms of dollars and cents.

   A key observation here: being a professional is only a starting point. It can never wholly describe a person's *ikigai*.

- *Vocation* describes the intersection of what you're paid to do and what you sense the world needs from you. Sometimes it's the same as what you're good at doing, but that's not always the case. Often a clear sense of vocation is what compels people to go back to school for specialized training. Rather than being motivated by money, they want to apply their skills to something they sense they're called to do in the world. Pastors and nurses, firefighters and military personnel, teachers and mental health professionals—these are the people who choose a vocation not necessarily for what it pays but rather because they sense it's their place in the world to meet particular needs.

The same observation applies here. Although a strong sense of vocation gets us much closer to *ikigai* than being a professional does, it's not an adequate substitute.

• *Mission* describes the intersection of what you think the world needs from you and what you love to do. It's that point where you sense what the world's calling is for you and, at the same time, will bring you tremendous fulfillment. While you might choose it for yourself, it's also something the world needs.

A mission can be the same as your vocation, and it can be something you get paid to do, but neither of these is necessarily the case. In fact, some people love doing what might be unrelated to either what they're good at or what the world pays them to do. People who volunteer in the community often do so out of a sense of mission. For instance, an accountant might spend his weekends working with troubled youth at his church. Or, an artist might be a leader for her local scout troop. Such activities have little if any bearing on the professional or vocational work these people do, but they're critical to their sense of identity.

Nevertheless, mission is still not the same as *Ikigai*.

* *Passion* describes the intersection of what you love to do and what you're good at doing, which brings us full circle. We say someone is passionate about something that they are good at doing because they love doing it. It could be a raw talent—like music or art—that is cultivated through disciplined practice for the pure love of creative expression. Or it could be a skill acquired entirely because of a desire to do something, like the ability to defend oneself and others from harm (the passion of the martial artist).

    Discovering your inner passion is vital if you want to understand your *Ikigai*, but passion alone won't do it.

I hope you're starting to get the picture. *Ikigai* isn't about any of these qualities in isolation or even in combinations of two or three. It's about all four working in tandem:

Profession + Vocation + Mission + Passion = *Ikigai*

Let me articulate that for you. Your *Ikigai* is the four-way intersection of what you are good at doing, what you could probably get paid to do (even if you don't), what you sense the world needs from you, and what you truly love to do. It's the professional vocation you choose that becomes your passionate personal mission (even if you're never paid to do it).

So there you have it. That's the secret of *Ikigai* that keeps Sardinians and Okinawans plugged into their communities and stubbornly refusing to give up well into their 90s at a rate five times that of most of us in the U.S. It's important for us to realize that *Ikigai* transcends the concepts of passion, vocation and mission. So much of the self-help literature and countless radio and television's guests talk about one or more of these, but rarely do they speak of all four working together in the highly integrated sense. They only have part of the picture right.

Some people believe that the two most dangerous years of your life are the day you're born because of infant mortality risks and the day you retire, assuming you do. The latter is because retirement is largely an illusion. You never really stop working. You just have to ask yourself difficult questions about where to go and what to do with yourself in a new leg of your life's ongoing journey. I think it's a mistake to make retirement a goal for our lives. Too often people reach that coveted day only to realize that the work they did for much of their lives is only vaguely connected with their sense of life purpose (assuming they even have one). That's why I suggest eliminating the myth of retirement from your consciousness.

The quest to be chronologically gifted begins with discovering and articulating your *Ikigai* as early in life as possible. In that way, it can be the engine of longevity that carries you into the many good years still ahead of you.

Let's get to work!

Discovering a sense of life purpose necessitates honest introspection about the future. It requires you to get up out of your daily grind and look hard at whether what you're spending most of your time doing is contributing to the kind of future you most want. "If you don't have long-term goals," warns psychologist Art Markman, "you run the risk of doing lots of little things every day—cleaning the house, sending emails, catching up on TV—without ever making a contribution to your future. That can leave you feeling restless and unfulfilled."[32]

People who never take the time to discover their personal *ikigai* (or who never take deliberate steps toward actualizing it) are in danger of mindlessly drifting toward (and through) their later years of life in a relatively meaningless and purposeless existence. Before learning some practical ideas to help you build a more fulfilling lifestyle, you need to explore some ways you can tap into your inner survivalist—the part of you that wants to "keep on keeping on" so you can have more opportunities to do what you want to do.

Suggestion #1: Revisit a favorite memory.

Schedule some time this coming week to be deliberately, selfishly introspective. Selfish is good. Let your mind revert to a time—recently or from an earlier season in your life—when you felt especially happy. Live in the moment and experience the memory at a deep, sensory level. Remember not only *what* happened, but also the circumstances—the sights, the smells, and the tastes. Focus on the part you played in creating the circumstances of your happiness.

Now, in this state of immersive memory, begin asking yourself questions. What is it that you're happiest about? What could you do today to reclaim a piece of that happiness? Are you doing something that brings special joy to your life in this memory? What would it look like to do that today? Are there people you associate with this happy memory who are still a part of your life? If so, what could you do to strengthen those relationships? If not, what could you do to kindle new relationships of that kind?

The point of this exercise is to take a mindful ride down memory lane. Most of us can remember a time in our lives when we were generally happier than we are today—at least in some facet. It can be fruitful for us to explore these memories to determine whether the happiness we think we were experiencing in the past is accurate. The goal is not to dwell on the circumstances of the past or present but instead to think critically about the extent to which we still have control or influence over those conditions.

But circumstances are only a small aspect of this exercise. The most important part involves an attempt to discover the real source of our happiness in these memories. For many, the source of happiness is proximity to and intimate relationships with family members. For others, it may involve doing something they rarely get to do now, since it's not a part of their work life. For still others, it may involve a time before a particular conflict or obstacle prevented them from enjoying the intimacy of personal relationships with certain people in their lives.

Don't take any action on these memories just yet. Let them simmer for a while. Journal about what seems especially significant, and make it a point to revisit your journal entries two or three weeks later. Let these observations fuel new explorations. The areas of passion that emerge as you traverse "memory lane" are often good starting points for exploring and discovering your *ikigai*.

Suggestion #2: Find an activity that gives you an outlet or "release" from the stresses of everyday life.

There is a psychological phenomenon called "flow" that describes a Zen-like, total immersion in an activity. While in a state of "flow," people experience a peculiar sense of freedom, enjoyment, fulfillment, and skill as they go about their work.[33] As long as they're engaged in this particular activity, it's easy for them to forget about temporal concerns and to open themselves to the "big picture." They become so absorbed in what they're doing that they can only focus on the task in front of them. Nothing else seems to matter.

Everyone has some kind of activity that enables them to experience "flow." I've known people who describe fishing in these terms. I've met others who talk about reading and writing this way—like "falling down the rabbit hole" and wondering where they'll end up. Still others experience this kind of immersion in cooking or yard work or Zumba classes. It doesn't really matter what the activity is. What matters is that while you're engaged in it, all the other potentially stressing concerns seem to take a backseat. It's the closest you can come to "zoning out" from life.

Chronologically gifted people cultivate hobbies and side pursuits that capitalize on their personal sense of "flow." Those are their coping mechanisms for the longevity-diminishing effects of stress in their lives. They use these activities as a self-imposed retreat, available to them as often as they desire—a way of getting back to basics and letting their minds re-center and find oasis in the midst of all kinds of challenges and concerns. So this month, make it a point to pay special attention to the activities that you sink into most easily. They should be activities that you feel especially skilled at, during which time your mind is occupied with thoughts of little more than accomplishing the task at hand—and accomplishing it well.

One of the most obvious signs that you're having a "flow" moment is when you suddenly look up at the clock and realize you've been working on something for hours and hardly noticed the time passing. Or someone summons you away from the activity and your heart aches a little because you really wanted to keep going. Or you find yourself eagerly willing to compromise other options you like equally well in order to carve out time for the activity (e.g., exercise done at the gym) at hand.

Once you get a handle on which activities help you "zone out," make it a point to incorporate them more regularly into your weekly routines. Instead of mindlessly carrying out these tasks, try deliberately relaxing into them. Cultivate a sense of joyous anticipation of the "selfish" time you'll spend doing them. Make it your goal to emerge feeling more relaxed than you were when you began. Chronologically gifted people treasure their "flow" moments, and they know how to draw energy from them to sustain their active participation in an otherwise challenged life.

Suggestion #3: Get some perspective on your per-sonality traits.

Most people have very subjective opinions of them-selves. That is, they see themselves through the lens of their own experiences—not others' impressions. Even when people have a certain amount of candid self-awareness, they often lack the ability to truly and objectively assess the activities that they're hardwired to do best. This is where an outside perspective can really help develop a more well-rounded picture of oneself.

There are a number of routes you can take to get started. My suggestion is to begin with a couple of free personality inventories.[34] Among many accomplishments, the psychologist, Carl Jung, is famous for proposing the theory that people experience the world according to four basic functions: sensation, intuition, feeling, and thinking. One of the better-known applications of Jung's typology theory is the Myers-Briggs Personality Inventory. This is an introspective questionnaire designed to generate a four-letter code that describes an individual's personality type according to the Jungian typology scheme (see Appendix). Without getting overly technical here, let's just say that it can describe in relatively broad terms the way introversion and extroversion play out in how people experience and interact with the world. It uses these factors to offer a basic personality description, much the way a professional psychologist would report on his or her observations of a patient in a traditional counseling office.

By modern scientific standards, the Myers-Briggs Inventory is considered imperfect, but it's still a popular starting point for discovering the personality type you fit into. Most online assessments that you'll discover are in some form based upon this personality theory, and many employers like to use it as part of their pre-screening of job candidates. It helps them get a better portrait of a person's suitability for a particular role in their organizations.

Another more rigorous personality inventory relies on something called "five-factor" analysis.[35] It describes how people interact with the world in terms of their: 1) openness to experience (curious vs. cautious); 2) conscientiousness (organized vs. careless); 3) extroversion (outgoing vs. solitary); 4) agreeableness (compassionate vs. detached); and 5) neuroticism (nervous vs. confident). It can be helpful to compare the descriptions that this assessment generates against the Myers-Briggs typology. Some people relate better to one over the other.

No matter which combination of inventories you use, the goal should be to start thinking more introspectively about what you're naturally attracted to in life and to understand better why certain things turn you off. Even more importantly, these assessments provide you with the knowledge and discovery of what makes you want to get up in the morning. They can suggest the type of life that's worth preserving for the years you have left. For instance, highly analytical, introverted people won't thrive by taking others' well-intentioned but misguided advice to get out more often in large crowds. They do better finding new subjects to research in private, connecting with special interest groups that share their level of interest and passion for particular subjects.

By the same token, highly extroverted people with strong leadership skills wither in isolated living environments that deprive them of opportunities to meet new people, spearhead new initiatives, and restructure the world around them. With the dizzying array of self-help advice for those who want to live longer (and I include this book among them), it's good to have a personality compass. It will point you toward those suggestions that are most likely to yield fruit in your pursuit of new activities and circumstances for your personal Blue Zone.

For those with the means to do so, it may even be helpful to get in touch with a professional life coach. Such individuals have special gifts for discerning and articulating others' passions and helping them discover resources for tapping into those passions in new, meaningful ways. Unfortunately, life coaching is a poorly regulated and increasingly trendy business opportunity that attracts some charlatans. They sell people on hopeless ideals and "get happy quick" schemes. Don't be fooled.

A legitimate life coach may not have the same credentials as a clinical counselor or psychologist, but neither does a good life coach take a one-size-fits-all approach to other people's affairs. Responsible practitioners use evidence-based methods and spend a lot of time getting to know their clients before trying to make suggestions for their future. They demonstrate willingness to challenge, rather than feed, the answers they want to hear.[36] They protect them from their self-destructive or self-obstructive tendencies, but they do so in a way that inspires them to reach their full potential—not someone else's.

BE GIFTED – Volunteer for a good cause.

Buettner (the Blue Zone expert) has observed that voluntarism, or the social obligation to charitably serve one another for the good of the community, plays a very important role in Adventist culture. This is one of the engines that drives the purposeful life characteristic of residents in the Loma Linda Blue Zone. It helps stave off depression and gives the older members of the community a sense of meaningful contribution well after their most productive labor years. Crowley & Lodge concur:

Altruism is a biological need. You will feel good about yourself if you give back, and you will pay a biological price if you don't. You are wired for it, to give when you don't need to, so the tribe grows and flourishes...and so it is there for you when you need it.[37]

In Jewish culture, we believe in tikun olam, or making the world a better place for others. We consider it a noble duty to take up the cause of others, to do our part—however small—in making the world a little better for our families, communities, and the world at large. I often say that apathy is the worst of human traits. We are our brothers' and sisters' keepers! We're all citizens of the world, more alike than different. All of us have a role to play in making this world a little more habitable and friendly for our neighbors and for the next generation. We all have gifts and talents. If we thoughtfully put them to use, we could alleviate suffering or improve opportunities for others.

Have you ever done something that you knew beyond the shadow of a doubt made a difference in someone else's life? If so, it probably made you feel proud. If not, you're missing out on one of the greatest natural highs that life has to offer. And so here's the challenge for those who want to be chronologically gifted: look for some way to plug in to an organization or get involved with an activity that is truly improves the lives of others. Make it your goal to find some way to align your gifts and passions in order to make a difference.

The ideal effort is one that puts you alongside like-minded individuals in a socially nourishing setting. In this way, you have an opportunity to do good for the world and to build and cultivate new friendships. Volunteering doesn't need to involve something elaborate. It might be as simple as meeting weekly with a quilting group at the local church or synagogue to bond with others over the creation of beautiful works of art that will be donated to local charities or sold in a fundraiser for a benevolent cause.

Or it could be something as elaborate and formal as getting involved with a local fraternal organization, the Chamber of Commerce, or even a national charity. A good way to get started is to think about the causes that you're really passionate about—the issues that you care about most deeply, what you would do just for the love of doing it, or causes you would advocate purely from personal conviction. Give no thought to any reward other than the satisfaction of accomplishing what you set out to do. Chances are, if you look hard enough, you'll find either a local or national organization already involved in precisely that kind of work. You only need to find out when and how you can participate.

I don't want to suggest any specific path because chronologically gifted people are open to many opportunities in their desire to give back. Some lean toward their own age group, while others are eager to serve their parents' or children's generation. Some need to see the outcome in concrete ways, while others are content to do unseen background activities that empower others to be in the forefront. What matters is that you appreciate the life-enhancing and longevity-promoting benefits of making a difference in others' lives.

At the same time, be proactive and don't wait around for someone else to suggest something you could be doing. Instead, go out and actively look for opportunities to make the world a better place for others. Nothing wards off the negative effects of senescence quite like discovering a way to do something you care deeply about for the benefit of someone else.

The bottom line

The modern picture of the typical senior's life is troublesome. We condition ourselves to think that sometime within the first twenty years after this phase we call "retirement"—assuming we choose to retire at all—we'll settle into a blessedly quiet life. Typically, it consists of little more than getting up early in the morning, eating three meals, maybe visiting with some friends or running a few errands, and then settling back in to watch a favorite show or two before calling it a night at 8:00 p.m.

In contrast to the high-demand, fast-pace, and stressful nature of the modern work culture, such a portrait initially sounds heavenly. But given a few months of this kind of mundane existence, the soul begins to long for something more, for fresh adventures and new avenues of personal growth and fulfillment. If we don't heed this survival instinct—this summons to discover a reason for getting up in the morning—then our bodies begin to concede to the reality of nature. We're just taking up space, and it's time to move on.

Don't let that be you. Before proceeding to the other exercises in this book, do yourself a favor by being deliberately introspective about what makes you want to live longer in the first place. Spend a few days mulling the question over because fear of death isn't the reason chronologically gifted people are determined to live longer and better.

Maybe you won't have perfect clarity right away. That's okay. Take your time. As you continue reading, revisit this question often: How does this choice make me want to get up every morning?

Personal Journal Pages

I have, I am, and I will choose new and old ways to promote feelings of self-worth and live life with passion and purpose:

_____

_____

_____

_____

_____

_____

_____

_____

_____

_____

_____

_____

_____

_____

_____

_____

_____

- 3 -

First Things First

By now, you've probably guessed that at some point we're going to have to talk about the nuts and bolts of a healthy lifestyle if we're going to be successful in prolonging our years. After all, there's a good reason why so many books on healthy aging focus almost exclusively on this aspect of getting older. As Dr. Edward Creagan of the Mayo Clinic asserts, "For the most part, how quickly or slowly you age is influenced by how well you take care of yourself throughout your life. Changes commonly attributed to aging are actually due to inactivity, smoking, an unhealthy diet and other lifestyle choices."[38] Or, to put it another way, how long and how well you live are, in many ways, reflections of how healthy you've been for most of your life. Chronically unhealthy people tend to die younger than those who take care of themselves. To most of us, that sounds obvious.

Yet, we indulge ourselves in life-shortening activities and consume toxic substances year after year as though we're immortal and expect no consequences from such behavior. Worse, the younger you are now, the more likely it is that you're thinking very little about how the choices you make today will affect the quality of your life many years from now. This has to change if you want to become chronologically gifted. People determined to live well into their 90s or 100s understand the processes that contribute to aging, and so they take their health very seriously—right now, before it begins to fail.

The choices we make each and every day and the lifestyle habits we engage in on a routine basis make a tangible difference in how long we may live and what our quality of life will be as we age. It's never too late to start making positive changes in our lives. The younger we are when we decide to be proactive about such decisions, the more positive impact our efforts will have. Similarly, the more likely it is that we'll stick with our improved lifestyle habits for the long haul. Far too many people wait until they're already feeling the effects of their age to begin thinking about what they need to do about it. And that's a grave mistake—literally!

In this chapter, I will paint a portrait of the kind of healthy lifestyle that characterizes the chronologically gifted. We're going to look at the way healthy aging is largely a matter of common-sense that will carry us into our later years. This awareness enables us to delay the onset of age-related illness, eliminate premature risks to our independence and mobility, and draw greater satisfaction from the activities we pursue. This will not be a detail-laden discussion of the "perfect" fitness regime and the "optimum" diet plan. (If you're interested in those subjects, there are countless books that elaborate on them.) What we're pursuing in this chapter is one simple goal: getting our priorities straight with respect to how we take care of our bodies. It's not the first concept we need to talk about in becoming chronologically gifted, which is why it's not the first chapter in this book. It is, however, the solid foundation upon which all of the other concepts we'll address must be built. So it's still a matter of putting first things first.

When you begin taking your physical health more seriously, you begin feeling better in a very palpable way. Simply put, your body is able to function better, and that frees up valuable physical resources for other activities. And when you feel better, you naturally want to do more to actualize your dreams.

Getting started is often the hardest part. It's surprising, but a great many of us have only the vaguest idea of what it truly takes to live healthfully. What's more, many of our instincts are likely to be misguided as a result of our popular culture's fixation with athletic body types, all-or-nothing fitness programs, easy-fix dietary schemes, and overly reductionist lifestyle mantras like "you are what you eat." In this chapter, we're going to stick to the basics—to those steps that anyone can take right now to begin feeling better about themselves and to take better care of their bodies.

Before we get started, I want to offer a word of caution. Especially among older audiences, it can be tremendously disheartening for those who haven't taken the best care of themselves to realize that they've potentially sabotaged themselves as a result of their decisions from their younger days. For instance, heavy smokers—even those who quit years ago—often find that the lingering effects haunt them well after they've kicked the habit. They may find it harder to sustain physical activity and resist the early onset of lung disease. What's more, often those who suffer from chronic diseases and physical maladies, over which they have limited control, focus too heavily on the personal fitness side of the equation. As a result, they may feel like slowing the effects of aging is a near-Herculean endeavor, and concepts like this can be more demoralizing than inspiring.

We want to avoid that pitfall at all costs. The goal of living a longer and more fulfilled life is not something we're going to actively pursue if it seems like far too much work with a minimal chance for success. So, readers, no matter what your current age or state of physical health may be—whether you're in your early twenties and fit-as-a-fiddle or rounding sixty and struggling with multiple chronic maladies—I encourage you to hear me out on this point: *no matter how positive you do (or don't) feel about yourself right now, it's never too late to start feeling better.* The only realization we need to arrive at in this chapter is the decision that our bodies are worth caring for. They're worth it because they're the vehicles that will propel us forward in the years to come. That's why we need them to last a long time to keep up with all that we have planned for them!

Two simple concepts

First, we need to eliminate the psychological baggage our society attaches to diet and exercise. We have a serious problem when we associate a moral value with our physical fitness, often equating being physically unfit with laziness and gluttony. We all have bad habits, and we can work to change them. But right from the beginning, we have to disengage ourselves from guilt as a motivation for making positive lifestyle changes. Even when the net effect is otherwise the same, the simple fact is: it's harder to sustain a lifestyle motivated by bad feelings than it is to sustain one motivated by hope and determination. So let's make a deal. From here on out, let's agree that getting healthier isn't a matter of making up for bad habits. It's a matter of training ourselves to achieve our personal lifestyle goals. At the risk of oversimplification, I'd like to suggest that the healthful lifestyle of the chronologically gifted is characterized by two basic principles: *Get moving. Stay fueled.*

That's it! People who want to live longer, healthier lives simply find ways to keep active and eat well. (No surprises there.) But there's more to it than just exercise and diet. Notice the order of the principles—exercise comes before diet. There's a very specific reason for that—one that often gets too little emphasis in the "how to" health manuals on the market today. Here it is: *the healthful lifestyle you're most likely to sustain is the one that enables you to get up and do what you most like to do.*

Exercising purely for the sake of fitness is very difficult to sustain as a lifestyle habit. Even well-intentioned people who genuinely care about their health and well-being get started on an exercise regimen only for it to peter out a few weeks or months later. Inevitably they will find it a little harder after each failure to start over again. They're guided too much by the thought, "I need to do this because it's what healthy people do."

That's an unhelpful mindset. Ironically, the people who exercise the hardest and most regularly can be those who think the least about their physical health—except inasmuch as it contributes to their progress toward a meaningful fitness goal. This could be completing a half-marathon, enjoying a long hike, or obtaining self-confidence through rigorous self-defense classes. These are the people who exercise hard and love every minute of it, precisely because they're not focused on exercise for its own sake. They're focused on an activity that just happens to include exercise along the way. It's worth noting here that one of the many benefits of exercise is the way it increases oxygen flow to the brain. This boosts energy and helps explain the natural high so many athletes experience from their demanding physical activity. Exercise makes our bodies feel alive in a way that few other activities do.

The same is true when it comes to how we eat. Too many people focus on negative diet plans that deny them the food they crave. They convince themselves that the key to eating better is gaining control over their ability to refrain from "bad" foods and to fill up on "good" foods. A moral approach to eating just doesn't work because it operates from a place of deprivation rather than a platform of empowerment.

You'll find that people who eat well tend to have a different, longer-range perspective when it comes to their eating habits. They aim to fuel their bodies for movement and the activities they most like to do. Healthy eaters don't deny themselves an extra helping of dessert because it's bad for them. They do it because they don't want to feel sluggish when they go for their morning jog. They don't eat a healthy assortment of fruits and vegetables because they're supposed to. They do it because they've found that such foods help them go a few extra rounds in Tae-kwon-do. Over time, they've trained their bodies to crave—yes, truly crave—the health-promoting foods that fuel their participation in an active lifestyle. Eventually they don't sense they are denying themselves anything.

In other words, people who are chronologically gifted are more active than their peers, and they tend to eat better, too. This is not just because they're stronger-willed or more stubbornly disciplined than others. It's because they've adopted a lifestyle that keeps them moving well into their later years. It's a routine they've become passionate about, and one that motivates them to stay physically fit. Also, they have learned to adjust their dietary habits to accommodate their bodies' enhanced demand for nutritious energy. That's why, whenever I talk to people about making a meaningful lifestyle change, I begin with exercise and then move on to diet. I'm cautious about using the words "exercise" and "diet" because in our culture they come with negative connotations. It's more instructive simply to think in terms of *getting moving and staying fueled.*

So let's get started.

Get moving!

There's an organic connection between longevity and exercise. That is, people live demonstrably longer in environments where they spend much of their time moving, engaging in mild to moderate physical activity for a significant portion of each day. Consider that in Sardinia, where the rocky terrain is the foundation for a thriving shepherding profession, many residents walk five miles or more every day as they perform their daily work routines. As a result of this regular, low-intensity but moderately challenging physical activity, Sardinian shepherds realize the cardiovascular benefits of aerobic exercise and the coordination-enhancing benefits of muscle-building treks through uneven terrain.[39]

In other words, the Sardinian lifestyle tends to promote healthy longevity by developing physical attributes, like balance and cardiovascular fitness that preserve bodies in old age when regular events like falls and heart disease are the leading causes of debilitation. And it does so by keeping Sardinians moving for much of their lives—not in some contrived gym-like setting, but in the organic context of everyday work and play.

What's more, the physical activity that Sardinians engage in is not nearly as demanding on their bodies as the high-intensity exercise that Westerners usually associate with associate with staying fit. As in so many cases, we overcompensate for our sedentary inclinations by engaging in hyperactive exercise regimens. Yet we wouldn't need that much activity if our lifestyles were more active to begin with! Sardinians don't ask more of their bodies than their lifestyles demand. They simply live a lifestyle that asks more of their bodies than ours do.

There's a lesson for us in this. The kind of exercise that is most likely to sustain us into old age is not the sweaty hyper-workout regimen of an Olympic athlete or Tour de France cyclist. It's the regular, low-intensity activity of getting up and moving around in the course of everyday life. Unfortunately, we live in a world that seems almost systematically opposed to this kind of lifestyle. We live in a day when many of the most lucrative career options and leisurely pastimes—including my writing of this book—demand many hours at a time spent seated in front of an electronic screen.

Far from the five-mile-a-day hike that shepherding requires, today's busy working mom will likely spend up to two hours daily seated behind the wheel of a car. Then add another four to six hours sitting in front of an electronic screen, straining eyes and wrists, but otherwise moving very little. At the end of a stressful workday, she'll be tempted—even conditioned—to recline for another hour or two in front of yet another electronic screen instead of taking a leisurely stroll or bike ride.

Our bodies aren't designed for this sort of protracted inactivity. Although we've become accustomed to ignoring or even suppressing it, there is a basic part of our physiology that craves and thrives on regular movement. Our bodies long to get up and move around. Activity helps us to sleep more restfully. It increases our circulation, which stimulates brain function and helps ward off age-related maladies like dementia and Alzheimer's disease. It even boosts our sexuality. After all, people who feel good tend to feel sexy!

When it comes to staying active, there's another obstacle to consider. Culturally, we're programmed to think that intensity is what counts, and that running a marathon is more impressive than walking half a mile several times a week. But experts disagree, at least when it comes to longevity. "Nature's rule is simple," experts Crowley & Lodge remark. "Do something real every day. [...] Whether the exercise is long, slow and steady [...] or shorter and more intense [...] is a lot less important than the 'dailyness' of it."[40] One of the fundamental keys to becoming chronologically gifted, therefore, lies in committing to a more active daily lifestyle—one that routinely involves walking, climbing, pushing and pulling, bending and twisting, jumping, and lifting—but not necessarily one that will put undue strain on our physiology.

The good news is that the more we program our bodies to expect steady, low-level activity throughout life (and the earlier in life we begin, the better), the less our bodies tend to fail us as we get older. Our brains become engaged at the subconscious level, sending out messages that stimulate the sustenance of muscle tone and bone density. All of this is in response to an evolutionary cue that the very body these bones and muscles are supporting cannot survive if it's allowed (or forced) to stop moving for very long.

Moreover, it has been abundantly well-demonstrated how low-intensity exercise can powerfully impact the brain, mitigating and sometimes even reversing the effects of certain contributors to the aging process. Athletic biographer, Bruce Grierson, offers one of the best summaries I've found on this topic:

> Exercise is a wonderful paradox, in the sense that it's both a stressor [...] and a stress reliever—maybe the best one known. It grows the hippocampus—the brain region that senses stress and reacts to it, marshaling a stress response. So quite apart from producing happy

neurochemistry that bleeds off stress in the short run, exercise renovates the part of the brain that actually manages stress. [...] Exercise buys us a chance at long life by lowering the risk of a variety of ailments—heart disease chief among them. It can reverse the effects of a genetic bad hand—by, for instance, switching off genes that predispose you to obesity. It seems to slow aging through such measures as promoting the growth of stem cells and even lengthening telomeres. That doesn't mean the lifelong exerciser has a hope of reaching 125. But it does mean that he or she is just younger, every step of the way, than someone who doesn't exercise. [...] Exercise just makes every good habit you have more potent.[41]

Grierson ought to know. He spent years profiling the life of the famous Canadian nonagenarian track-and-field star, Olga Kotelko, an amazing woman who earned hundreds of gold medals and was breaking world records well into her 90s. Kotelko passed away in 2014, only months before her 95th birthday. Writers have observed that a number of her accolades were owed at least partially to lack of competition in Kotelko's age group. Far from diminishing her accomplishments, however, this serves to remind us that she was making a name for herself. It wasn't so much for being the fastest or strongest—though she did break records for her age group in those races too—but merely by being a participant in activities from which her peers had long since retired. Her story, more than anyone's, ought to encourage us to consider physical activity as anything but a young person's game.

Our bodies are wired to reinforce healthful exercise habits. We just have to get them moving. "Don't think of it as exercise," Crowley & Lodge suggest. "Think of it as telling your body to get stronger, more limber, functionally younger, in the only language your body understands."[42] Give our bodies a chance, and our brains, muscles and bones will remind us how good it feels to be in shape!

So let's talk about some practical considerations. It's important that we understand that not all physical activity works the same way for our bodies. There are several kinds of exercise, and a balanced lifestyle includes a little of each:

- Endurance activities increase cardiovascular function by raising the heart rate and improving the body's capacity for processing oxygen. Important in staving off heart disease, they also promote weight loss by burning excess calories and forcing the body to regulate its temperature under adverse circumstances. (That's one of the reasons you sometimes hear people say that you have to sweat to make exercise count. Unless you're sweating, your body isn't burning a lot of calories to maintain its internal homeostasis. Nevertheless, this is one of those exercise one-liners we need to avoid memorizing, precisely because aerobic and endurance exercise is only one small part of a healthfully active lifestyle.)

- Strength-training activities (or other forms of resistance) work against the effect of gravity, stimulating muscle growth and improving bone density. Your body is engineered to accommodate the routine demands placed on it, which is why athletes have larger and more toned muscles. They use them more and have to deal with higher levels of routine resistance than others. Strength-training exercises are important throughout life. Also, they are helpful for those who want to combat the effects of osteoporosis and muscle atrophy that are common in old age. They improve overall resistance to the wear and tear of an active lifestyle, too, which makes it easier for us to sustain and recover from injuries and illnesses.

- **Balance and flexibility activities help improve coordination and agility.** This is important in our younger years because it helps us avoid premature death from accidents. Also, it is tremendously important in our later years because it helps us avoid falls—a major problem for the elderly and one of the fastest tickets to immobility and compromised independence.

Many activities encompass more than one type of exercise. For instance, walking is both an aerobic and strength-training activity because it raises the heart rate to accommodate the pace of movement, while also requiring the legs to support the body against the downward pull of gravity. Turn that walk into a hike across variable terrain, and you have added balance and coordination to the mix as well. (You see what I mean? We often think of walking as being a passive form of exercise, but it's actually one of the most well-rounded activities we can do on a daily basis.) Yoga and Tai-Chi are simultaneously weight-training and coordination-building activities because they require practitioners to support their body weight in multiple poses that stretch muscles and train reflexes. Add the adverse condition of doing yoga or Pilates in a heated room—a common preference among serious practitioners—and you have an endurance component. Increased heat forces the body to self-regulate and cool itself in a manner not all that different from when it's being forced to walk at a brisk pace for several minutes at a time.

For those who are feeling more adventurous, neurologist, Daniel Amen, recommends activities that incorporate both coordination and aerobic activity, like dancing and tennis. "The aerobic activity spawns new brain cells," he explains, "while the coordination moves strengthen the connections between those new cells so your brain can recruit them for other purposes, such as thinking, learning, and remembering."[43]

Remember what we talked about earlier? The activities you're most likely to do regularly—and regularly is the most important word here—are the activities that you already enjoy doing or always wanted to learn. I've met people who have an insatiable passion to run, and they are caught up in their identity as a runner. I've met others for whom outdoor gardening, which requires a lot more physical activity than most would imagine, is more than a hobby—it's practically a religious experience. I know individuals who are avid cyclists, but not so much for the exercise as for the thrill of the ride and the sense of freedom it gives them. In my case, I attribute my high energy level and passion for life to my five times per week workouts at my local gym. Some people get stressed out just stepping inside a gym, so what works for one person isn't necessarily going to work for another. What really matters most is for people to become comfortable in their own skin and remain committed participants in an active lifestyle of their own making.

If I can do it, then so can you. All it takes is the will to get started. Go ahead! I'm with you all the way!

Stay fueled!

Many of us have an unhealthy relationship with food. I'm not just talking about those with clinical eating disorders, which are a serious problem in our country. And simply resolving to eat more healthfully will not overcome them. Eating disorders manifest outwardly as physical problems, but they are actually serious psychological maladies that should be treated with counseling and ongoing group support. Attempting to self-regulate an eating disorder is unwise. If you suspect that you have a chronic problem with overeating, an unusual preoccupation with weight loss, or an uncontrollable urge to "binge and purge," seek professional advice before proceeding with any of the suggestions in this book. Because we unconsciously imbibe a host of false cultural messages about the significance of food in our lives—whether, when, and how to enjoy it (or not to enjoy it)—we forget that food is essentially meant to fuel our bodies for activity. Here are just a few of the messages I'm talking about:

- *Food as entertainment.*

  Eating is an enjoyable activity, and rightly so. One of life's many gifts is the ability to enjoy the basic physical pleasure of good food. But too much of anything edible is not wise. We push the limit and turn eating into a form of entertainment—a diversionary activity to alleviate boredom and enhance good times. The fact that we have options like concession stands in movie theaters and ballparks is evidence of how closely we associate food with having fun. This wouldn't be so harmful if it weren't for our tendency to get the messaging backwards. We begin to think that eating can stimulate good times, and so we eat when we're not really hungry.

Also, we eat food more for the stimulation of flavor than for the nutritional content it offers. Worse, we begin to worry that without food and drink, we won't be able to have as much fun. Without quite realizing what's happening, we move from a place of associating food with entertainment to a place where food has become entertainment. And that's an important distinction. There's no harm in enjoying the act of eating. There is, however, tremendous harm in confusing the purpose of eating with the purpose of other diversionary activities like going to the movies.

- *Food as a social mechanism.*

    In nearly all cultures, food is linked inextricably to the social bonds that human beings enjoy with one another. In most cases, these are important traditions. Sharing a meal is one of the most intimate activities in which we can engage. In welcoming others to our table, we invite them to experience kinship with us as living creatures in need of nourishment. Whatever differences we might otherwise bring to the table, eating together can become an occasion for strengthening relationships on the basis of what we have in common. Yet, many of us have a penchant for perverting this daily routine into something destructive.

Over time, we tend to assign food a significance that goes beyond its mere association with social occasions. It's a subtle but very real problem, and perhaps a few examples would be helpful. Have you ever felt "guilted" into having dessert because you didn't want to disappoint a friend who had baked something special for the occasion? Or have you felt compelled to finish your entire portion for fear of insulting the cook at a meal? Or maybe you secretly eat less in front of others, but binge in private because you don't want to be thought of as a glutton. It's not that it's wrong for us to associate enjoying a special dessert with a memorable social occasion, nor is it problematic that we eat more or less at any particular meal. It's when the food itself comes with social strings attached that it becomes an issue. Eating can be an occasion for relationship-building, but it shouldn't add social baggage to our lives. When you think about it, you'll realize that many of your choices about where, when, and what you eat are motivated less by nutritional preferences than they are by social considerations.

• *Food as a coping mechanism.*

So many of our food cravings are not as they seem. They're emotional cravings. We snack between meals in response to boredom, stress, and life calamities that have nothing to do with genuine hunger. Keep in mind that there are only four basic emotions—happiness, sadness, anger, and fear—and three of them are unpleasant. We look for ways to mitigate these unpleasant feelings. Because of the immediate pleasure we associate with certain kinds of food (especially junk food), we often turn to them for a dose of emotional satisfaction. More insidiously, we come to associate pleasant feelings with the experience of eating certain meals.

There's a good reason why restaurants that are known for large servings of high-carb dishes, like chicken fried steak and mashed potatoes, call their fare "comfort food." Such dishes are linked in many people's minds with home cooking, of being full and satisfied, as well as being loved and cared for. Likewise, there's a good reason why so many restaurants have appetizer and drink specials during a "happy hour" that usually takes place when people are leaving work. They like to reward themselves with refreshments such as beer and nachos (or in my case a mango margarita) for putting in a hard day at the office. Don't misunderstand what I'm saying, though. There's nothing inherently wrong with associating food with good feelings. It simply becomes a problem when we begin to think of food—especially the unhealthful food choices—as the provider of those feelings.

- *Food obsession.*

Sometimes we go too far in the other direction. In our fear of having unhealthy eating habits, we become "health nuts" who fixate on particular kinds of food as though we're navigating a well-disguised minefield of potentially deadly options. We let our dieting habits become more than a simple preoccupation. They become an obsession. This is the seductive lure of fad diets. It's easier for us to focus on following a list of what to eat and what not to eat than it is for us to make our own well-reasoned decisions about what our bodies need.

As with the other disordered thinking patterns we've been discussing, there's an important distinction here. It's good to be mindful of our eating habits. Often, this is the first step in making positive changes in our nutritional decisions. But there's a world of difference between mindfulness and obsession. People who are mindful tend to savor their food, while ironically, people who obsess over their food enjoy it less. Both tend to be in better physical shape, but food-obsessed people get less intrinsic reward for all their hard work. Food is not meant to be eaten without attention, but neither is it meant to become an all-important facet of our lifestyle.

If you're noticing how all these considerations tend to overlap, then you're well on your way to understanding the basic problem. When it comes to food and nutrition, we bring a whole lot of baggage to the table. Our instincts about what, when, where, and how to eat are being dictated to us by people who don't necessarily have our longevity in mind.

If you're going to become chronologically gifted, you're going to have to get back to basics. *Food is fuel for our bodies, not for our souls.* Got that? It doesn't matter that there's supposedly such a thing as "soul food." Having a healthy relationship with food means putting it back where it belongs: as the engine of activity that allows us to incorporate the "get moving" lifestyle we talked about earlier. The people who live the longest like to eat, but they've come to crave the foods that their bodies need to stay active. I'm not talking about taking all the fun out of eating. I'm suggesting you forgo the illusory, temporary pleasure of chronically bad eating habits in order to embrace a wholesale approach to nutrition that will energizes you for long-term lifestyle fulfillment.

The word "chronic" is key. Periodically indulging in our favorite junk foods is a very different issue than making it a mindless daily habit. I've been known to eat a lot of dark chocolate or a whole bag of honey mustard pretzels in one sitting. And you know what? I don't feel guilty about that. It's part of seizing the moment—once in a while. As long as it's the exception rather than the rule, the occasional planned binge is one of life's sweetest gifts to enjoy.

Having said that, I want to emphasize a few basic guidelines for healthy eating that you would do well to take to heart. I'm not talking about a diet plan. Rather, it's basic nutritional biology—a subject that (let's face it) most of us remember little about from school. What follows isn't a laundry list of food options. There are many books by more reputable authors than I who can point out the kinds of foods that make the most sense for you. At the same time, here are guiding principles for making healthful food choices so that your body stays more consistently fueled for the active centenarian lifestyle you're preparing to enjoy.

- *There are no "quick fixes" for weight management.*

  One of the most seductive messages we hear in main-stream media is the promise that losing or managing weight will be easy and simple, and results will follow with little or no major effort on our part. This is simply a lie, and it's not just a lie about the hard work that dietary change entails. It's a lie about the way that our nutritional habits relate to lifestyle choices. Essentially, the world wants us to believe that it's possible to go on living an unhealthful, nutritionally reckless lifestyle while suffering few or none of the adverse health effects that go along with it.

  Don't be fooled. I'm going to tell you the truth. *Good nutrition takes discipline and hard work.* It isn't easy because it's not just about what you do or don't eat. It is about how you live and how you train your brain to think about the way you eat in response to social and environmental cues. It takes determination, commit-ment, practice, and time. Yes, time. It takes a long time.

  Okay, that's the bad news. Ready for the good news? Here it is: *good nutrition also has a way of reinforcing itself over time.* That's right! As we repeatedly make different lifestyle choices that result in more healthful eating, our bodies re-calibrate themselves and begin saying, in effect, "Yes! This is what I need. Give me more, please." With enough time, the self-discipline requires less conscious attention because the benefits of good nutrition begin to diminish the appeal of poor nutritional choices.

Here's a simple example of what I'm talking about. Most of us over-season our food and use excessive condiments. In doing so, we have unwittingly lost any distinct sense of what the food we eat actually tastes like by itself. If we were to eat unseasoned food, we would find it bland and unsavory. That's not the way it should be. Seasoning ought to merely complement and enhance the natural flavors already present in food. When we get to the point that we forget what food tastes like in its most natural form, something about our enjoyment at mealtimes is diminished rather than enhanced by these condiments.

People who choose to limit their intake of additives like salt and sugar often report how, after a period of several months, their tolerance for these substances changes. Suddenly, for instance, a soda seems too sweet—so sweet that it compels us to take smaller sips and experience deeper enjoyment between sips. More importantly, one soda seems like plenty for one sitting—no refills necessary. And rather than being the complement to a meal, soda seems more like an appropriate dessert or leisurely beverage to be savored for a special occasion. Notice the lifestyle and attitudinal changes that such biochemistry entails. Soda has assumed a dramatically different place, almost of its own accord. The combination of overall reduction of sugar intake and enhanced enjoyment of the calories consumed tend to naturally reinforce the new lifestyle habits of moderation.

So hang in there. If it seems like a difficult adjustment at first, remind yourself that your body will compensate for the hard work by delivering new, healthful cravings over time. A huge part of nutritional adjustment is undoing the biochemical lies we've told our bodies by feeding them junk for so long. But deep down, our bodies know what they need—and that's what they want, too.

- *Eat mindfully.*

  This is the single most important piece of dietary advice you'll ever hear. Whether you're trying to lose weight or simply feel more energetic as a result of the calories you consume, deliberately pay more attention to the nutrients you're putting in your body. "We gain weight insidiously," observes one expert, "not stuffing ourselves, but eating a little bit too much each day—mindlessly."[44] If you think you're not guilty of mindless eating, there's an easy way to find out. Start keeping a food journal for a few weeks. Be ruthlessly honest with yourself. Note every single item you put in your mouth every day. After a few days of brutal self-examination, you may find that you're already motivated to make some changes to your eating habits.

  Mindfulness simply means paying attention to something. It doesn't mean obsessing over it, but it does mean being thoughtful about the choices you make and giving consideration to the reasons you're eating something. It means deliberating over your food options and then savoring the choices you make for all they're worth. Have you ever finished a package of cookies or chips and suddenly realized that you hardly even tasted them because you were distracted by something else at the time—something like a TV program or a sporting event? This is exactly what I mean by mindless eating. It is imbibing in calories without a clear sense of need and drawing relatively little enjoyment from it. Also, it might include doing so as an accompaniment to another activity that wasn't enhanced by the consumption of those calories in the first place.

Now let's consider an alternative. Instead of grabbing a bag of chips while watching TV, turn off the TV during a commercial break and sit at your kitchen table with a handful of the same chips. You eat one, slowly, savoring the crunchy texture and salty-spicy flavor. You pause between bites, reflecting on memories the taste conjures up, relationships that you associate with enjoying this particular snack. After a few moments, you take another bite, and you reflect a little more. After five or six bites, you begin to realize that you're reaching a saturation point in your enjoyment. As a result, finish the chip in your hand, put the rest away, and resume watching TV. You will find that you're more focused on program now than you were before.

That's mindful eating. It's choosing to make eating an activity worthy of attention and deliberate enjoyment. Notice that merely taking the time to savor something can enhance its enjoyment, so much that you actually crave it less. Remember the occasional planned binge we discussed earlier? These are opportunities for deeply savoring your favorite foods, precisely because they involve rich flavors that arise less frequently in the eating habits of the chronologically gifted. So be sure to enjoy them for all they're worth. As long as you're going to indulge yourself, why not make the most of it? Occasionally, truly mindful indulgence is a celebration of life!

- *Pacing is key.*

   This advice goes hand-in-hand with the previous one: take your time when you eat. "No matter what you heard from your parents as a child," Creagan explains, "you don't have to finish all the food on your plate. Eat slowly, savor every bite and stop when you're full. It takes time for your stomach and the processes of digestion to signal to your brain that you're full."[45]

   Creagan also warns about how easily we under-estimate the number of servings we habitually consume each day. "Unfortunately, the eye can be deceiving. Most people habitually, and unintentionally,... consume more calories than they think, and they can't understand why they're gaining weight, or not losing any."[46] Excess calories from any source, he stresses, will contribute to weight gain—and that includes excess calories from supposedly "healthy" or low-fat alternatives to junk foods."[47] It also includes excess calories from overeating even otherwise healthful foods like organic peanut butter and whole wheat bread. In other words, part of good nutrition is training ourselves to let our bodies eat until they're full and no more.

This is one of the areas where conscientious eaters will notice one of the most rewarding self-reinforcing qualities of healthful nutrition. The first few weeks of cutting back on portion sizes will be tough. Your body will want to scarf up as many calories as possible. (Have you ever caught yourself eating faster than you needed to because you didn't want to feel full before you were finished enjoying what you had on your plate?) That's because your body is accustomed to this kind of intake. As you discipline yourself to put your fork down between bites, take a drink of water, and have conversation with your dinner companions, you'll find that over the first few months your "fullness equilibrium" will reach a new homeostasis at a lower level than before. That is, you'll feel full sooner than you used to, and you'll be able to consume smaller portions without feeling like you want more. It's just a mindset. I'm working on mine. So can you.

The secret is training your eyes to match your nutritional needs. This is especially difficult when you're eating out frequently because restaurants want to deliver value. They know customers will pay more when they get larger portions. But the items restaurants fill the plate with are less healthful and include cheaper sides like potatoes and other starches. So if you feel like you have to finish your plate to get your money's worth, you're actually more likely to take in a significantly higher volume of unhealthy calories than you otherwise would. As a result, your body will begin craving larger volumes of food than it requires to stay active.

So here are two recommendations. First, cut back on eating out. Make your meals at home in order to gain the optimal level of control over what and how much you consume at each meal. And secondly, when you eat out, do yourself a favor and immediately set aside some of the food you're served to take home and enjoy later. Ask for a to-go box right after your food is served. Doing this early in the meal puts those extra calories out of sight and out of mind. When you finish, your eyes and stomach are satisfied that you've eaten enough, but not too much. My freezer is full of half-portions of food I've brought back from restaurants, which make me feel like I'm getting two meals for the price of one when I eat out!

Also, let's spend a little time talking about what it really means to savor our food. Savoring is more than just tasting the food. It's thoughtfully enjoying our food and really paying attention to the complexity of flavors, textures, colors, and sensations that go along with consuming our favorite foods. It's about relishing the memories those flavors kindle for us and allowing them to create new ones in the company of others. The opposite of savoring is what we're accustomed to doing. For example, eating "on the go," eating while doing mindless activities like watching TV or checking social media updates, eating behind the wheel (when we should really be focused on driving), or eating at work without taking a forma meal break. The more distracted we are at mealtimes—even when the distractions are otherwise enjoyable—the more unmemorable and ultimately unsavory our food becomes. The food just becomes a source of unnecessary and unhealthful calories.

So take your time when you eat. Eliminate the distractions. Savor your food. And over time, you'll find that *less* truly is *more* when it comes to good nutrition.

- *Drink more water.*

This is a simple step you can take no matter what the rest of your food intake looks like. A healthful, active lifestyle will make you very thirsty—and that's. People who drink a lot of water are continually flushing their bodies of toxins that would otherwise accumulate in their systems and slow them down. "Proper hydration is a very important rule of good nutrition," Dr. Amen says. "Even slight dehydration increases the body's stress hormones. When this happens, you get irritable, and you don't think as well. Over time, increased levels of stress hormones are associated with memory problems and obesity."[48]

The recommendations vary, but one common and very memorable guideline is called the "8 x 8 Rule:" the average adult should drink no fewer than eight 8-ounce glasses of water daily. That's an intake of about a half a gallon. Too much water can lead to health problems, but most of us are so chronically under-hydrated that we don't need to worry about ever reaching that limit. Besides, active people tend to use the water they take in more rapidly than sedentary people who simply drink water mechanically because someone told them they should.

Many people have no idea how much water they're actually drinking daily. I've found it helpful for these people to use visual cues. Take an empty half-gallon jug and fill it with water at the beginning of the day. Place in conspicuously where it will remind you of how much water you still need to consume before going to bed. You might be surprised how much is left at the end of the day. The first time I tried this, I had better than half the jug left, and yet I didn't feel thirsty. After a couple of days, I began disciplining myself to drink water instead of tea or juice when I was truly thirsty. Over time, I also came to better appreciate what a dramatic impact my physical activity had on my desire for water. The more active I was during the day, the more quickly I would consume that half-gallon of water—and still want more!

Most of us go about our lives mildly dehydrated all the time. We drink soda, tea, juice and coffee. As long as our thirst seems quenched at the time, we assume we're good to go. But we're not. We're carrying more weight and laboring with less energy than we should be. What we really need is just plain water to clean us out—and not just at those times when we're consciously experiencing thirst. Most of the beverages we enjoy with and between meals contain empty calories that we'd do better without, and some might contribute to dehydration. For example, caffeinated beverages are diuretics and therefore promote frequent urination that evacuates our bodies of water. On the whole, it's easier to drink mindless calories than it is to eat them. So, I find that a helpful rule of thumb is to drink a glass of water before you consume any other beverage. It's become a habit for me. What's interesting is how often I find that, after drinking the water, I no longer really even want whatever beverage I was reaching for instead.

Although this rule may not apply to you, others who are trying to lose weight need to consume a lot of water for a few important reasons. First, water is a great way to reduce cravings. It's a calorie-free belly-filler that can dramatically curb your appetite. One good way to determine if you're really hungry is to force yourself to drink a tall glass of water when you're tempted to snack between meals. Likewise, drinking a glass of water immediately before meals can help reduce your overall portion consumption, enabling you to feel full while eating less than you normally might. Over time, as you consume fewer calories at meals, your body learns to be satisfied sooner. Because water is evacuated relatively quickly from the body, it's a great filler to give you that immediate "I'm full" sensation without the long-term sluggishness that comes from overeating.

The second reason water helps with weight management has to do with the way cells retain water when they're dehydrated. Your body has a remarkable fluid regulation mechanism that causes excess water to be quickly eliminated in the form of urine, but when fluid intake is reduced, it tends to retain water. This allows the body to have a relatively constant fluid level, regardless of how much water is consumed. At the same time, gross irregularities in fluid intake can upset the balance of this mechanism and cause it to retain excess water. Most people who have poor eating habits and those who are chronically dehydrated likely suffer from diminished energy and an overall "blah" feeling that they're not even fully aware of until they begin drinking more water.

Retaining water makes you feel bloated and uncomfortable, but it's easy to cure: drink more water! As our bodies take in more fluids, they also flush more out along with the toxins those old fluids contain. A steady supply of fresh water helps many conscientious eaters drop five to ten pounds within the first few weeks. This is "water weight," and it provides a relatively immediate boost in energy, stimulating the positive hormones that make your body want to get moving again. And once you get moving, you're going to get thirsty.

- *Eat smaller meals, and eat more frequently.*

Our bodies go into survival mode when we consume empty calories. Though we eat until we're full—or overeat till we're past full—we tend to get hungry again sooner than we should. As Grierson observes, "Commercial voices drown out the body's own little voice asking for what it needs."[49] We eat more and more while giving our bodies less and less of what they need to thrive. Combine that vicious cycle with the dysfunctional eating patterns we talked about and you have a sure recipe for disaster.

One powerful way to combat this tendency is by eating smaller meals, spread out over more frequent intervals throughout the day. Consume less at each meal, but eat more frequently than you would normally. This method helps you discipline yourself to go lighter while making more healthful choices about the type of calories you eat. Because this type of eating introduces regularity and substance into our bodies' dietary expectations, it's like we're telling them, "It's okay. I know you need energy, and I'm making sure you're getting what you need. Don't panic." And so they don't. Instead of craving more food, they self-regulate to crave the nutrition that we're giving them and on the schedule we've chosen. Meanwhile, because what we're providing is a nutrient-rich supply of calories, our bodies are energized to do the work we're conditioning them to do.

Those two considerations—smaller portions that contain more "bang" for our calories, coupled with more consistent water intake throughout the day—encourage our bodies to get out of survival mode and to begin dropping the excess fat they're retaining. This is another one of those principles that seems counter-intuitive at first. We're accustomed to smaller portions when we want to lose weight, but the idea of eating more frequently seems contradictory to our goal.

When you think about it, Americans have some strange eating habits. They like to have their biggest meal of the day—and usually their "heaviest," too—only a few hours before bedtime. This routine floods their systems with calories right at the time when they are least likely to be active. Meanwhile, they tend to eat lunches "on the go," often at the expense of balanced nutrition, during the times of the day when they're most likely to need healthful calories. But, as we know, our bodies need a steady supply of nutrients throughout the day. Yet, arbitrarily, we limit ourselves to two or three relatively large meals at specific times, instead of letting our bodies' nutritional needs dictate when and what we eat. On this point it's worth noting that in many European countries, the main meal is served around 3:00 pm, at the peak of daily activity. It's something to think about when you're planning your own daily meal schedule.

Of course, if we're going to be eating smaller meals, we'll need to make sure that they pack a lot of punch. Instead of snacking on crackers or candy, we'll want to munch on apple slices or fresh granola. Instead of ordering a double cheeseburger for lunch, we'll choose to fill up on a turkey avocado salad. Keep in mind, making the adjustment to smaller, more frequent meals isn't easy at first. Your body is conditioned to crave what it's accustomed to receiving. So, when you have a small piece of fruit and a cup of yogurt in the morning instead of loading up on pancakes and sausage, you're inevitably going to feel under-satisfied. This will make you grumpy and eager to load up on unhealthy "fillers." If, however, you can resist that temptation for a short period, you'll find that your body will adjust. Over time, it will learn that the nutrient-rich calories contained in that fruit and yogurt energize your body longer than the pancakes and sausage do. Then, you will start craving the healthier foods in place of the less healthy ones.

In fact, I'd be willing to bet that after a few weeks of eating a heathier breakfast, you'll find that you couldn't even finish a stack of pancakes. You'll feel full sooner than expected with less food than you were accustomed to before. Or, if fruit and yogurt isn't your thing (it isn't mine), try other options like oatmeal, a slice of cheese, fresh fruit or whole grain toast. Experimentation and variety make all the difference, and that's one of the wonderful gifts our bodies provide. They tend to reinforce the good work we do to keep them healthy.

- *Variety and balance make a difference.*

"Because your body is a complex machine," Dr. Creagan observes, "it needs a variety of foods to operate at its best."[50] Unfortunately, most of us don't incorporate a healthful variety in our diets. We're creatures of habit, and so we choose the foods we like, and we stick with them. As a result, many of us don't even know what we're missing, and we're okay with that.

Not if I can help it! I'm here to inspire you because chronologically gifted individuals know that variety is the spice of life. It's not just a cliché when it comes to longevity-promoting nutrition. The more variety you put in your diet, the more interesting your meals will be. And the more interesting your meals are from week to week, the more you'll enjoy them. The more you enjoy your healthful meals, the more likely you are to continue exploring wholesome new foods as an alternative to junk foods and empty calories. And the more you explore new foods, the more variety you'll introduce into your diet over the long run—and so the cycle continues.

But variety alone isn't enough. We also need balance. Regrettably, most of us have only a vague idea of what it means to eat a balanced diet. We know we should eat from the four basic food groups, and we know we should eat more vegetables (of all shapes and colors) and fewer fats and sugars, but we don't necessarily know why.

While this isn't the place for an extensive discussion on nutritional science, the Mayo Clinic Healthy Weight Pyramid offers a comprehensive summary in a simple and visually powerful way. I strongly encourage you to review this resource[51] and to study it carefully. It organizes the various categories of food according to the concept of energy density—that is, the amount of energy (as expressed in calories) contained in one gram of food. Fruits and vegetables are at the bottom and are permitted in unlimited amounts. Next come your carbohydrates, like whole grain bread and pasta (4-8 daily servings), followed by protein and dairy products like fish, meat, eggs, tofu, milk, and cheese (3-7 daily servings). At the top of the pyramid are fats (3-5 daily servings) and sweets (up to 75 calories per day). Mayo Clinic Physician Dr. Creagan explains the diagram's logic as follows: *Foods high in energy density are at the top of the pyramid—you want to eat less of these. Those low in energy density are at the bottom of the pyramid— you want to eat more of these. Foods that are low in energy density are generally healthier, and you get a lot more food for the calories.*

When you look at the foods that appear at the top and bottom of the pyramid, it begins to make sense. Fruits and vegetables form the foundation of a balanced diet and should be consumed in relatively high proportion to other food groups like protein and dairy. That's because you can eat a whole lot of salad before you reach the level of energy saturation that you get from a single serving of meat or cheese. Or, to put it another way, you can fill up on vegetables like lettuce, celery, and cucumbers that contain a large amount of water and fiber to dilute their calories. That way, when you get up from the table, fully satisfied, you will have consumed fewer calories in a single sitting than if you filled up on calorie-rich foods like meat and cheese.

We already know foods like candy and ice cream are basically unhealthy, but it's not always so easy to pick out other energy-dense foods. Some so-called "health foods" are actually quite high in calories. They're just drawing their energy from more healthful sources, like nuts and dried fruit, instead of sugar and saturated fats. Nevertheless, consuming too much of an otherwise healthy, but energy-dense food like peanut butter, (near the top of the pyramid) will contribute to weight gain unless it is matched by a level of physical activity that demands that kind of energy. This is why you hear of athletes consuming energy-dense foods prior to major sporting events. They truly need the burst of energy to perform well under those circumstances, but they wouldn't consider it healthy to eat that way on a routine basis.

Less energy-dense foods like salad and steamed vegetables are the ones you want to fill up on at mealtimes. This is why it's a good idea to eat a side salad and drink a glass of water before a meal. You'll experience fullness sooner and consume less of the energy-dense main course. And later, if you're in the mood for dessert, substituting some fresh fruit for energy-dense sweets can help satisfy your sweet tooth at a far lower calorie intake.

So now that we've seen what a balanced diet looks like, we're in a better position to appreciate the kind of variety I was talking about earlier. Basically, you want to increase your dietary variety as you get lower on the pyramid, and limit your selections to a few occasional favorite indulgences as you get toward the top. Rather than becoming a cheesecake connoisseur, become a vegetable snob. Try foods like bok choy and leeks just for a change. Read up on recipes that incorporate ingredients such as purple cabbage and kale in place of more common vegetables like broccoli and cauliflower. Develop a taste for perfectly ripened fruits like papaya and nectarines, and pride yourself on knowing exactly when they're in season. Experiment with fresh mushrooms, or try substituting tofu for meat in your favorite dishes.

So there you have it: balance and variety. A healthy diet is a colorful one. Literally.

- *Sugar is not your friend.*

  Neurologist Daniel Amen is very adamant on this point. "Sugar increases inflammation in your body, increases erratic brain cell firing, and sends your blood sugar levels on a roller-coaster ride. Moreover, new research shows that sugar is addictive and can even be *more* addictive than cocaine."[52] I'm always a bit reluctant to talk about limiting sugar intake because there's simply no fun in taking people's desserts away from them. But that's not what I'm trying to do in this section. I'm simply trying to arm you with a powerful truth: *the less refined sugar you include in your diet, the longer your body's hardware will tolerate the increasing biological adversity that aging sometimes involves.* This is a serious problem. As research suggests, Americans, in particular, consume an almost ludicrous amount of sugar—the equivalent of three cans of cola daily.[53]

  I'll avoid getting too technical here, but the metabolism of sugar is a surprisingly complex process that wreaks havoc on your body's metabolism. Sugars (and other simple carbohydrates like wheat) are broken down into the molecule known as glucose. These cells absorb from the bloodstream after the pancreas triggers the release of a hormone called insulin. The inability to metabolize sugar properly is precisely what makes diabetics require insulin injections and careful monitoring of their blood-sugar levels throughout the day.

  Consistently high intake of sugar can overload the body's natural self-regulatory mechanisms, with obese individuals becoming especially susceptible to adult-onset diabetes. And here's the really interesting part. This sugar absorption process also causes tryptophan molecules to be converted to serotonin—what psychologists call the "happiness molecule." That's why, in low amounts, sugar can actually have a calming effect on the body, and it's part of why we crave sugar and other high-carbohydrate foods for comfort. Unfortunately, too much sugar can lead to a condition known as hypoglycemia—a "sugar low" caused by insulin being kicked into overdrive when the bloodstream is flooded with excess glucose molecules. Hypoglycemia leads to moderate to severe fatigue, and it has emotional overtones as well. Some report feeling sad or even chronically depressed as a result.

So a little sugar from time to time isn't bad. But on average, Americans don't usually consume only a *little* sugar. Most of us consume more than three times the recommended amount, which means that all of us can afford to severely reduce our sugar intake habits. Our bodies will thank us for it. Unfortunately, reducing sugar intake is not as simple as skipping dessert and avoiding junk food between meals. The next time you go grocery shopping, take a few moments to read the ingredients listed on some of your staple foods and condiments. You might be surprised to see sugar (or its common alternatives like high-fructose corn syrup) listed within the first several items (indicating a high amount relative to other ingredients). That means if you're serious about cutting back on sugar, you'll have to take the time to investigate what the less-obvious sources of sugar are in your diet. Condiments like ketchup and even some varieties of healthful foods like yogurt may have to be consumed in moderation.

Many of us will be tempted to turn to alternative sweeteners, but these should be used with caution. Almost without exception, the major artificial sweeteners like saccharin, aspartame, and sucralose have been linked with potentially serious health concerns (though the jury is still out on how serious these concerns are).[54] Rather than trying to simply replace full-sugar products with diet alternatives, it's better to cut back on sweets altogether—from any source—and to explore natural alternative sweeteners like stevia and local honey whenever possible. (I use stevia or honey with my breakfast coffee—very satisfying!)

Some experts suggest that, if you're already committed to limiting your sugar intake, it's actually easier on your body to simply let yourself have the occasional pure cane sugar treat than to consume a similar product loaded with artificial sweeteners. That's a win-win for you because you get the full flavor of the dessert you crave, and your body gets the benefit of reduced overall sugar intake.

Of course, the very best sources of sugar are found naturally in whole fruits. Whenever possible, reach for these in place of refined sugar. The more of natural sources of sugar we consume, the less our bodies crave the high-intensity sweetness of refined sugar. This makes it easier for us to have dessert items like cake and ice cream in smaller portions.

- *Purge the temptations.* It's easy to routinely and mindlessly snack on unhealthful foods when you keep them in plain sight and easy reach. For that simple reason, do yourself (and your sanity) a favor by choosing not to keep your favorite indulgences stocked in the pantry. Don't buy those empty calorie items at the store, and you won't have them available to mess with your head during the week! Fill your refrigerator and cabinets with whole grains, fresh fruits and vegetables, and energy-rich snacks. When you're truly hungry—and not just looking for food to alleviate boredom or stress—you'll find that your body will soon want to snack on the healthful foods with which you've surrounded yourself. Within a matter of weeks, you'll find that your cravings for the unhealthful foods you used to make a routine part of your shopping trips are diminishing.

You may find that it helps to plan your shopping trips more deliberately in advance. Instead of wandering the aisles at the grocery store, waiting to see what catches your eye, take some time at home to think through two or three specific meals you would like to prepare for yourself in the coming week. Then, jot down the ingredients you'll need. You don't need an exhaustive shopping list, but simply having a basic road map can help anchor you during a shopping trip by giving you something to guide your progress through the store with a more concrete goal in mind. This gives you the flexibility to take advantage of sales and in-store coupons while helping prevent unnecessary distractions on aisles that you don't need to go down—like the ones with chips, cookies, and candy. The principle here is simple: it's a lot easier to avoid temptation if you don't walk down those aisles.

One of the perks of deliberately leaving the indulgences out of your house is that when you have a strong urge to have a treat, you'll have to get out of the house to satisfy it. Just getting out of the house can build tremendous momentum toward doing something good for yourself, if you'll take advantage of those occasions. Meet a friend at a coffee shop for conversation over a latte, or take a jog in the park before stopping by the yogurt shop for a reward. By creating these lifestyle-reinforcing habits around your indulgences, you'll find it easier to pace yourself and savor them, preventing them from becoming mindless stumbling blocks along the road toward becoming chronologically gifted.

- *"Everything in moderation, including moderation."*[55]

Wiser words may have never been spoken. Moderation has long been recognized as one of the principal virtues of human existence. The ancient Greek temple to the god Apollo at Delphi bore an inscription to the same effect: "Nothing in excess." Or, as Aristotle (384-322 BC) is said to have put it, "It is better to rise from life as from a banquet—neither thirsty nor drunken." The idea here is that even good things can become problematic when used to excess, and even seemingly bad things can occasionally be all right. Wisdom comes as we learn to recognize the difference and learn to control our behavior before it gets out of hand.

I bring this up because the principle of moderation is a huge part of the chronologically gifted mindset, and one of its clearest applications is in our nutritional habits. Specifically, we do well to avoid eating anything in excess—especially those foods that have been proven to contribute to life-shortening ailments like cancer, diabetes, and heart disease. "There is something about humans that is inherently self-destructive, at least when it comes to eating," observes one expert. "The best diet is basically one of moderation."[56]

The reason we prefer the foods that tend to reduce our chances of living a longer, healthier life is that they taste good! Just reflect for a moment. We eat junk food because it brings us pleasure, but this is precisely the point where moderation becomes so important. Pleasure is one of those emotions that bends to a law of human nature called diminishing returns. In economics, this describes how the additional costs of a production input (like hiring an extra worker) are eventually no longer justified by the marginal outputs that the input generated. In other words, when the work you do isn't clearly linked to increased profitability, you can be sure your job will be on the chopping block before long— unless you happen to work for a company that doesn't manage its cost of sales well.

The application to psychology is a bit simpler, but no less important: *the more you experience something pleasurable, the less pleasure it seems to provide in each instance.* Take one bite of chocolate mousse, and it's delectable. Take a second bite, and it's almost just as good as the first. By the fifth or sixth bite, though, you're just piling on the calories. This is part of why addicts often explain their spiraling downward behavior in terms of needing more of whatever it is they're addicted to in order to get the same "fix" as they used to be able to achieve with less.

The truth of this observation tends to sink in the more you think about it. Why, for instance, do we expect to receive such large portions at mealtimes? Is it that we're really still hungry, or is it that we're enjoying the flavor and want to experience it more? If it's the latter, then we need to take more time to savor the food, not consume more of it. And that's the point I'm trying to make: so many of our unhealthy eating habits stem from chronic immoderation. We don't know when enough is enough. Or we have not yet sufficiently mastered our self-control to stop when we've reached the *enough is enough* point, and so we overdo it.

Ironically, when we're feeling motivated to correct our immoderate eating habits, we tend to swing to the opposite extreme. We try cutting sugar and flour out of our diets altogether. We make dessert a sin. We avoid some category of food with almost puritanical commitment, only to find that our choices demand unnecessarily rigid and ultimately unsustainable levels of self-control.

That's why I tell audiences that moderation itself must be done with moderation. Contrary to what some nutritionists will tell you about healthy aging, I'm inclined to endorse the occasional lapse from a rigid dietary plan. Even though I fully recognize that such actions can have deleterious effects when practiced in excess, I think "reward days" and occasional binges on sweet or salty treats are preferable to an obsessive attempt to constrain one's desire for junk food altogether.

Part of the joy of living is experiencing these genuine sources of pleasure. But remember, eating more of something unhealthy won't increase our ability to enjoy it. It will only multiply the negative consequences of consuming it. So we need wisdom to recognize our individual saturation points of pleasure, coupled with self-control to cut ourselves off once we've reached those points. It takes practice, but over time, our bodies will reward our efforts with lower, more easily achieved saturation points. It will take less of the unhealthful foods to bring us to the same place of pleasure.

As with so many challenges, it's a mindset—a decision to make and keep. YOU CAN DO IT!

Just avoid going to extremes. Don't be a health nut, but don't be careless about your health, either. Resist turning dessert into a sin, but also refrain from turning your good habits into a license to indulge in junk food all the time. And if you have an occasional, planned "binge day," it is empowering. But don't let that become an occasion for despair. You were in control! Get up the next day determined to pick up where you left off, and savor the memories of your indulgence for all they're worth. Let that experience be the fuel that propels you forward in your desire to eat more healthfully. Know that your self-control will make your next indulgence that much more memorable when the time comes.

And remember, your brain is your ally in this battle. Brain plasticity is such that, over time, new behaviors become the norm. They override old behaviors, because we are not bound by our past. We can change!

- *Incorporate a few age-defying super-foods.*

  Make no mistake. There are no miracle foods that will reverse the aging process or add years to your life. Sometimes, you'll hear these claims, but they're usually nothing more than overstating common nutritional facts. Nevertheless, there are a few proven foods that lend a much-needed helping hand for longevity. Incorporating these into your overall diet is a good idea because they help your body (at any age) better weather the trauma of getting older.

  1. *Goat's milk.* It provides 13% more calcium, 25% more Vitamin B6, 46% more Vitamin A, 134% more potassium, and three times the niacin of traditional cow's milk. Such ingredients help your body fight osteoporosis, increase cognitive ability, promote healthy vision and immune function, and increase energy conversion. Developing a taste for goat's milk may be a big contributor to the longevity of

people living in Blue Zones like Sardinia, Italy and Ikaria, Greece.

2. *Red wine.* Moderate consumption has been linked to a number of positive health benefits. Those include a reduced risk of heart disease as a result of the artery-scrubbing qualities of flavonoids contained in the wine and the overall calming effect (i.e., lower stress levels) associated with regular, moderate consumption. Also, red wine may help protect against certain cancers and slow the progress of memory loss later in life. Though the jury is still out on whether the long-term effects of alcohol outweigh its short-term benefits, all studies emphasize that moderation is the key. Immoderate alcohol consumption—drinking to the point of intoxication—is a dangerous health risk, not to be confused with the one-glass-a-day habit of the health-minded person.

3. *Fish.* This is an excellent source of protein that is also rich in omega-3 fatty acids, which have been solidly linked to increased cognitive function. Anchovies, cod, halibut, mackerel, salmon, sardines, scallops, shrimp, snapper, trout, and tuna are all excellent choices. According to Dr. Amen, a team of Danish researchers who studied the diets of 5,386 healthy older individuals, found that the more fish in a person's diet, the longer that person was able to maintain his or her memory and ward off the effects of dementia.[57] In other words, substituting fish as the major source of protein in two or three meals a week is a great brain-booster. You might

also supplement your routine food intake with a salmon oil supplement. But if you're one of those who just cannot tolerate the flavor of fish very well, don't worry. There are a number of other foods that are high in omega-3 fatty acids that also can be incorporated into your diet. These include broccoli, Brussels sprouts, cabbage, cauliflower, flaxseed, tofu, and walnuts.

4. *Soy products.* Researchers who study the Okinawan Blue Zone are linking real health benefits to a number of traditional Asian foods. One of these is soy. Consider experimenting with soy products like tofu and edamame to reap the benefits of lower LDL ("bad") cholesterol and reduced risk of heart disease.

5. *Turmeric.* Try incorporating this spice into some of your favorite recipes for an exotic flavor twist. This spice has long been used in ancient Chinese medicine because curcumin (the most active component of turmeric) has strong antioxidant properties and may help decrease brain plaque.

6. *Green tea.* Drink this tea from time to time. It has half the calories of coffee and cream, and Chinese researchers have found that two to three cups daily actually make DNA look younger under the microscope.[58]

7. *Nuts.* You can never go wrong snacking (in moderation) on nuts, which multiple studies suggest help significantly reduce the risk of heart disease.[59] Most nuts contain at least one of several health-promoting substances—like unsaturated fats (which

lower LDL cholesterol), fiber (which promotes fullness and reduces overall food intake), vitamin E (which counteracts the development of plaque in the arteries), and l-arginine (which helps improve artery flexibility and reduces the risk of blood clots). Walnuts are especially well-studied and known to be high in omega-3 fatty acids, but almonds, hazelnuts, pecans, cashews, and even peanuts (which are technically legumes rather than nuts) all have health benefits in their unsalted, raw forms. A handful of nuts makes a great snack, but keep in mind that nuts—and their corresponding nut butters—are also high in fat and calories. A tablespoon of peanut butter, for example, contains nearly 100 calories by itself, so be careful not to overdo it.

8. *Berries.* Some types have been shown to protect the brain from the effects of aging. Because they contain an antioxidant called anthocyanidin that can cross the blood-brain barrier, they benefit the portions of the brain responsible for memory and learning.[60] Blueberries are one of the best choices for this, but be sure to select organic varieties. They're one of the so-called "dirty dozen" fruits and vegetables known to be especially subject to industrial chemical contamination. The "dirty dozen" also include celery, peaches, strawberries, apples, nectarines, bell peppers, spinach, cherries, collard greens, kale, potatoes, and grapes. It's usually safer to pay a little extra for the organic varieties of these common foods, since the potentially detrimental

effects of pesticides and other contaminants may cancel out the health benefits of their increased consumption in your diet.

- *Consider the wisdom of the vegetarian lifestyle.*

  I've deliberately saved this point for last, because many readers will find this to be a step they're unwilling to take. That's okay. Not everyone needs to be a vegetarian. But it would be irresponsible for me to overlook this option just because it might not be right for everyone.

  "Protein is essential to human life," writes Dr. Creagan. "But despite what you may have heard, it's not necessary or even desirable to eat meat every day. Although rich in protein, many cuts of beef, pork, lamb, chicken and turkey are too high in saturated fat and cholesterol." Dr. Creagan recommends a number of alternatives to meat-based protein—choices like low-fat dairy products, seafood, and plant foods like beans, lentils and peas.[61]

  While he might not advocate strict vegetarianism, his wisdom lends credence to the observation that the health-promoting benefits of the vegetarian lifestyle practiced by many of the Adventists who reside in Loma Linda is a highly significant factor in their longevity. In fact, it's the only Blue Zone in the United States. There is talk that new Blue Zones are emerging in California. Researchers at Loma Linda University studied more than 70,000 Adventists who followed the church's nutritional counsel of a plant-based diet over a six-year period. Some participants were strict vegans (eating no animal products whatsoever), while others ate fish, eggs and dairy products, and still others even ate meat occasionally. According to the results of their study, those who followed strict vegetarian diets experienced 12 percent fewer deaths during the study period.[62] In other words, the less meat, the lower the risk of death in general. It's not hard to understand why: vegetarians still get their protein, but without the heart disease and other health risks that go along with eating meat.

There's an important caveat to this finding, though. For many Adventists—unlike for many of the rest of us—a vegetarian diet is part of a traditional religious upbringing. For them, it's part and parcel to life in the church, where healthiness is considered akin to godliness. So for those who have been raised to believe that adhering to a plant-based diet helps them honor their religious commitments, such a diet may be less of a sacrifice than it would be for people long accustomed to eating meat-based protein at every meal.

Whether to adopt a vegetarian lifestyle—in whole or in part—is a decision that readers will have to make for themselves. As a pescatarian, a person who avoids the consumption of any meat besides fish, I would simply say this: the evidence is there, and the vegetarian/pescatarian lifestyle can add years to your life. Personally, I eat salmon about three times a week. It's flavorful and fulfilling.

And even if you decide against vegetarianism, you owe it to yourself to limit your meat intake, remembering that the more meat-based proteins that you replace with fish and plant-based alternatives, the more your diet will cooperate with and reinforce your body's desire to live longer. And the longer you live, the more opportunities you'll have—if you're so inclined—to savor those indulgent occasions when you have meat or chicken with your salad instead of fish or tofu.

Whew! That's a lot of information to process at once. So don't try. Go back and read over these sections several times. Pick one dietary habit and work on it for a few weeks before trying to adopt another. If you try making a wholesale lifestyle change all at once, you're more likely to fail in the long-term than you are if you make smaller, incremental lifestyle changes over several months. Mindful eating is a process—a work in progress. Recognize that we're hardwired to hunger for the foods that in the past have given us the greatest satisfaction, even if it comes at the cost of healthful longevity. Take heart in the fact that, as we get moving more in our daily lives, the nutritional recommendations from this chapter gradually will become more intuitive, and our bodies will reinforce our commitments as we go along. A body that is actively in motion will quickly learn to crave the nutrients that keep it lean and fueled for daily activity.

Before we go on, here's a quick discussion of body image. If you follow these healthful eating recommendations and commit to a more active lifestyle, it's very likely that you will lose a substantial amount of weight in the process. You'll feel more energetic, and you'll feel sexier than ever before. But none of those choices are good reasons—by themselves—for making the kind of lifestyle adjustments I've shared. The desire to look good won't sustain your commitment, but the desire to live well should. People need to learn to accept their bodies as they are right now in order to appreciate the changes in their bodies once they get moving and stay fueled. Unfortunately, there are some for whom no amount of diet and exercise can cure unhappiness with their bodies.

Fringe benefits

Before we leave the topic of physical health, I'm going to mention some perks that often come with the get *moving, stay fueled* lifestyle concepts described in this chapter. One is better sleep. The other is better sex—at any age. Both are important to the chronologically gifted way of life, so let's talk about them.

An active lifestyle, coupled with good nutrition, tends to promote more healthful, regular sleep cycles. And that's important because, as Dr. Amen explains, "One of the fastest ways to age is by getting less than seven or eight hours of sleep at night." He cites research that shows how getting less than eight hours of sleep is associated with cognitive decline and chronic insomnia can triple your risk of death from all causes.[63]

It's hard for younger people to appreciate this, and our culture doesn't help. In an increasingly 24-hour society, where it's possible (and often expected) that we work and play late into the night, sleep begins to feel wasteful and we do whatever we can to minimize our dependence on it. When you're in your twenties and thirties, sometimes it's possible to get by on four hours of sleep and plenty of caffeine, but that doesn't mean it doesn't take its toll on your physiology. When you don't get enough sleep, the blood flow to the brain decreases, which means your brain functions less effectively afterward. Not that it's a good idea to sleep all day, either. But think hard about the physical cost of the all-nighters some pull on a routine basis. Each time you burn the midnight oil, for any reason, you spend a little of your longevity on that activity. That's okay, as long as it's an occasional indulgence—but it had better be worth it!

And now a discussion on sex. I already mentioned how a healthful lifestyle tends to promote a better self-image, because people who feel good about their bodies—and how they're taking care of them—tend to feel more confident in the bedroom, too. And that's essential because sex has been shown to be an excellent longevity-promoter. An average lovemaking session can burn about 200 calories (or the equivalent of running vigorously for 30 minutes). It causes the release of endorphins that reduce anxiety better than prescription antidepressants.

Some research suggests that regular sex boosts the immune system, and people who have frequent sex have been shown to eat better and exercise more regularly than those who don't. This makes intuitive sense. As you feel better about yourself, you tend to enjoy sex more. As you enjoy sex more, the activity makes you want to maintain the habits that make you feel good about yourself. And the cycle continues.

But what's even more important than all of these considerations is the fact that our bodies crave touch. We know that touch-deprived babies fail to develop normally, and this basic human necessity persists even as we age. Unfortunately, older people tend to enjoy fewer opportunities to give and receive the kind of intimate touch that they crave. This is regrettable because as Dr. Weil observes, "Many seniors say that the capacity for sexual pleasure increases with age, even if frequency and intensity of sexual activity do not."[64]

By learning in our younger years to really enjoy our sexuality for all its worth—that is, to experience the fulfillment of physical intimacy with our partners as we explore new expressions of love in the bedroom—we actually help our bodies set the stage for enjoying sex well into our golden years, too. The idea that seniors are disengaged sexually from their partners is nothing but a myth, and by learning to have better sex now, we're preparing to have better sex at any age. And we'll live longer to enjoy it as well.

That said, we need to remember that both sleep and sex are bedroom activities, and experts recommend keeping them that way. Too many of us turn our bedrooms into second offices, playrooms, or storage closets, and this interferes with our bodies' interpretation of cues. Sleep is an activity that doesn't combine well with other endeavors. You can't work and sleep at the same time, so don't try. Remove the stigma from falling asleep by making it an intentional effort and delaying it no longer than necessary. Instead of just watching TV until you're too tired to keep your eyes open, pick a stopping point for your day and head to the bedroom—the one place in your home where your body should associate consistently with sleep.

Be wary of insomnia. It's not helpful to go to bed and remain awake for hours before you fall asleep. It's okay to relax in anticipation of sleep, reading in bed, for example. If, however, after half an hour, you can't fall asleep, it's a good idea to get up and do something else in another room (preferably low-intensity, relaxing activities like assembling a puzzle or doing some late-night yoga). The goal is not to energize yourself but to coax your body into a state of sleep-readiness. Sometimes your body needs to be reminded of how tired it really is. Then, when you go back to bed, help your body get the signaling straight by keeping the room dark and quiet. No electronic screens allowed!

Let's get to work!

Have you ever watched a late-night TV infomercial advertising a special dietary supplement that claims to make you want to eat less? Or some expensive, gimmicky piece of exercise equipment that promises to give you results in a matter of weeks? These are brilliant marketing ploys because they appeal to everyone's negative self-images. They portray people who achieved unbelievable results by making one *simple* change in their lifestyles. (Never mind the "results not typical" disclaimer that flashes along the bottom of the screen, right?) When you're feeling especially motivated to make a change—particularly when those motivations stem from guilt and poor body image— you're especially susceptible to empty promises of quick solutions.

Don't be a victim. Remember one simple rule that consistently applies: *lifestyle change is hard*. But just because it's hard doesn't mean you can't do it. It simply means that each single step you take toward your goal will be that much more satisfying as you achieve it.

This has been a long chapter, with a lot of information to absorb. If you're feeling overwhelmed at this point, I would stress again: *don't try to get it all done at once!* Don't run out and buy a gym membership on impulse. Don't try to become a vegetarian or pescetarian overnight. Instead, think about very simple, concrete steps you can take right now to help you make incremental progress toward the long-term goal of enjoying a more healthful lifestyle. These suggestions can give you the necessary momentum to let your body take over and do the rest.

Suggestion #1: Keep a simple food journal.

An important first step in any lifestyle change is taking stock of where you are now. It all starts with an honest inventory of your lifestyle habits. Most of us have a very poor estimation of how unbalanced our diets are. A journal can help with this, but keep it simple. When you begin, you may think it's best to write down every single item you eat and then count the calories accordingly. But do it knowing that even the most disciplined people have a hard time sustaining that kind of willful effort. As a result, many will simply give up after missing a few days' worth of information. You'll do yourself a tremendous favor by sticking to the basics, which are:

- *What you ate (in general terms)*
- *Where you ate it (i.e., at home, at work, at a restaurant, etc.)*
- *When you ate it (i.e., morning, midday, late night, etc.)*

You'll probably find this exercise is easier if you make your journal entries as you eat or shortly thereafter. Then you won't forget about your choices earlier in the day or overlook little snacks between meals. Also, it will help you avoid thinking of this as end-of-the-day homework if you integrate it with mealtimes.

You won't want to record every single detail about the meals. Entries like "baked fish and mashed potatoes with canned fruit, home, early evening" or "apple slices with peanut butter, work, around 2:00 p.m." are sufficient. The goal is to have enough information to begin making substantial observations about your choices. Many people find it helpful to keep a small notebook handy throughout the day just for this purpose.

There are a number of viable smartphone apps that can help you with this process. My one reservation with digital apps for a basic food journal is the relative complexity of some of them. Browse the app stores for your Android or iOS phone and you'll find dozens of options. And, most of them are data-rich. In fact, they might distract you from becoming more mindful of your daily eating habits. What's important is developing a routine that what works for you. Pick a day of the week when you'll review what you've written over the past several days, and ask yourself questions like these:

- *How many fresh fruits and vegetables did I eat this week?*
- *What kind of protein sources have I consumed this week?*
- *What time of day do I intake the most calories?*
- *How much sugar did I consume this week?*
- *How many meals am I preparing for myself at home?*
- *How often am I eating out?*
- *How do I feel about the choices I've made this week?*
- *How has my energy level been?*
- *Have I been eating mindfully?*
- *What can I do next week to improve the overall balance of my eating?*

Of course, this is not an exhaustive list. It's just an example of the kind of self-reflection you'll want to engage in as you take stock of your eating habits. And the point of doing this several days after journal entries is that you will have a more objective perspective about your choices. Keeping a journal helps you become aware of how often you are eating out or how many sugar-loaded snacks you consume in a day. It's much easier to make incremental changes to your dietary habits based on conscious observations.

Notice—and this is important—that I'm not asking you to make any specific changes. How you process and respond to this information is entirely your decision. This chapter has armed you with information to make wise choices about the degree and scope of dietary changes that are right for your lifestyle. Remember, being chronologically gifted doesn't necessarily mean being a "health nut" in or out of the kitchen. It simply means being mindful and deliberate about what you put into your body. That way, you don't consume those foods inadvertently in a way that would shortcut your chance to living a longer and more energetic life.

Suggestion #2: Look for ways to increase your daily activity level incrementally.

No matter what your current level of physical activity is, chances are good that with just a few simple adjustments, you can significantly increase the work you're asking your body to do on a daily basis. These simple changes can amount to the equivalent (in terms of health benefits) of five to ten minutes' worth of vigorous exercise each day, so it's definitely worth exploring. Here are a few examples:

- *Drive only when necessary.*

  You probably drive to places you could just as easily reach by foot or bike, unless you live in a rural area. And even if you do live someplace where driving is necessary, there are steps you can take to minimize your dependence on your vehicle for getting around. For instance, instead of driving from store to store in a strip mall, consider parking in a more central location and walking the stores.

- *Take the long way.*

  People are accustomed to seeking the shortest path to their destinations to save time. It's just human nature to prefer the path of least resistance. But when you're trying to increase your activity level, look for opportunities to get more out of it. Instead of parking close to the front of the store, try parking near the back, which requires you to walk an extra 50 to 100 steps than you otherwise would not. Plan your grocery trip so that you walk from one side of the store to the other to get the items you need. If the place you're headed is near a greenbelt or hike-and-bike trail, consider parking a few blocks away from your destination, and walking or jogging along the path. Even if you are shopping for a few items, walking back to the car while carrying them adds upper body strength-conditioning to the mix!

If you're working on a particular health goal like losing weight, consider getting a pedometer or Fitbit™ and challenge yourself to increase steps your steps by five percent each week. A pedometer is a small, relatively inexpensive electronic device that is wearable, senses body motion, and tracks the number of steps you take. Many are surprisingly accurate. Also, there are smartphone apps that can emulate this function, though often with less accuracy than wearable devices. A Fitbit™ is a popular device worn on the wrist that pairs with other wireless devices to help you track biometric data like your heart rate, estimated calories burned, etc. Over time, it can be a helpful tool for tracking your overall activity level.

- *Take the stairs.*

  Climbing is good for building leg muscles and improving balance. This extra exertion helps burn calories. Avoid elevators when you have the option of stairs—it can make a big impact over time.

- *Turn passive activities into active ones.*

  Watching TV and reading a book can be relaxing, and that's okay. They should be. But we don't always have to be sitting for them, right? Who says we can't jog in place while watching a favorite show, or take a little stroll while we're chatting on the phone? For that matter, simply standing for these activities can burn extra calories without making them any more difficult. Be creative with this suggestion. When you're about to do something sedentary for a while, look for ways to keep moving while you're doing it. You might be surprised at what you discover.

Suggestion #3: Enlist the help of friends.

Research from the Blue Zones demonstrates consistently the power of community support in the longevity equation. We'll talk about this in detail in a later chapter, but for now simply know that people live longer and sustain healthier lives when they're in consistent, mutually beneficial relationships. You may already have some great friendships, or you may be one of the many people who could benefit from some deliberate and conscious friend-making activities.

Either way, the choice to engage in healthier lifestyle habits is an occasion for bonding with others who have similar interests. Find a walking or exercise group to join, and make some new friends while burning your calories. Or maybe you've decided to begin incorporating more whole foods into your diet. If you're not sure where to begin, online social media now offer many ways to connect with people who are eager to share their wisdom and experience, too. You need not even be in the same city to benefit from the habit-sustaining relationships that such friendships can engender over time.

Develop a list of your favorite activities and hobbies—the ones that are most likely to keep you moving if you had more opportunities to engage in them. Then do a little research at your library, community center, or popular community gathering places. Find groups that share your interests, and reach out to them. Go to a community yoga event or sign up for a 5K run-walk. One of the best ways to meet people who will help reinforce your healthy lifestyle commitments is to get out there and do what you love with people who are already doing them. Once you get to know a few, you'll find that positive peer pressure and a sense of belonging can be powerful motivators on the path toward living a longer and better life.

BE GIFTED – Try something new. You might like it.

We talked about this earlier, but it's worth repeating here: *the healthful lifestyle you're most likely to sustain is the one that enables you to get up and do what you most like to do.* Healthy eating and weight loss goals are much easier to achieve when they're set in the context of an active lifestyle—one that demands solid fuel for performance while bringing genuine joy and fulfillment. Unfortunately, too many of us wander through life never fully appreciating what we most like to do. Worse, we settle for our present activities and rarely make an effort to discover new ones. It's never too late to start. The older you get, however, the harder it gets to coax yourself out of your routine. So don't wait until you imagine that you'll have more time to do it than you do now. Now's the time! Today's the day!

The chronologically gifted are eager to try anything that might support their forward-looking lifestyle goals. As we come to the end of our discussion of healthy lifestyle habits, I challenge you to choose a new activity and give it your best effort. It should be something physical—something that requires you to get up and move around. Ideally it will be something that brings you out of your comfort zone and promotes new friendships (or strengthen existing ones).

Moreover, it should be something that requires a long-term commitment if it is to become a routine part of your life. The reward for making that decision will be the improvement of some skill or talent that's important to you. Taking a few self-defense classes, for instance, isn't just good exercise. It can help improve self-esteem and personal confidence. Learning to swing dance can help you meet fun new people to enjoy even off the dance floor. Or, taking up gardening might help you discover an untapped passion for the outdoors.

And, if you are one of my older readers, you have an advantage over your younger peers on this one. One of the perks of getting older is having less to lose by trying something new and everything to gain by discovering something that can help you live longer and better. For example, I belong to a local gym where, five times a week, I experience a natural high from participating in aerobic classes and weight training. I love the company of my peers there, and the level of energy I leave with at the end of each class is amazing!

How about you?

Zumba, anyone?

The bottom line

Chronologically gifted individuals live active, healthy lifestyles. It's that simple. But they don't do it in order to live longer. They just happen to live longer because they already have meaningful, healthy lifestyles. "The older you get, the healthier you've been," says Dr. Thomas Perls, founding director of The New England Centenarian Study. We've talked about how an active lifestyle, fueled by nutritious eating habits, is an important key to longevity. Also, we've learned how important it is to become mindful about our habits and to make incremental changes as we take ownership of particular areas of concern.

This chapter isn't about a sudden "shock and awe" adjustment to our lives. It's about getting serious with our minds and bodies because they're the only vehicles we have to carry us into our 100s—and beyond. And if we get serious now, before it's too late, we can change our personal forecasts for how we'll weather our later years. According to Crowley & Lodge, "If we had the will to do it, we could eliminate more than half of all disease in men and women over fifty. ... Instead, we have made these problems invisible by making them part of the 'normal' landscape of aging."[65] Whether young or old, chronologically gifted people refuse to be inert all the time. They simply have too much to see and do, and they're certainly not going to let preventable health challenges slow them down!

I consider myself chronologically gifted. Please join me on my journey—living long and living well, with purpose and passion to 100 and beyond. YOU CAN DO IT!

Personal Journal Pages

These are my lifestyle choices that promote longevity...like moving and staying fueled:

_____

_____

_____

_____

_____

_____

_____

_____

_____

_____

_____

_____

_____

_____

_____

_____

_____

_____

_____

_____

_____

_____

_____

_____

_____

_____

_____

_____

_____

_____

_____

_____

_____

– 4 –

Looking on the Bright Side

In many ways, optimism is the most important subject we're going to talk about in this book. If I had to ask readers to skim just one chapter, I would direct them to this one. If I could ask them to internalize just one principle from everything I have to say in this book, it would be the one I will emphasize here: *a positive attitude and a hopeful outlook are everything if you want to live well.*

Notice that I didn't say "...if you want to live longer." We've just talked about healthy lifestyle options that can improve the chances of becoming chronologically gifted, not than just living longer. In fact, I would argue that the chronologically gifted don't necessarily have to live a long time. They simply need to live *well* for as long as they can. And that means facing a certain harsh reality: even the healthiest person can drop dead from an undetected, asymptomatic brain aneurysm or get broadsided by a drunk driver. Life is full of risks and uncertainties, even for the ones determined to live the longest.

Most people know these truths, but not everybody reacts to them the same way. Some people dwell on such facts and feel hopeless, but others (like me), think that death gives meaning to life. The chronologically gifted don't fear death because they know that life is not infinite. The past is gone, and the future may never be, so we have to live in the moment—as if we'll live forever. So while some people live in the shadow of death, others live in the light of the present, determined to make the most of whatever time they have left. Which group would you rather be a part of?

Living well begins with a positive outlook on life. We addressed this in Chapter Two when we talked about the concept of *Ikigai*. But, even when you know what makes you want to get out of bed in the morning and feel highly motivated to take good care of yourself, you still need a certain set of basic, hopeful assumptions about how the world works. This is the only way you're going to consistently achieve your goals. These assumptions, often made at the subconscious level, will frame how you plan and pursue major life objectives. More importantly, they have a tremendous impact on how good you feel about your life from one moment to the next. Some outwardly successful people are profoundly miserable, while those who might seem stuck in a rut feel hopeful and energetic. It's the people in that second group who have a better shot at living to a ripe, old age.

In recent years, psychologists have begun addressing their patients' search for happiness and fulfillment using a novel approach. Instead of studying people who are depressed and chronically under-fulfilled and trying to determine what's wrong with them, increasingly counselors are studying those who are happy and fulfilled. This includes asking what it is about the second group and their outlook on life that makes them react differently to the same circumstances as the first group. Whereas psychologists have traditionally sought to understand why some people get depressed, now they're more interested in why others flourish. It's a movement known in professional circles as "positive psychology," and the initial findings are astounding.

It turns out that "looking on the bright side" is more than just a cliché. It truly can add years to your life and life to your years (which is also more than just a cliché). From this point forward, everything you do (or don't do) to better your overall health and prolong your years, as well as to discover a sense of meaningful purpose for your days, depends on whether you've conditioned yourself to see your glass as half empty or half full.

Actually, for some of us, it's even more dire than that. When you're living under the weight of tremendous life challenges, it's tempting to see the glass as almost completely empty. But the chronologically gifted know that when you find yourself crossing a seemingly endless desert, even a few drops of water can mean the difference between life and death. And so they savor every drop, dig a little deeper, and discover that they're able to keep going when others drop out. That's my philosophy, and I hope it can become yours too!

This chapter is about viewing our lives through a lens of gratitude and hopefulness—both now and in the future. But it's about more than just talking ourselves into adopting a happy state of mind. That kind of mental gymnastics is a fool's errand, sure to disappoint. We're not talking about an easy fix for people who have spent most of their lives as chronic pessimists. We can't change a worldview overnight. Still, there are steps we can take right now to begin molding a new, more hopeful outlook, no matter where we are in our life journey at the moment. The plasticity of our amazing brains is such that with time and effort, we can shed our half-empty perspective and begin living rich, fulfilling lives.

Seligman's big idea

The field of positive psychology was pioneered in the late 1990s by Martin Seligman, who described an important concept called "learned helplessness." Seligman wanted to better understand the causes of depression, and so he conducted a series of adversity studies on animal subjects during his early years of research at the University of Pennsylvania. In the first part of his most famous experiment, two sets of dogs were given painful electric shocks. The dogs in Group A could immediately terminate the shock by pressing a lever. The dogs in Group B could also press a lever, but doing so had no immediate effect for them. Instead, the shock could only be terminated for dogs in Group B when the "paired" dog in Group A happened to press its lever—at which point the shock would terminate for both dogs.

To put it another way, a Group A dog had the power to end its own suffering as well as the suffering of a Group B dog. A Group B dog, however, had no power even to end its own suffering. Group A dogs were conditioned to believe they had control over the adversity they experienced, while Group B dogs were conditioned to believe they had no control.

In the second part of the experiment, the dogs from both groups were placed upon electrified grids, which they could easily escape by jumping over a small partition. What Seligman and his colleagues observed was that dogs from Group A—the ones conditioned to feel in control over their adversity—quickly learned how to escape the grid. Meanwhile, dogs from Group B would simply lie down and whimper. They wouldn't even try to escape. No amount of cajoling or threatening would compel them to jump the barrier on their own. The experimenters had to physically move them across the partition (more than once) in order to demonstrate that there was an escape route that they could take and that they had the ability to do it on their own. Only then would they begin to independently act to alleviate their suffering.

Subsequent studies by Seligman and others have shown similar results. Around the same time that Seligman was experimenting with animals, two child behaviorists conducted an experiment involving separate groups of human babies who were placed in cribs with an overhead mobile. The babies were delighted when they watched the mobile. But, whereas Group A babies had sensory pillows that allowed them to control the movement of the mobile, Group B babies had pillows that had no effect on the mobile. It just moved and stopped on its own. When both groups of babies were later placed in cribs with active sensory pillows—that is, when both sets were given control over the movement of the mobile—only those from Group A even attempted to use them. Group B babies would just lie there, staring at the inert mobile. Although Group A babies had been conditioned to understand they had control of the mobile, Group B babies had not been, and this assumption of powerlessness carried over into an entirely new environment.

Seligman described this state of conditioned tolerance as "learned helplessness." Basically, he reasoned, when someone is subjected to unpleasant circumstances and denied the ability to control them, that person shuts down and succumbs to a sort of crippling despair that dominates his or her perception of future circumstances. Because that person has been conditioned to feel out of control in previous situations, he or she will do little or nothing to escape the unpleasantness of future occurrences. The helplessness learned in the past carries into the future and becomes a chronic pessimism that, coupled with other exacerbating factors, can drive even an otherwise healthy individual into the depths of clinical depression.

But there's a good side to Seligman's findings, too. (What optimism study would be complete without a bright side?) Another important concept that Seligman described is called "explanatory style." His studies revealed that optimism is not merely something that some people are born with while others are not. Instead, optimism is a *learned* condition. We may think that some people just wake up naturally bright and cheery while others are destined to be gloomy, but that's not true. What's really going on is that some people have been conditioned (or have conditioned themselves) to wake up believing they have control over their environment, while others have been conditioned to believe just the opposite. This holds true despite the complex web of personality factors that play into how intensely we respond to various environmental stimuli, too.

The messages that people send themselves in the face of adversity—that is, the way the way cope with or make sense of difficulty and trauma—are what constitute their "explanatory style." Those who use a positive explanatory style consistently (seeing the bright side and looking for growth opportunities from adversity) feel empowered. They take proactive steps to alleviate their suffering and feel in control of their lives, even when they encounter painful circumstances that truly are beyond their immediate control.

On the other hand, people who use a negative explanatory style regularly (wallowing in feelings of helplessness, focusing on the problem rather than looking for solutions) wither in the face of adversity. Rather than seeking ways to escape or change their circumstances, they shut down. For them, adversity is not a temporary circumstance they have control of, nor is it something that will go away soon. For them, each new bit of adversity is just further confirmation of how helpless they really are, or how useless it is for them to try to do anything to feel better. And so they do nothing.

It's not hard to figure out which group the chronologically gifted belong to.

Adversity isn't necessarily bad

Of course, a positive explanatory style (or optimism) won't spare you from the difficulties and occasional traumas of life. But it can help you appreciate how adversity isn't necessarily bad in the first place. Optimists recognize that adversity is actually a biological need, something that promotes human thriving. Sometimes, philosophers talk about the "adversity hypothesis," which describes the way human beings need setbacks and obstacles in order to reach their highest potential and to achieve their greatest levels of personal fulfillment. The reasoning says: if everything in life was easy, then our enjoyment would be diminished substantially. Experiencing and overcoming pain are more empowering than avoiding the discomfort altogether.

The logic of this philosophy is intuitive enough. Just ask any cancer survivor about how they experience life differently in the aftermath. They'll tell you that resilience is a learned trait that comes from facing hardship and overcoming it. Food tastes better. Time spent with friends is a little sweeter. Simple joys like an evening sunset or a midsummer rain shower are intoxicating. And when the next hardship comes along, the determination to overcome it is a little stronger than the time before.

I know this scenario first-hand. Having survived the horrors of a Nazi concentration camp, I've seen and experienced some of the greatest atrocities that human beings are capable of. I know what it's like to go to bed at night wondering whether tomorrow would come. I've gone hungry, naked, scorned, and humiliated—all for belonging to a Jewish family. I've seen streets littered with bodies and watched as people around me literally went insane with fear.

Because I was given the opportunity to *live* through such horrific times, I also learned how to strive to live more abundantly afterward. In fact, when I look back at my life—all eighty-something years of it—I'm perfectly confident that a significant part of what keeps me ticking today is the war-forged resilience I was forced to endure in order to survive the horrors of being a Jewish girl in Nazi territory. And today I'm sincerely thankful, if not for the war, then for who I became as a result of having endured it. In addition, I'm thankful that from an early age, overcoming adversity has been part and parcel of what it means to be me—to be able to look others squarely in the eye and say, *"Don't tell me I can't do it! I know that I can, and I most certainly will."*

Also, I know that my periods of adversity have made me a more interesting, well-rounded person, with meaningful stories to share and time-tested wisdom to pass on. Not everything in my life has been as dramatic as surviving the Holocaust. Many of the hardships I've endured include pursuing graduate education in spite of my family's lack of support and nearly being ejected from the program over a gross misunderstanding with one of my professors. These types of hardships are not all that different from those that all of us face. When I look back today, I realize that the woman I see in the mirror is shaped by having overcome those challenges. It helps me appreciate what Dr. Weil means when he says, "Many of the oldest trees are not conventionally beautiful. They are scarred, ragged, twisted, and gnarled, and we love them for it, because their imperfections only reinforce the fact of their endurance."[66]

So how can we learn and grow from our experiences of adversity? Here are three ideas to ponder in the midst of our difficulties—including the trials sometimes associated with growing older—in order to glean new resources for facing tomorrow[67]:

1. *What does this experience teach me about myself?*

   Overcoming, or at least enduring, a hardship often reveals some aspect of our character about which we were unaware previously or that we under-appreciated. One of the dubious benefits of going through something difficult is getting to see in ourselves some quality that can help us cope with future adversity. Qualities like assertiveness, resourcefulness, leadership, and courage often emerge under fire. Pay attention and see what otherwise recessive personality traits you show most clearly during these difficult times.

2. *How is this experience changing my relationships with others?*

   Adverse circumstances have a way of drawing out friends and allies we either never knew we had or whom we previously underestimated. Often, we relate differently to the people in our lives in the aftermath of trauma— sometimes positively and other times negatively. We may even face the loss of close friends as a result of something difficult, but there's one certainty: adversity invites, and sometimes forces, us to reexamine and reprioritize our relationships. It prompts us to consider whether we should have spent more time cultivating intimacy with others. Also, it helps us appreciate the relationships we've already cultivated that are yielding longevity-promoting dividends. The kind of people we draw close to in times of adversity are exactly those who make good traveling companions along the journey to our golden years.

3. *How does my outlook on life differ as a result of this experience?*

Adversity, if it does nothing else, should force us to reexamine our lives and to gauge whether our personal priorities are in alignment with our deepest desires for self-fulfillment. Many readers may be motivated to become chronologically gifted as a result of some life-changing experience—one that makes living a longer and more fulfilling life more important now than it has been in the past. Again, we should be very mindful of such beliefs. This is the gateway to making wholesale lifestyle changes that can propel us into a better life than the one we've lived up to this point. It ensures that whatever years we have left—whether it's twenty or eighty—will be the best they can possibly be.

Considering these concepts, perhaps you'll see that there are some real benefits to experiencing adversity in life. Then maybe you can allow these thoughts to impact your self-talk the next time you're facing difficult circumstances. But before we move on, let me be clear: *it's not healthy or longevity-promoting for us to seek out adversity or to deny the pain we feel as though it wasn't there.* I don't want to be misunderstood. I am not suggesting that we should invite new problems or refuse to allow ourselves to feel frustrated by the ones that we face, despite our best efforts to avoid them. Some people do that, and regardless of what they say about themselves, they're profoundly miserable and more likely to die young than some of their more outwardly frustrated peers.

Well-adjusted people get mad, and they get sad. They feel fearful at times, and they have their bad days when they retreat from the world a little more than usual. But what makes them different in the long run is how they routinely cope with adversity by simply doing what needs to be done. They remind themselves that they are accruing real benefits to support their determination to persevere.

That's a quality of the chronologically gifted, too. After all, for those determined to live longer, better lives, adversity will most definitely become a familiar traveling companion—even if not always a welcome one. It's worth noting here that the chronologically gifted don't let adversity become their only traveling companion. They know that life takes courage and support from their family, friends, and community ties, and so they travel in good company with like-minded people. The sooner in life they learn to adapt, the better equipped they'll be for the rockier times ahead.

Understanding the stress factor

While we're on the subject of adversity, let's spend just a little time discussing the effect that stress has on our bodies, both good and bad. Stress is the mental and emotional tension we experience in response to adverse circumstances. It can arise from physical trauma, like an injury or intense workout, or it can derive from concrete circumstances like having a fender-bender on your drive to work in the morning. And not all stress is bad. Stress drives us to improve our situations, recover from injuries and illnesses, and protect ourselves against future adversity. But chronic stress can become disordered, and it leads to uncontrolled inflammation, forcing our bodies to turn against themselves.

Especially, disordered stress leads to post-traumatic stress disorder (PTSD). In the aftermath of a pronounced traumatic experience, PTSD leaves a person functionally debilitated in the face of subsequent adversity. It's a serious mental health issue, requiring professional psychiatric intervention and it represents the exact opposite of the kind of resilience I'm talking about here. As such, PTSD is a concrete example of why it's dangerous to make unqualified statements like, "What doesn't kill us makes us stronger."

Inflammation is one of those medical words that most of us don't understand well. We know it's bad, but if asked to define exactly how it manifests itself, we'd be at a loss. So here's a simple working definition: inflammation is the body's attempt to repair damage, especially as it refers to our autoimmune response to injury, infection, and other stressors. The most obvious kinds of inflammation are the ones you can see—like when you leave a splinter under your skin and the whole area becomes red and tender to the touch, or when your skin swells after a mosquito bite. Even fever is an inflammatory response (the body's attempt to fight off infection).

The less obvious kinds of inflammation are the ones taking place internally (the production of white blood cells, changes in metabolism, etc.). It's important to realize that inflammation can be triggered in response to emotional stimuli, like the loss of a loved one. Although the circumstances and responses to such events take place primarily in our heads, the body's response is similar to physical trauma: hormonal overdrive, elevated blood pressure, decreased autoimmune functioning, etc.

We don't have to understand the nuanced biochemistry of inflammation in order to appreciate that it's a biological response to stress. Inflammation only becomes problematic when it's a chronic condition—that is, when the source of whatever is triggering the body's inflammatory response goes unrelieved persistently. Chronic stress is such a big deal because it takes a physical toll on our bodies. People who are subjected to the same kind of adversity for a long time experience physical symptoms that actually shorten their lifespans. Whereas relatively short bursts of adversity can help us live longer by stimulating new growth, prolonged adversity has the opposite effect. Unrelieved stress taxes our survival resources beyond the replenishment threshold. It literally saps the life out of us.

So here's why we're talking about this now. Our routine thought patterns play a big role in the amount of chronic stress we experience. People with a negative explanatory style (pessimists) tend to experience stress at a much higher rate than those who encounter the same circumstances but use a positive explanatory style to cope with them. That's because learned helplessness trains pessimists to believe they have no control over their circumstances, and so their bodies must adapt to living in a state of perpetual psychological strain. Optimists, on the other hand, tend to view their adversity as a temporary problem, and their bodies respond by marshaling their energies to help cope with present circumstances until the problem has abated. Pessimists' bodies have a much harder time obtaining a healthy homeostasis (or equilibrium state) than optimists' do, and so their bodies tend to wear down (and wear out) at a faster rate.

It's just that simple. "Whenever you experience depression, grief, or chronic stress, think of it as a health emergency," Dr. Amen says. "Unless treated aggressively, [these things] will rob your ability to live a long, healthy life."[68] Stress may even be worse for longevity than smoking or a bad diet. Part of what the chronologically gifted do is look for ways to cope with and shed unnecessary stress in their lives. They relentlessly target the adverse conditions that they have control over, and they do something about them. "If you think you are being given the gift of extended, prosperous life for your mind and body," Dr. Amen continues, "you will start to vigilantly protect your health from all those people [and things] in your life who are actively trying to steal it."[69] That's what the chronologically gifted do. They focus on what they *can* do rather than what they *can't*, recognizing that resilience is a choice. They cope by controlling their lives as much as possible and surrendering the rest to destiny.

So optimism is more than just a strategy for enjoying life. It's also a strategy for living longer and better than you can as a pessimist. It's a trait that characterizes survivors—those who still have a few miles left in them, while others are throwing in the towel. Unfortunately, cultivating optimism while getting older can be an uphill battle, primarily as a result of the cultural messaging we've been fed over the years.

What's in an analogy?

When it comes to a more subtle kind of messaging, let's consider how writers have compared phases of the typical lifespan to the seasons of the year. I have no objections to that analogy because there's something beautiful about thinking of life in this way. Spring is an apt parallel for youth—the most delightful season of life, when the world is seemingly limitless in all it has to offer. It's also the gateway to summer (our early adult years) that is typically the most productive season of life, when the days are long and the nights are short.

We love summer's opportunities for basking in the sun, splashing around in our favorite watering holes, sowing our fields, and making preparations for a good harvest. Of course, there's much to love about autumn—the season of middle-adulthood. This is the time when the leaves begin changing, and the world is cast in an almost surreal beauty. It is characterized by unwinding after the hard summer labor and enjoying the fruits of an abundant harvest. The days are shorter and the nights are growing longer. Also, the climate is more favorable to leisure and new adventures. For those who have enjoyed a prosperous youth and gainful young adulthood, this period brings many of life's gifts.

The only problem with autumn, however, is how quickly it passes into winter. Very soon, it seems, the nights grow longer than the days, and the highs begin leveling out. Soon the early winter holidays we look forward to all year have come and gone, and all we're left with are the harshest, coldest days of the year. This is the time when it's tempting to remain indoors, to socialize relatively little, and to ponder plans introspectively for the next year.

Except in life, there isn't always a new year to look forward to. Once the year we've been given passes away, that's it. And that's where an otherwise beautiful analogy begins to break down because it's profoundly depressing to associate the end of our lives with the harshest, most forbidding of all seasons. If we buy into this analogy too much, we'll feel consigned to see our lives come to a relatively sudden, underwhelming end shortly after the winter holidays. No sooner will we have finished our holiday shopping than we'll find our living rooms are empty, the presents opened, the family gone, and the last week of the year upon us.

Unfortunately, that's the picture of getting older that our society conditions us to see. The world is a fascinating place in our childhood, full of promise for us as young adults, ripe with fruit for those of us who have worked hard throughout our middle years. But sometime shortly after age 65, all that fun comes to a relatively abrupt end, if we let it. In this scenario, increasingly, the short days and foreboding weather keep us from the activities we used to enjoy. All that's left to do is hunker down and make ourselves comfortable until eventually we drift off into a very long hibernation.

Many of you are still in the spring or summer of your lives, and so winter may seem far off and may occupy relatively few of your thoughts. But like all of us, one day you'll feel the winds shift. You'll shiver as the cool breezes of autumn give way to the first winter frost. In that moment, the way you've conditioned yourself to respond will either excite or deflate you. It will make you either pull out your blankets or polish your skis.

Personally, I love the winter. I look forward to it. Sure, the weather's colder and the days are shorter, but I can't help noticing that the sun shines so much more brightly in the winter than it does in the summer.[70] It's not lost on me that fruits harvested after the kiss of the first winter frost are so much sweeter than the ones harvested at peak—delicacies practically begging to be savored, even if in small batches. I look forward to gathering with friends around the hearth of a well stoked fireplace when the biting winds forbid outdoor activities.

Here's the point I'm driving at: if we choose, we can enjoy the winter of our lives as much as (if not more than) any other season. The key is remembering that it's winter, not spring—and that the same climate that's unsuitable for certain activities is perfect for others. The chronologically gifted use the power of positive thinking to focus on enjoying their winter years for all their glorious worth. Even now, they prepare for how they'll spend those years—not hunkered down waiting for another spring that will never come, but out jet-skiing in Bora Bora or climbing the Inca trails in Peru. (Yes, I've done both!) The world says, "Remember what we did last summer? That was a lot of fun." The chronologically gifted reply, "Yes, it was. But just wait until you hear about what I'm planning for this winter."

Changing perspectives

The chronologically gifted perspective on winter is hopeful and determined. That is why I'm convinced that the concept of retirement is one of the most unhelpful notions we identify with when we think about getting older. It cultivates the sense that we should be spending the majority of our younger years working up to some magical point in time when we can just stop working and sit back and enjoy life. That would be fine, if it were true. But it's not.

Even people who save substantial money for retirement and attempt to "live it up" in their golden years sometimes describe feelings of depression. This happens when they become increasingly aware that they're running out of activities to do with the vast amount of free time they suddenly have. (Vacation, after all, is only enjoyable when you're taking a break from something, right?) Unless this population finds ways to tap into new, rewarding activities, they will not experience the satisfaction that comes from a full day's work. As a result, they may grow pessimistic about the value of their remaining years and end up spending more time than they ever imagined in an inert state—retreating inward instead of reaching outward. And who says that a person can't switch professions late in life or boldly take on new personal projects they've always wanted to do?

The chronologically gifted have what psychologists call a "growth mindset." This is an attitude of continual self-improvement, always preparing today for a better tomorrow. Remember Olga Kotelko, the nonagenarian athlete? Her biographer observed this indefatigable quality in her, both on and off the track:

> When people think of themselves as capable of continual improvement, they improve. ... It is a bit like that "remove grid" function on some desktop publishing programs. With a push of that key, the lines and boundaries that defined your work space vanish. The growth mind-set is about first learning that the key exists, then thinking to push it, and then pushing it. Life becomes limitless.[71]

I'm convinced that if we simply set our minds to it, we can discover creative ways to live our lives without limitations—not even the supposed limitations of getting older. That's why I'd like to spend a little time talking about a few facets of aging that our culture tells us we need to dread. I want you to see that, when framed from the proper perspective—a growth mindset—such notions are not really as dreadful as others want us to believe. In essence, it's a practical exercise in cultivating a positive explanatory style for the unchangeable realities of senescence. Someday these will come upon all of us, regardless of which season of life we find ourselves in now.

Problem #1: Changing bodies means a loss of beauty and attractiveness.

A lot of people accuse us of being overly superficial when we talk about this problem, but I think it's an important topic for us to think about. We like to feel attractive. It's part of our biology. It's not always fun to realize that age tends to endow us with wrinkles and mature our appearance. Even when we're happily married or otherwise disinterested in seeking a mate, there's a part of us that can't deny that each passing year brings us closer to the point when we're no longer "out there," "hip," "in," or otherwise part of the youthful society we are programmed to cherish. But we don't have to buy into what our ageist society is trying to sell us!

Another perspective: Attractiveness, at any age, goes far beyond outward appearances.

We've talked about this perspective already in Chapter One, when we described some of the positive words and phrases that we associate with aging. Here, I want to emphasize the basic idea of complexity and interest. It's a mistake for older people to feel less attractive than younger people. They're actually considerably more attractive in terms of what they have to offer others. This is a result of the experiences they had during their lifetimes—especially when their journeys reflect the kind of purposeful, fulfilled life the chronologically gifted seek.

And physical attractiveness is not age-related! It's simply not true that good looks belong solely to the domain of youth. (Jane Fonda and Robert Redford come to mind!) In the final analysis, attractiveness at any age is really a function of being in good shape, well-groomed, and fully engaged in life. How you feel about yourself and how you take care of yourself are far more important than how old you are on this measure. That said, there are a few cosmetic touch-ups that can help anyone! I made the decision to have cosmetic surgery, and I am happy with the results. My point is that we have far more control over attractiveness than an ageist society leads us to believe. For the chronologically gifted, age enriches rather than diminishes attractiveness.

Problem #2: Aches and pains can make life difficult.

Let's be real with each other for a moment. Some realities the self-help experts don't talk about much are the very real aches and pains associated with getting older. It's as though people who experience unpleasant symptoms are expected just to think themselves out of their discomforts. I don't think it's healthy to minimize and ignore them. The simple fact is that as our bodies begin wearing down with age, they won't work as well as they used to. For some people many routine activities may become more difficult than they used to be. There are age-related diseases and physiological maladies that can overtake even healthy individuals as they get older. The chronologically gifted learn to cope positively with those ills, if and when they arise. But—and this is important—most of the aches and pains that people think inevitably come with getting older are imaginary and wholly preventable! Those who stay active and maintain healthy lifestyles the way the chronologically gifted do have every reason to expect to die healthy, with minimal pain or none at all.

Another perspective: We can be realistic about life's challenges without becoming pessimistic about them.

As a group, optimists tend to be less realistic about their circumstances than pessimists. That is, optimists are likely to perceive their situation more favorably than, in fact, it is. Pessimists are likely to make a more accurate (if hopeless) assessment of their condition. The chronologically gifted lean toward optimism in all situations, but one of their more subtle characteristics is the ability to strike a balance between optimism and realism. They don't attempt to deny the unpleasantness of certain aspects of senescence. Instead, they simply use a positive explanatory style to cope with its occasional symptoms. When they feel winded earlier than they might otherwise like, they tell themselves, "Wow, that was a good little burst. I've earned the privilege of getting to savor this moment of satisfaction, and when I'm done, I'm going to see if I've got a little more left in me."

That kind of perspective takes training. It doesn't just happen overnight. We experience pain at all ages, (e.g., sports injuries) and it's always unpleasant. The chronologically gifted choose to see it as an opportunity for growth. For them, occasional pain is an invitation to pause and to breathe in the world around them a little more deeply than normal. After savoring their experience of the moment, they simply challenge themselves to recover and try again. And the earlier in life they adopt this perspective, the longer they find they can last before experiencing any of the typical aches and pains of getting older.

Problem #3: For some people, getting older means realizing how many opportunities they've squandered over the years.

Moments of *regrets* and *should-haves* are not uncommon. Some are petty, like wishing you would have tried skiing at least once before it became too dangerous to make it a hobby. Others are profound—like failing to take steps to repair a broken relationship before someone you were once close to passed away. Experts believe that these feelings are designed to impel us to action, especially in our youth—an evolutionary benefit to promote life-changing decisions.

But as we get older and the opportunities for second chances diminish, these regrets lose their evolutionary advantage, and they can actually shorten our lifespans by miring us in self-defeating thought patterns.

In other words, regrets are only helpful when they give us an opportunity to do something about the situation causing us sorrow. When that opportunity has passed, regrets are like thought-poison. If we don't take control of those thoughts, we'll face our final years with pervasive hopelessness. Living a fulfilled life in the moment is about empowering ourselves to focus on what we can do rather than what we cannot.

Another perspective: There's no time like the present to seize the day and make new memories.

The chronologically gifted don't experience a lot of regrets about missed opportunities in life. If they do, they accept that they can't get those opportunities back, and they know that the longer they spend dwelling on missed opportunities, the less time they're leaving for new opportunities in the present.[72] Framed from a proper perspective, getting older can mean living with fewer and fewer regrets. That's because age blunts the edge of regret by narrowing the window of opportunity for making dramatic life changes. Instead of succumbing to the risky decisions that are associated with youth, the chronologically gifted focus more on making little changes that have a more subtle and more sustainable impact on the way they feel each morning when they get out of bed.

Regardless of where we are on the age spectrum right now, we might as well decide to accept and appreciate ourselves. The chronologically gifted do, even if they see room for improvement. And because they use a positive explanatory style to cope with their shortcomings, they're convinced they have the power to become better tomorrow than they are today. That mindset enables them to live without regrets, even when they feel they have missed opportunities in the past. The question for them isn't as much, "What do I wish I had done differently with my life?" as "How am I going to make the most of today and the many tomorrows of my life?"

One of my favorite stories to share with audiences comes from reflecting back over my own life and thinking about what I would have done differently. If I had foreseen the consequences, I would have realized that *life is a gift*. Life is a precious journey that we began the day we were born. It consists of a million mini-journeys bounded by the start and finish of each day we live in between our birthdays and our funerals. Every time we squander one of those days working toward a future that could never realistically be—or, worse, anytime we spend one of those days wallowing in regret over a past we can never change—we age a little faster than is necessary. We succumb inwardly to the soul-decay that senescence isn't supposed to bring, even if we live well past 100. We bring ourselves one step closer to the grave, living as though we're ready to die or are already dead.

So the chronologically gifted seize the day. That's not to say they embrace unnecessarily risky behaviors like people who have no thought for tomorrow. But they do discipline themselves to spend time thinking hard about what matters the most to them in the here and now. In that way, they savor all of what their present moments have to offer. They leave it to others to worry about what might have been or what could be if only they had more time. And that leads to a profound state of gratitude—sincere thankfulness for the life journeys that have brought them to the unique places they are now, in spite of and because of the bumps of life along the way.

You get the idea, right? This is the way longevity all-stars think about life—as something for which they can be authentically grateful, treasuring past memories while looking forward to making new ones, savoring the pleasures of today while optimistically preparing for many more years to come.[73] We've only begun to scratch the surface of how these positive thinking patterns can form the basis for a cultivated discipline of optimism that, quite literally, can change our world.

As we think it, so we create it. I, for one, choose to construct a world in which getting older is a privilege to be cherished and grateful for!

Let's get to work!

No one goes from being a pessimist to being an optimist overnight. It simply doesn't happen that way because thought patterns are ingrained habits tied to our environment and personality. But the good news is that even the most ingrained habits can be changed. Personality is only 15 to 20 percent the work of genetics; 75 to 80 percent of it is determined over time by the deliberate choices we make and the thoughts and ideas we preoccupy our minds with each day. That means if you're unhappy with the routine thoughts that fill your head today, you can bend your will toward becoming the kind of thinker who consistently opts for hope, where others settle for despair. In time, you'll find that your routine thoughts—your equilibrium state—will have changed to reflect a more optimistic outlook on life, and you'll have more resources for dealing with adversity.

Here are a few ideas for increasing your optimism.

Suggestion #1: Keep a thought journal.

Get yourself a simple spiral notebook and make one entry at the end of each day. Focus on one incident that happened during the day that made an impact on you—especially if it was something negative. Your entry need not be very long, three or four sentences will suffice. Make sure you don't simply narrate what happened. Assume you're writing to someone who was there and saw it, too. Instead, write about how you feel in response to what happened.

Do this exercise for several weeks. Choose a day at the end of each week when you'll go back and review your entries. During your review, note whether you feel the same way today as you did when you wrote your entries. Circle any words that jump out at you, especially words that help elucidate whether you're using a positive or negative explanatory style to describe your feelings. Do you find that you blame others consistently, use victim-like statements, or resort to negative assessments of ambivalent situations? If so, try writing in the margin of your previous entry at least one positive thought (in hindsight) that might help you re-frame your perspective on what happened that day. That way, you'll remember it the next time you encounter a similar circumstance.

The point of this exercise is to get you thinking critically about your thought patterns. You may be more optimistic than you realize, in which case a thought journal may help you replicate more positive thoughts throughout the coming weeks. But you might discover that you're far more pessimistic than you imagined. In that case, your thought journal can be documentary evidence to motivate you to look for new ways to frame the way you deal with your world.

After several weeks, you might find it helpful to share your thought journal with a trusted friend. If you do, be sure to explain that you're trying to uncover any unhelpful pessimism in your attitude about your life circumstances so that you can find healthier ways to think about adverse situations. Enlist your friend's help in seeing the bright side in situations, where they catch you using a negative explanatory style. Obviously, you'll want to use your own colloquial language to express these thoughts. Don't be clinical. Just lean on the strength of your friendship for help in doing something that friends naturally do for each other: help one another live happier, more fulfilled lives.

Suggestion #2: Inventory the chronic stressors in your life.

As we discussed earlier, chronic stress is toxic and will short-circuit your goal of becoming chrono-logically gifted. Take some time in coming weeks to develop a list of the people, places, and things that routinely create tension in your life. The key word is "routinely." I'm not talking about those occasional circumstances that come and go with the ebb and flow of life. I'm talking about the stuff you encounter at least monthly, on a fairly predictable basis.

It might be helpful to make three columns to help keep your list organized: people who create tension in your life, places where you feel tense, and *things* that stress you out. The "things" column could include tangible objects you see and touch as well as intangibles like ideas, categories, and discussion topics. For example, if religious discussions stress you out, that would go in this column. But if a particular pastor, rabbi, or community member stresses you out, that person would go in the "people" column.

This exercise demands brutal honesty. Inevitably, there are a number of stressors most people can name with very little thought, and they're happy to list them because they're eager to be rid of them. But, there are likely others that we know about deep inside but are reluctant to list because the thought of releasing them is itself a source of stress.

This is especially true about the stressors that appear in the "people" column. Often we have relationships with people who are toxic to our goals of living longer, better lives—people who drag us down emotionally. These people demand more from us than they're willing to give in return, elicit unsavory qualities in us that make us feel uncomfortable with ourselves, or otherwise make it difficult for us to stay on track toward achieving our personal goals. Sometimes these are people we've known a very long time. Sometimes they're even members of our own family. For instance, if you've recently adopted a faith that brings purpose to your life—one you're unwilling to give up—but your siblings are dismissive, you might have to become assertive about acceptance of your beliefs as a condition for continuing the relationship.

You're getting the picture now. The purpose of making this list is to get the stressors in your life organized so that you can begin tackling them one by one. Start with the ones that are easiest to do something about—like getting rid of that clutter in the spare bedroom that makes you nuts every time you walk in there—before tackling the really difficult ones. You might find that there are some stressors you can't simply eliminate but must find healthy ways to deal with instead. In those cases, try coming up with a concrete way of coping that you haven't tried before.

Your list doesn't need to be comprehensive. The goal isn't to get rid of all the stress in your life. No one can achieve that. You simply want to become more aware of the sources of your stress, and then make decisions about which can be eliminated and which you can do a better job of addressing.

Suggestion #3: Smile more often.

It has become a cliché at this point, but it's actually true: laughter is powerful medicine for the body as well as the soul. According to researchers at the University of Maryland, laughter and a well-developed sense of humor actually help stave off the risk of heart disease, the number one cause of premature death in American men and women.[74] You've probably also heard that the simple, physical act of smiling can literally make you feel better, and that's true as well. "Each time you smile," writes psychologist Sarah Stevenson, "you throw a little feel-good party for your brain." She goes on to explain that smiling activates neuropeptides that combat stress and release endorphins that help relax your body, lower your blood pressure, act as a natural pain reliever, and stimulate the imitation reflex in others around you—promoting happiness in others as well.[75]

That means that whether you consider yourself an optimist or a pessimist, you stand to benefit from finding ways to smile and laugh more often. It means that if you're in the middle of something difficult, forcing yourself to smile—no matter how badly you want to frown—can physically improve your mood and lift your spirits. It means that spending time watching romantic comedies may actually be better for your health than you imagined.

So your challenge, should you choose to accept it, is to make a concerted effort this week to smile more than you did last week. I won't make it any more specific than that, other than to ask that whenever you have occasion to smile—whether it's a natural or a forced smile—remind yourself of this simple fact: you're helping yourself live just a little bit longer by choosing to look on the bright side of life in that moment. That said—Dr. Miller's order: Smile at me right now, and I'll smile back at you.

BE GIFTED. Set a lofty (but achievable) personal goal, and get started on it today.

One of the surest ways to feel better about yourself and more hopeful about the future is to accomplish something important that you've always wanted to do. The chronologically gifted have no shortage of personal goals they're constantly working to attain, and achieving one only stimulates their desire to set another.

Make your goal lofty—that is, something that you know would be challenging, but worth the effort. At the same time, be sure it's reasonable, too—something you can actually achieve. Put your goal in writing, and make sure that you're being specific. Give yourself a timeframe for achieving it (and permission to reevaluate that timeframe along the way), as well as some concrete terms to measure your progress toward the goal. A good goal statement, for instance, would be something like, "Run a 5K, without having to walk any portion of it, by the end of next year." It's not enough to simply say, "Run a 5K," because that's too vague to keep you on-task, and it leaves you with no concrete way to evaluate your progress toward achieving what you set out to do.

It might be helpful to start by stating a smaller goal that will help you make progress toward a larger one. Using the 5K example, an ancillary goal on the way to achieving the larger goal might be something like, "Run half a mile, without walking, by the end of next month." For those who have a tendency to procrastinate, identifying multiple smaller goals that lead to a larger goal is the way to achieve success. It will focus your efforts and reward you in smaller increments as you progress. And then, with each smaller achievement, you'll feel that much more empowered and motivated to set your sights a little higher.

People who live longer, better lives know that pursuing personal goals regularly is a huge secret to longevity. It removes chronological age from your mind and calls attention to the better person you're becoming. And that helps keep your thoughts optimistically focused toward realizing your inner potential, something that age only refines the longer you live. How about a new adventure, like a start-up business by yourself or with someone? How about it? Any ideas?

The bottom line

It's not difficult to work out the profound behavioral ramifications of learned helplessness and explanatory style. Optimists are the ones who can "take the hit" of adversity without missing a beat, while pessimists will be defeated every time. Optimists may experience a temporary setback, but before long they will be back in the game—playing for keeps. Pessimists will just want to stay in bed after their first strike-out. For pessimists, adversity is the norm, and even the biggest victories are just exceptions to the rule. For optimists, victory is normal, and adversity is just a challenge to overcome.

What kind of person do you want to be?

Decide now, because your life depends on it.

Personal Journal Pages

My ideas for incorporating and promoting a positive, hopeful perspective on life—an essential step in becoming chronologically gifted:

_____

_____

_____

_____

_____

_____

_____

_____

_____

_____

_____

_____

_____

_____

_____

_____

_____

_____

_____

_____

_____

_____

_____

_____

_____

_____

_____

_____

_____

_____

_____

_____

_____

_____

_____

_____

_____

_____

_____

_____

_____

_____

_____

_____

_____

_____

_____

_____

_____

_____

– 5 –

Leap of Faith

Would it surprise you to learn that "finding God" (in whatever sense that concept is most meaningful to you) can actually help you live longer? It's true. Studies have shown that, on average, people in developed countries who attend religious services at least once weekly tend to live about seven years longer[76] than people who never participate in such activities. That means that, all other factors being equal, people who get up and go to church, synagogue, or mosque services each week are more likely to live into their nineties (and beyond) than those who sleep in on their day off. To hear the way some experts describe it, religious habits are second only to healthy eating and exercise in any longevity regimen. The correlation between vibrant spirituality and long life is that strong.

Of course, it's also tempting to make too much of the connection between spirituality and longevity. We should be aware that, while it's clear that there is a demonstrable correlation between religious involvement and healthy longevity, the proper interpretation of the evidence—including whether and how the findings apply to different circumstances—is anything but clear.[77] So in this chapter, I'd like to explore the positive ramifications of a healthy spirituality, without attempting to sound like I have all the answers. As many of us who are privileged to reach beyond eighty know all too well, spiritual growth is much more about the journey than the final destination.

But before we get started, I'd like to clear up a common misconception about what I mean when I refer to "spirituality." I try to use precise language when discussing this concept because it's easy for us to use the words "religion" and "spirituality" as though they mean essentially the same thing. They most certainly do not.

Spirituality is a bigger and more comprehensive subject than religion. We often hear that a person can be spiritual without being religious, and a person can be religious without being spiritual. There's a lot of truth to that. Spirituality is concerned with our sense of fulfillment and purpose in life. It's related to our ability to align ourselves with our fellow citizens of the world and with whatever higher power we believe is responsible for overseeing the disorder of life. Spirituality is achieved when we can, at least in some vague sense, answer the greatest question of life: why am I here?

Religion, on the other hand, refers to the various, more specific ways that people articulate their spiritual convictions and apply them to their daily lives. Christianity, Judaism, Islam, Buddhism, Hinduism—these are all religions. Each brings its own peculiar understanding of a higher power to bear on the world. The adherents of each use their peculiar terminology and lenses of experience to describe what it means to achieve life's ultimate goals. A Roman Catholic will not see life the same way as a Sunni Muslim; nor will an Orthodox Jew go through life the same way as a Tibetan monk. That may seem obvious, but we have to consider the profound importance of religion in shaping how we live out our pursuit of spirituality. It is tragic that many people spend their lives devoutly and piously practicing some religion without ever discovering the life-affirming, life-elongating power of real spirituality within those practices.

Spirituality, in other words, is something more than just religion. That's why I dare to write about it. I'm a Jew, and I'm not afraid to let others know that. It's part of who I am, and my ethnic and religious heritage are very important to me. They form my identity as a woman, as a wife and mother, and perhaps, most importantly, as a *bubbe* (a grandmother, culturally charged with passing on my own distilled wisdom and that of previous generations of my people). Still, over the course of my life I've discovered a rich spirituality that transcends my Jewishness—something that lends significant meaning to my life beyond merely supplying a particular set of stories and ritual behaviors for expressing it. And it's this aspect of my spirituality that I share with others because I'm convinced that it's common to all meaningful religious systems and explains why those who live longer, more fulfilled lives tend to be people of faith in the first place.

As we go forward in this chapter, we'll talk a lot about religious practices and religious services. Undoubtedly, those phrases will have different meanings to different readers, depending on the particular faith communities they belong to. But in discussing these topics, I hope you'll understand that we're not saying it's the religious practices themselves that are linked to longevity as much as the underlying spirituality they represent. Even without a clearly defined religion to go along with it, the pursuit of a meaningful sense of spirituality can help anyone live better, right now. That alone makes it worth the effort. But along the way it just might help you live longer, too.

How does it work?

One of the more obvious reasons why people of faith live longer surely lies in the fact that communities of faith usually foster a culture of mutual accountability and multi-generational collaboration. Participating in the life of a local church or synagogue, for instance, means becoming part of a fellowship of like-minded peers who watch out for and take care of one another, spiritually and otherwise. Besides praying for one another, younger members may care for the elderly in very tangible ways. They might help with meal preparation or supply rides for medical and other errands, enabling their elders to remain more independent in their old age than they otherwise might.

And should it become necessary for an individual to enter a long-term care facility, being a member of a local community of faith can supply a meaningful connection to life "on the outside." Meanwhile, elders in their faith communities become models of wisdom and pillars of instruction charged with preparing younger generations to bring spiritual resources to bear on life's most intransigent problems. If for no other consideration, actively participating in the life of a spiritual community makes good sense to those who hope someday to enter their winter years in good company. But this only scratches the surface.

As we'll discuss in more detail in the next chapter, meaningful social connection is a critical factor in promoting Blue Zone longevity. Religious communities of any type provide an invaluable means for their members to forge and nurture these fraternal bonds. People who participate in the give-and-take exchange of a religious community feel loved and cared for, and they tend to love and care for others in return. Such institutions are usually bastions of service and outreach, offering myriad opportunities for those with the time and energy to get involved in direct, hands-on activities that yield measurable results in their communities. Whether it's volunteering at the local food pantry, providing childcare for young families during religious services, or going overseas on a mission, such opportunities are tremendously life-affirming—and the social connections shaped in the midst of them are life-sustaining.

Perhaps more intrinsic to the issue of faith and longevity is the way many belief systems explicitly promote healthy lifestyle habits. Codified in a combination of formal and informal rules (which vary in strictness of enforcement, depending on the faith tradition in question), these habits become ingrained world views overtime, prompting adherents to stay on track pursuing their particular vision of the "good life" with the largely positive support of peer influence. They might abstain from excessive alcohol use or avoid reckless behaviors in order to honor the social mores of their religious friends, for instance. They might self-consciously undertake more wholesome eating habits and exercise more diligently as a way of honoring their creator and of modeling responsible behavior for the next generation of believers.

However, there is a corollary caution warranted. Not all religious communities exert positive peer influence, especially when it comes to lifestyle rules. Some communities of faith are overly legalistic about their religious practices, effectively measuring and communicating the worth of individuals by their evidenced ability to keep the "social code" of the religious organization—or to at least put on a pretty façade and make people believe they have their lives in perfect order. These groups have the opposite effect on longevity. They create unnecessary stress in a person's life and promote self-defeating attitudes about one's ability to achieve a religious ideal. For the rest of this chapter, I'm assuming the faith community you choose to associate with is a healthfully functioning one.

What's more, there are a number of specific practices common to various religious systems that are effective stress-reducers. Meditation and prayer, for instance, can redirect worrisome thought patterns toward a big picture perspective. They enable people of faith to more easily assess the control they have over their lives—and, more importantly, what they must surrender to a divine higher power.

Other religious practices, like singing favorite congregational songs and studying sacred texts in organized settings, stimulate a sense of solidarity with fellow believers that prompts positive emotional responses to trauma and hardship. That is, religious life tends to supply a positive explanatory style to help members more effectively cope with the adversities they face. Many religious communities invite their members to share specific needs and concerns. They also provide means for the community to come together in tangible expressions of solidarity with those who are suffering. In the midst of the most challenging circumstances of life these individuals immediately and powerfully receive life-giving social affirmation.

Moreover, people of faith often practice the discipline of forgiveness—the selfless decision to forgo the prerogative of punishment against someone who has injured them in some way. Forgiveness isn't about blithely pardoning someone's reckless behavior, nor does it mean we condone what they have done. It means that we choose to support their well-being over their destruction, and we work to that end rather than take our revenge.

Forgiveness is something wholly foreign to the way most of us view the world. When we think of forgiveness, we usually expect an apology first. We want the person to do something appropriately contrite to merit our decision to withhold condemnation. But many faith communities promote forgiveness even in the absence of apology (and sometimes even in the absence of remorse). The moral reasoning for the decision may vary, but one trait that faith communities share is a focus on how forgiveness of this kind is uniquely healing for the person who forgives, often even more than for the person who receives forgiveness.

But there's a much more important reason than any of these linking spirituality to longevity. Simply put, people tend to live longer and more fulfilling lives when they sense that their efforts to do so are connected with something bigger than themselves. Dr. Creagan of the Mayo Clinic offers one major explanation why. "When you believe in something larger than yourself, you strengthen your ability to cope with whatever life hands you."[78] When all we know is our own little corner of space and time, we're sure to atrophy—physically, mentally and emotionally.

We sense the world's preoccupation with youth and begin to believe the lie of our diminishing significance as we get older. Then, as we begin seeing the signs of our age, we focus so much on approaching the end of our lives that we lose sight of the possibility that our persisting breath has a purpose—a purpose that didn't begin with us and won't end with us, either. So one of the greatest benefits of spirituality is its ability to help believers make sense of the end of life in a way that offers hope and assurance rather than sadness and anxiety. As Dr. Weil observes:

> "Contemplation of [aging] can catalyze the awakening of the self and propel spiritual growth and development. One way it does so is by forcing us to consider what aspect of the self does not change, even as time alters our bodies and minds. Furthermore, awareness of aging and mortality can inspire us to engage more with life, to live it to the fullest, and to fulfill our potential for accomplishment."[79]

Spiritually fulfilled individuals don't fear death. They embrace it as part of the circle of life, which is precisely why they tend to enjoy more of life.

A world of spiritual options

The sheer number of religious movements is mind-boggling. Fortunately, all of them can be thought of in broad categories, based on common features. To help you navigate and think critically about your spirituality, let's spend time looking at some of the better-known and more influential religious movements of the world—with an obvious emphasis on the ones you're most likely to encounter in America. In absolutely no way do I intend for this list to be considered an authoritative statement about the movements described. While I've done my best not to misrepresent the beliefs of these groups, my primary focus is to highlight specific aspects of their beliefs and practices that the chronologically gifted may find useful in pursuing their longevity goals.

I'd also like to say something that I realize is somewhat controversial. *I believe there's something worthwhile for the chronologically gifted to learn from all faiths, even if they choose to practice one or none.* In my experience, individuals who adopt this perspective enjoy a more grounded and well-rounded spirituality than those who feel threatened by people who believe differently than they do. Most of the chronologically gifted people I've met say that expanding their spiritual horizons has brought them considerably more peace as they contemplate the realities of senescence.

- *Atheism.*

Let's start with what many would say is the opposite of religion. In the 21st century, atheists are a growing subset of society, and their world view is guided by the principles of methodological naturalism and scientific empiricism. Those are two very academic-sounding phrases that essentially mean that atheists frame their beliefs according to what they can see, smell, taste, and touch. They describe the world not in terms of possibilities, but in terms of what can be consistently demonstrated through repeated experimentation and objective observation as they actually occur under normal circumstances.

For this reason, most reject the concept of the supernatural outright, believing it to be an unhelpful encumbrance to living authentically in the here and now. In some of its more codified forms, like Marxism, atheism asserts that religion is an illusory veil that we pull over our eyes to make the world easier to deal with. The more courageous act is to pull back the veil and see and cope with the world as it really is, rather than what we would like to believe it is.

To many, atheism sounds like a negative, even depressing world view. And in some respects, it is. That's because it comes without many of the comforting spiritual overtones of other religious perspectives— like an afterlife, a means of spiritual redemption, or connection with a cosmic power greater than ourselves. But for those who find atheism attractive, it also offers tremendous resources for living well. For one, it doesn't merely encourage, but outright insists that our best life is right in front of us, not in some nebulous "hereafter" that we can't see. It teaches us, whatever may in fact be true about what happens after we die, to live today in a way that honors the resources we still have left. For most, that means taking good care of their bodies in order to preserve them for as many good years as possible.

This is precisely the perspective of the chronologically gifted, regardless of their religious beliefs. Unlike much of America, few atheists are living in denial about the realities of getting older, and they look to no higher power than themselves to do something to prevent and mitigate its unpleasant symptoms. For them, this is an empowering thought that urges them to take action, not a depressing invitation to give up early as though they're already defeated.

Atheism also teaches mindful deliberation about our spiritual habits. Rejection of the existence of any supernatural deity is, at least for them, a profoundly religious assertion that they've arrived at with due consideration of the consequences for their well-being. They don't have time to waste on what they believe are fruitless spiritual pursuits, and so they devote themselves to whatever alternative ideas they believe help them grow into the better selves they envision.

To this end, some atheists have formed "churches" in their communities, though these are often little more than disciplined weekly meetings for encouragement and social engagement with like-minded individuals. If you're attracted to the atheist's perspective on life, then connecting with one of these groups[80] in your community could be an excellent way to form meaningful, longevity-promoting relationships with people who are just as determined as you to make the most of their here-and-now existence.[81]

- *Hinduism.*

  The most diverse and one of the oldest of all world religions, Hinduism is largely a polytheistic world view—one that posits the existence of a panoply of gods who influence specific realms of existence, as opposed to a single god who runs the whole show. Well-known gods include Shiva, Brahma, and Vishnu. Hindus believe that each of these gods visited the earth in various incarnations (they call them "avatars") to aid humanity in its perpetual struggle. Among the more important teachings of Hinduism is the idea that the world we experience is an illusion. The goal of life is to free one's soul from entrapment in the cycle of birth and rebirth (or reincarnation), in order to be absorbed into the Ultimate Principle of the universe (Brahman). This is achieved by different means, the most popular route being devotion to one of the Hindu gods or goddesses. Hinduism is also the religion from which we get the idea of *karma*, which stipulates that our thoughts and deeds in the present will come back either to reward or haunt us in the future.

The Hindu perspective on life emphasizes the way our choices about how to live today have real spiritual consequences for how we experience tomorrow. This is empowering because Hindus recognize that many of the circumstances that make them unhappy derive from poor decisions. This belief encourages them to do something about their lives rather than to hope that the fates will fall in their favor the next time.

Unlike spiritual perspectives that allow for "death bed reformations," Hinduism offers no hope for people unwilling to do something now about their spiritual condition. This is because the cycle of birth and rebirth is continual, and there is no better time than the present for securing a better future. This belief has the potential to reorient our perspective on death. Hindus recognize that the number of years we have left to live is irrelevant because one can be young and still unhappy. Likewise, one can be quite old and yet be living determinedly for the future.[82]

- *Buddhism.*

Now one of the more popular of world religions, Buddhism began as a movement within Hinduism in the sixth century BC, when Siddhartha Gautama claimed to have achieved "enlightenment" (nirvana) while sitting under a fig tree. He was subsequently called the Buddha (which means "enlightened one"), and his teachings became the basis for an entirely new religion. Like Hinduism, Buddhism teaches that the ultimate goal of life is to escape the cycle of birth and rebirth.

Additionally, Buddhism stresses that suffering in life comes as a result of our attachment to the world and our desire for worldly satisfaction. We eliminate our suffering by detaching ourselves from the world and its desires—largely through a studied moderation of habits. One stream of Buddhism (called Zen) has become popular in America, especially as a result of its connections to yoga and New Age mysticism. Many who are attracted to these ideologies are also attracted to Zen Buddhism's emphasis on self-salvation through meditation.

It would be difficult to overstate the potentially life-elongating benefits of Buddhism's meditative qualities or its abundant resources for coping with the unpleasant side effects that may come with getting older. In a recent study on intensive meditation training at a retreat center in Colorado—when blood samples taken from training participants were compared with those of individuals still on the waiting list for the retreat—telomerase activity was significantly higher.[83] Telomerase (as we discussed in Chapter One) plays a role in the preservation of chromosomes from damage during cell division, one of the factors that contribute to senescence and deteriorating body function over time.

Researchers believe that this process highlights the way meditation insulates the body from stress through intense inward focus. This is coupled with the way it prepares practitioners for coping better with the world around them as they emerge from a meditation session. Enhanced mental acuity and a more positive outlook are powerful antidotes to chronic stress. There is also clinical evidence linking meditation to improved inflammatory reflex[84], or the mental processes that set the body's physical response to trauma in motion. That means people who are in the habit of meditating— whether for religious or other reasons—tend to have better immune system function, lower blood pressure, and better recovery times from injury and illness.

But meditation is only one of the resources of Buddhism available to the chronologically gifted. Many practitioners discover that they are more content with their present lives as they discipline themselves to let go of the worldly things they cling to. This involves a conscious downsizing of their material possessions. It means mindful eating with minimal seasoning to avoid the temptation to overeat. Also it means regulating their preoccupation with physical attractiveness and reconciling differences with others to avoid nursing grudges and becoming emotionally encumbered. The simpler their lives are, the happier they are. Why? Because without the distraction of worldly possessions, they feel more intimately connected with hidden spiritual realities.

Meanwhile, this religious habit of intentional moderation yields tremendous health benefits, serving to correct the average American's greedy preoccupation with pleasure, possessions, and self-advancement. Few enter old age with the level of tranquility that Buddhists' religious habits cultivate for them. If you have an opportunity to explore Buddhist practice,[85] regardless of whether you choose to embrace the religious world view of Buddhism, you won't regret it.

- *Judaism.*

   This religion is the first to focus on the exclusive worship of one God. Judaism traces its origins to the story of Abraham, who lived around 2,000 BC and whose descendants ultimately would form the Semitic peoples of the world. The God of Judaism (like the God of Christianity) is viewed as loving, personal, and supremely good—the standard against which all human qualities are measured. According to this theology, God chose Abraham and his descendants from among the peoples of the world to be a light for salvation through worship and devotion to him. Jews celebrate stories of being miraculously saved and preserved from destruction by God, as in the exodus of the Hebrew people from Egypt under Moses' leadership and the settling of the Promised Land in what would come to be known as Israel.

   Jewish worship revolves around weekly observance of the Sabbath—a ritual day of rest, honoring God's own rest and enjoyment at the end of the creation story. From the time of Solomon until the destruction of their temple in Jerusalem under Roman rule in 70 AD, Jews made peace with their God via ritual animal sacrifice in accordance with the Law of Moses (called Torah). It represents a complex moral code that specifies how they are to conduct themselves in relation to one another as well as in relation to others outside of Israel.

Today, Jews worship at synagogues,[86] where they gather for recitation of the Law and encouragement to live out their faith in honor of God.

A traditional Jewish blessing says, "May you live to 120." According to Jewish lore, that's how old Moses was at the time of his death, on the boundaries of the Promised Land. Some fascinating DNA research[87] even suggests there may be some amount of genetic truth that ethnic Jews are biologically predisposed to live longer lives. But there are undoubtedly religious reinforcements to long life that stem from Jewish tradition. They put an emphasis on familial loyalty and strict adherence to very specific rules about behaviors such as what not to eat, what kind of company to keep, and how often one should pray (and about what).

In other words, Jewish religious practice tends to foster an intensely supportive, like-minded community of accountability for upholding the sometimes rigorous demands of kosher living. Technically, the word kosher refers to the rules of kashrut, or the dietary restrictions that Jews observe. However, in common parlance the word simply means "proper," as in conduct or attitude appropriate to shared Jewish cultural values and religious beliefs.

The eccentricities of an orthodox Jewish life are akin to the Adventist lifestyle that characterizes the people of Loma Linda—one of the Blue Zones where people routinely live well into their 90s and beyond. The Torah actually precludes mistreatment of one's parents as one of ten primary sins against God. Honoring one's parents—which tends to promote profound loyalty to one's family at all levels—is an extremely important emphasis of Jewish life. That means that eldership automatically confers a level of respect in the Jewish community, and families tend to be more supportive of their aging relatives.

Some believe that the inordinate number of rules rabbinic tradition applies to Jewish life inhibits their enjoyment of it. Others appreciate the way these rules provide firm boundaries and a dependable structure for an otherwise chaotic environment of myriad temptations. I'm inclined toward the latter perspective. I wouldn't say this is true for everybody, of course, but there are certainly those who thrive when they don't have to figure things out for themselves. There are clear guidelines that are lovingly enforced within a community of like-minded people. They "get" why they're so important in the first place, and this community thrives and finds spiritual fulfillment in the discipline of keeping them.

- *Christianity.*

This religion emerged out of Judaism in the first century, when Jesus, a rabbi (teacher) from Nazareth was proclaimed by his followers to be Christ (a Greek term for the Jewish word "Messiah" or savior). For political and religious reasons, Jesus was executed by crucifixion in what Christians regard as a miscarriage of justice. It's said to be the means by which God dealt once and for all with the problem of human rebellion. For Christians, Jesus's death on the cross is a final ritual sacrifice, eliminating the need for temple worship and opening the salvation of the Jews to all the peoples of the world.

Christians believe that Jesus was not merely a man, but the incarnate son of God, and he rose from the grave as proof that God was pleased with his sacrifice for humankind. Christian theology is unique among world religions in its trinity concept. Christians believe in one God—the Jewish God—but they also believe that this one God exists in three divine persons: Father, Son, and Spirit. They worship all three as God, including Jesus (the Son), emphasizing the way the three cooperate in the creation and redemption of humankind. Christians meet once weekly for worship on Sundays, during which time they encourage one another to live in accordance with Jesus's teachings and to spread the good news of this salvation to others.

At its core, Christianity is a spirituality of hope and gratitude. It is unique among world religions in its emphasis on the utter depravity of the human heart. Ultimately, nothing we do can please God. At the same time, Christians hold out hope in the divine person and goodness of God himself. Christians teach that God's love is such that he reaches down to his people with unmerited love and then empowers them to live in a way that is pleasing to him.

This religious life, however, isn't about following the rules in order to obtain salvation. Instead, it's about living out the remaining years of one's life in profound gratitude for the free gift of eternal salvation. Rightly perceived, Christianity offers a powerful impetus for living joyfully in the here and now of this chaotic world. It offers peace for the afterlife, allowing its practitioners to shed the stress of trying to be "good enough" for God and to exchange that fruitless pursuit for the hope of a better life with God after death.

But God's love also gives Christians permission to live at peace in the present. His love acknowledges that the troubles of this world are passing, and anything, no matter how small, that a Christian does to serve others after Jesus's example helps advance the kingdom of God on earth. That supplies Christians with a powerful reason for getting up in the morning. Forgiveness is heavily emphasized, too, along with love for one's neighbors and even one's enemies. This is because Jesus's example teaches Christians to give selflessly to others out of the abundance they have already received from God.

Christianity is an extremely diverse religion. Each denomination emphasizes different expressions of what it means to follow Jesus, some with elaborate liturgical ritual, others with very informal protocols. Some congregations meet in ornate cathedrals, while others meet in the privacy of their own homes. Some churches are global organizations, while others exist only within the bounds of their own neighborhoods.

But one of the greatest advantages of Christianity as a spiritual path is the abundance of communities available in local neighborhoods. Chances are there are multiple churches or gatherings of Christians that meet weekly within a few miles of your home. Because there are so many, it's possible for Christians to be discriminating in the kind of congregation they will choose to join and participate in. Many offer opportunities for spiritual fellowship outside of regular worship services, too. Small group meetings, such as those for Bible study, service projects, and topic-specific encouragement, provide intimate opportunities for expanding and enriching a circle of confidants. Members of these groups check in on and pray regularly for one another as they grow together.

- *Islam.*

Unfortunately, one of the most misunderstood and therefore under-appreciated religions in America, Islam is not the religion of terror that many make it out to be. It centers around the teaching that humankind is universally under obligation to "submit" (the concept that is the basis of the word "Islam") to the benevolent will of Allah. This is the same God worshiped by Jews and Christians, though understood somewhat differently as a result of different source materials.

Muslims look to the prophet Muhammad (c. 570-632) as their spiritual leader, and their devotional life revolves around a set of practices known as the Five Pillars. These include personal testimony to one's conviction that there is no god but Allah, ritual prayers performed five times daily, almsgiving in support of the poor, fasting from dawn to dusk during the month of Ramadan each year, and (resources permitting) a pilgrimage to the city of Mecca at least once in a Muslim's lifetime.

Practitioners live by a code of moral laws called Shari'ah, which are similar to the laws of Torah practiced by orthodox Jews. These rules frame the rights and responsibilities of the members of a Muslim community (including dietary restrictions, guidelines for gender-appropriate attire, and rules governing association with non-Muslims). Muhammad's example (as passed down in codified stories known as "hadith") serves to guide the devout as they pursue a lifetime of good works in the hope of final admission to Paradise at the time of judgment.

Rightly understood and reverently practiced, Islam provides a powerful moral structure to life. It inculcates surrender of one's life to the divine will, which Muslims trust is both wise and ultimately for their own good. Like Christians, they are skeptical of humans' ability to behave in a way that honors God apart from his special revelation of the principles that ought to characterize a holy life. Jihad is encouraged, but for the majority of the world's Muslims, that doesn't mean violence and political terrorism against non-Muslims. Jihad is simply one's ardent struggle against the powers, internal and external, that would thwart the realization of Allah's will in the world. Understood that way, jihad is a powerful metaphor for the priority that the chronologically gifted place on their sense of life purpose. For them, this kind of "all-in" submission to another's benevolent will is liberating. It lends significance to enduring difficult life circumstances, including those that may be brought on by getting older.

The ritualized prayers serve as continual reminders of one's dependence on Allah for breath and for opportunities to please him every day. Also, for Muslims, they become a source of meditative benefits like those associated with yoga and Zen Buddhism. Meanwhile, the emphasis on almsgiving promotes a tangible, mission-driven connection to other Muslims that is akin to the bond of *moai* in Okinawan culture. Okinawa, you'll recall, is one of the world's Blue Zones. Also, the discipline of fasting encourages Muslims to exercise greater mindfulness over their eating habits, placing their nutrition in subjection to the divine will (just like everything else). Though this might sound restrictive, Muslims believe fasting makes them feel empowered to control their dietary choices rather than become— as so many Americans have—slaves to their gluttonous appetites.

Muslims meet once weekly, usually on Fridays, at an area mosque. If you are attracted to Islam as your spiritual path, consider paying a visit to learn about this beautiful religious world view.

- *Indigenous mythology.*

  Mythologies revolve around stories—some passed down over many generations, some in spoken and others in textual form. Each has its variations among different groups and each is focused on explaining the world and social practices in terms of mythical heroes of the ancient past. Modern Native American spirituality revolves around such stories, and there are dozens—if not hundreds—of variations of this practice around the world.

  It would be difficult to do justice to the many facets of these different religious movements. Most of them are geographically localized and exert relatively little influence on American culture outside their spheres of indigenous origin. Most revolve around some form of ancestor worship and belief in a Great Spirit whose will guides believers through the vicissitudes of life. Dan Buettner spoke with a man in Okinawa for whom this spirituality was part of his daily prayer life: Innkeeper Ishikichi Takana prays every day. "My ancestors are watching over me," the 99-year-old told me. "I never pray for a long life, but I just express my gratitude for another day. It reminds me that every day is important."[88]

  Chances are, unless you're already a part of the indigenous group, you're not going to find the religious perspective compelling. But it would be a mistake to discount this mythology and ignore it, too.

  If you ever meet some of the older members of Native American communities—or other indigenous cultures who practice this form of spirituality—you'll discover that they are often revered as their community's storytellers. Younger people look to them for the passing on of the ancestral tales that give their communities meaning and vitality, and this is a tremendous honor for them. It fuels their *ikigai*. Whether the stories are true or merely legendary, based in actual events or religious elaborations of ancient history, the storytelling process is profoundly spiritual, and this reverence for one's ancestors is inspiring.

That's why I invite my readers to spend a little time exploring the indigenous spirituality of their regions. This may require some time at the local library combing through history books, or it might warrant a visit to a local museum. Perhaps there's a lecture at a nearby community college to audit, or better still, maybe you're fortunate enough to live near a Native American community you could visit. If so, make it one of your personal adventures to befriend people with Native American heritage and to listen to their stories—stories they likely heard from their grandparents, who heard them from their grandparents, and so on. You will be fascinated by the rich traditions that have arisen from these stories in their communities.

More importantly, let your explorations stimulate your thinking about your own stories— the traditions that have formed you—the ones that you would like to pass on to your grandchildren. Think about the way others' stories have shaped your journey to the present, the way the tapestry of your life intersecting with the lives of others has led you to where you are today. This may not sound like a very religious activity, but it can be a profoundly spiritual one. It may even prompt you to explore your own ancestry to better appreciate where you come from and to learn the previously untold stories of your own ancestral past. This can be a rather engaging hobby, especially in the Information Age. With the help of new technology—like DNA sampling and online archives accessible through internet services like Ancestry.com—it's easier now than ever to learn about your personal ancestral linkage and connect with the heroes of your family origins.

- *Modern paganism.*

  It's difficult to summarize the specific religious habits of those who would self-identify as pagans. That's because there are so many fringe groups that practice forms of contemporary witchcraft—the best known being Wicca. While it's true that there is a lot of negative baggage associated with sorcery and the occult, people who choose to keep an open mind will discover that modern paganism is rarely devoted to evil pursuits and black magic. Its practitioners tend to revere nature and other mystical entities like faeries. To the extent that they practice magic, it's intended to serve good ends like promoting healing and wellness, warding off malevolent spirits, and restoring balance and harmony to the universe.

  For many, witchcraft means little more than a close, spiritual connection to Mother Nature. This is a bond so intimate that, at times, it truly seems as though practitioners channel the very spirit of the earth and can harness it for the good of themselves and others. Though no common moral code exists among these groups, they frequently abide by a variant of the Golden Rule, as expressed in the Wiccan counsel: "Do what you will, so long as it harms none." In other words, shamelessly enjoy life and all it offers, as long as your choices are made with due consideration to the right of others around you to enjoy the same. Freedom for such individuals is not a license for recklessness, but a warrant for unbounded personal fulfillment.

For those who are turned off by organized religion and attracted to the unadulterated beauty of nature—who sense in nature a kind of power more profound than anything humankind has ever devised—a goodhearted exploration of the wisdom of modern paganism is neither dangerous nor evil. Most of us could stand a deeper immersion in the wonders of nature anyway to be reminded of how small we are and how much we depend on nature for the lives we enjoy.

Also, consider how that enjoyment entails a responsibility to give back to nature some of what we so often take for granted. This can stimulate that connection to something larger than ourselves that lends purpose to our existence. Also, it can promote an honest appreciation for the circle of life—of which aging and death are vital parts. It can help us take a step back and get a healthier perspective on what it means to get older and go through our senior years with grace and gratitude.

Even someone who ultimately rejects pagan understandings of the world can appreciate the sense of personal empowerment that witches and sorcerers feel over their lives. This includes the sense of intimate kinship they feel with their natural surroundings and the comfort they enjoy being authentic in their own skin. They're unafraid to enjoy life's pleasures, even to violate popular taboos, as long as they aren't hurting anyone. That opens them to new and exciting experiences that many people whose minds are unnecessarily constrained by moral codes will never appreciate.

Incidentally, many contemporary witchcraft practitioners also happen to be experts in applying homeopathic remedies to physical and psychological maladies. They delight in using obscure herbs, spices, elixirs, and tonics drawn from regional plant life. Their embrace of the natural healing powers of Mother Earth and their reluctance to do harm leads many of them to vegetarianism. In other words, their holistic remedies and dietary habits can provide an excellent model for the chronologically gifted to follow, regardless of whether they do or don't share the spiritual convictions that motivate the witches and sorcerers.

Obviously, this is far from a complete catalog of spiritual world views, but I hope that you're getting the picture of the diversity of spiritual options that are out there for the chronologically gifted to explore. Also, I hope that a common theme has emerged from our discussion of this topic: For those with the eyes to see, any spiritual path is better than none because all challenge us to become the best possible versions of ourselves.

This means to live with purpose in the here and now and to find cosmic significance even in the smallness of our existence in the universe. For those who want to learn more about the specific teachings and practices of any of these religious movements, any library is a great place to start. I highly recommend spending time reading on the subject of spirituality. The very act of learning more about comparative religions is intellectually stimulating. It challenges people to think hard about the spiritual lenses through which they view the world around them. That's precisely the kind of mental activity the chronologically gifted crave because it promotes brain plasticity and keeps them functionally younger even as their bodies get older.

Let's get to work!

Applying the insights and ideas from this chapter will require you to step out of your comfort zone more than in any previous part of this book. Now you're better prepared to take this leap of faith and make the commitment to live a longer and better life that honors and incorporates a new or renewed sense of a higher power. I want to emphasize once more that religion isn't what makes you chronologically gifted. It's the willingness to cultivate spirituality and a holistic world view that connects you with something larger than yourself that matters. Exploring religious perspectives is a highly practical way to go about that, but merely participating in a religious community isn't what makes you live longer. It's the other way around. If you're living longer, chances are good that going to church (or other places of worship) is already one of your habits. It is this activity that enables you to connect with your higher power and with the community that fuels your intimacy with that higher power.

If you already participate actively in a spiritual community, some of these suggestions may not apply to you. I'm addressing them more to those who either have no spiritual habits to speak of or who (like most of us) could benefit from practicing them more mindfully and intentionally.

Suggestion #1: Keep a prayer (or meditation) journal.

One of the most profound benefits of prayer and meditation is the way it diverts your attention from the distractions and noise of the outside world and then directs it inward. Prayer and meditation aren't quite the same. Prayer is about being spiritually present and communicating with a higher power, such as a deity, ancestor, or other entity. Meditation is about disciplined relaxation and self-focus, without any specific intention to communicate with anyone besides yourself. Often, people will describe how meditation leads naturally into prayer. It heightens their awareness of spiritual reflections. Also, it allows them to express deeply spiritual thoughts without having to focus on the articulation of those expressions the way they would in, say, a liturgical prayer during a worship service.

What I suggest is that, regardless of what your prayer or meditation habits are right now, you can benefit from disciplining yourself to write a few sentences in a journal each time you enter this inward state. Two options are possible. On the one hand, you could write a few sentences—more is okay from time to time— but try not to turn this into a diary.

Just before you pray or meditate, allow those sentences to frame the thoughts that you will take into this session. For instance, you might write about a particularly stressful situation you're facing or you might express gratitude for a special person in your life. Then, as you enter your prayer or meditation time, you let that thought preoccupy you and clear your mind of all other thoughts. If it's a positive thought, you let its warmth overwhelm you. You enjoy the way your mind gently wanders into tangential thoughts inspired by that warmth, wordlessly expressing your gratitude and petitions for the blessing it represents. If it's a negative thought, you slowly let it go as you relax more deeply into your spiritual zone of prayer or meditation. You seek to unburden yourself of this concern and ask for new resources for dealing gracefully with it as you emerge from your session.

Alternatively, you could go into your prayer or meditation session as you typically would. Then as you emerge, spend a few moments journaling (again, two or three sentences is enough) about something you want to take away from that session. Begin your next session by reading what you wrote the previous time, and see whether your time in prayer or meditation is enriched by reminding yourself of the takeaway from your last session.

Either way, the goal of this exercise—which can become a regular spiritual habit or an activity you do once in a while—is to cultivate a heightened awareness of the thoughts you're allowing to preoccupy you. As you draw your attention to these notions, you can become more mindful about what you're seeking to get out of your prayer or meditation practice. Perhaps it's a greater sense of peace with life circumstances beyond your control (including the challenges of growing older). Maybe it's a deeper sense of gratitude for life's gifts that you rarely stop to appreciate. Or maybe it's an assurance of divine presence as you go about the mundane (and not-so-mundane) facets of daily life. Whatever it is for you, the important idea is to focus on what helps you live with greater purpose and a richer spiritual connection to something bigger than yourself.

Suggestion #2: Add some variety to your faith life.

The chronologically gifted aren't satisfied with the status quo in any aspect of their lives, including their spiritual growth. If you've never explored a faith practice, there's no time like the present for plugging in and experiencing the many benefits of becoming a part of a local religious community. But even if you already practice one of the faiths we've discussed in this chapter, my challenge here would be to explore one or two creative ways to become more spiritually adventurous within the community and tradition in which you are already familiar. Spiritual complacency can sneak up on you unknowingly.

To counteract this trend, finding meaningful new ways to grow spiritually can ignite new fires that rekindle passions and cast life circumstances in a much warmer light. The chronologically gifted prize these opportunities for exploring and going deeper with new facets of their spirituality. They take comfort in much the same as they do from being a part of a closely knit religious "family" that nurtures and challenges them along the way. For example, I recently discovered Kabbalah philosophy, and I am intrigued.

Variety in your spiritual habits can take many forms. Perhaps it's as simple as committing to attending worship services more regularly. Or maybe it means joining a small group or class that your religious community offers. If you enjoy reading, consider perusing some of the spiritual classics in your faith tradition—connecting your own faith life to the grander picture of its historical development. You may want to advance particular causes in prayer, explore a previously unfamiliar spiritual practice like liturgical dance, or even make a pilgrimage to an especially sacred place (perhaps even a far-off land).

This is your tapestry. Weave it according to your heart.

As you do, keep in mind that growing your spiritual habits is an opportunity for deepening your most cherished relationships. Introspection of your spiritual habits has a way of helping you think more objectively about your connections. It enables you to determine more accurately which relationships are already potent sources of encouragement to you and which could use more investment on your part. As you act on these spiritual instincts and connect more deeply with the people in your lives, both inside and outside of your religious communities, you will move much further along the path toward becoming chronologically gifted.

Suggestion #3: Consider participating in a service project.

There are few activities that a religious organization provides that are more stimulating, meaningful and more longevity-promoting than community outreach opportunities. Some groups operate weekly food pantries for needy families in their areas, while others have mission teams that meet other local needs—like after-school programs for neighborhood children, employment assistance for job-hunters, computer literacy and English language classes, etc. Some organize teams to travel to areas recently affected by natural disasters and other crises in order to provide clean-up and relief services. Others even send short-term mission teams to foreign countries for building and development.

This kind of benevolent outreach extends naturally from the spiritual identity of community groups, from their desire to make the world a better place and to selflessly give to others out of the abundance they have already received. Also, you might look outside your religious organization for service opportunities within your community that aren't explicitly religious, but which might benefit from your expertise. For instance, consider volunteering as a board member for an area nonprofit organization or cultural enrichment group.

Volunteerism of this type feels good. The hard work can be tremendously rewarding for those who believe in the causes they are supporting. It is the experience of making a tangible difference in others' lives that results in deep satisfaction. But these service projects aren't just about helping others. They're about bonding more intimately with important people in your life—the people you serve and, more importantly, the people you serve alongside.

Shared missions tend to stimulate shared passions. This draws people who might otherwise never have the occasion to get to know each other into lasting bonds of friendship and camaraderie. What's more, doing something worthwhile in the company of like-minded people tends to promote the kind of lifestyle that keeps you moving physically and psychologically. Also, it keeps you focused on something tremendously life-affirming: the difference you're able to make in others' lives.

The easiest way to do something like this is to volunteer and connect with a group that already meets within your present religious organization (or within your community at large). Contact the religious leaders at a local area organization to find out about upcoming service opportunities, or look at the online event calendars of area churches and synagogues. Consider, too, checking in with your local chamber of commerce and city government. Often there are service opportunities that don't directly relate to a specific religious opportunity, but community members come together to staff volunteer efforts. For instance, there might be an area homeless outreach or domestic violence shelter in need of volunteer support.

BE GIFTED. Experiment with a spiritual tradition other than your own.

If you're a Christian, visit a Hindu temple. If you're a Muslim, participate in a service project with Christians. If you're an orthodox Jew, go to a Buddhist meditation center or attend a Catholic mass. The goal of this exercise is not to try converting to another religious tradition, nor to show any kind of disrespect toward those who believe differently than you do. On the contrary, it's intended to help you grow your appreciation for the rich variety of spiritual expressions across the world and to sense the spiritual kinship you may have with practitioners of unfamiliar religions. It's about deliberately stepping out of your comfort zone. It involves telling your limbic brain to grow a little and cultivate a more sociological intelligence by observing how others who face the same life circumstances and problems find spiritual answers to their deepest questions. It's an opportunity to view objectively the kind of purpose-filled lives others lead in response to their spiritual connections with particular religious traditions. Doing so will stimulate more thoughtful engagement with your own practices.

I'm fortunate to participate in a synagogue where interfaith prayers and dialogues are a common occurrence. It's an amazing opportunity to hear and learn from others who have followed different faith paths than I have in life. I encourage you to pursue similar opportunities within your own community. There's no need to feel intimidated by unfamiliar faiths or places of worship, as long as you conduct yourself with humility and deference. You may feel like an outsider at first, but soon you'll find that most places will welcome you openly and appreciate your visit. It will be regarded, not as an intrusion, but as a gesture of respectful interest. Don't be surprised if you're invited back.

Spiritually adventurous activities light the fires of the chronologically gifted. They expand their horizons, extend their generosity, and open themselves to new experiences of the divine in their own lives.

The bottom line

Olga Kotelko's biographer, Bruce Grierson, rightly perceived that his subject's spiritual habits were an engine of motivation for her, indispensably part of what kept her going and what made her tick even as she continued to run competitively into her 90s. Until the night she died, suddenly and unexpectedly, Kotelko was living each day of her life the way someone far younger than she might have lived. Her spiritual world view was big enough to encompass the possibility that age was just a number. It didn't have to prescribe the quality of her life or dictate what she would live for day-to-day. "The power of faith," Grierson summarizes, "is really the power of purpose."[89]

Do you want that power to fuel your journey, too? I should hope so. I believe that all of us covet a world perspective that helps us process the occasional challenges of getting older with more grace, to grow our spirits even as our bodies reach maturity. Regardless of what you believe about the relationship between our world and the spirit world, this life and the life to come, heaven and hell, or whether there is or isn't a God, the choices you make in response to your beliefs will make a meaningful difference in the quality of your life. You owe it to yourself to come to these decisions mindfully, after due consideration of your spiritual options. Remember, there are others out there who share your desire to exploit the riches of spirituality and to begin living the most fulfilling life imaginable, right here and right now. Finding those traveling companions ought to be one of your top priorities. It's certainly one of mine!

Personal Journal Pages

My thoughts about making God/spirituality a part of my daily life in order to achieve super-centenarian status:

_____

_____

_____

_____

_____

_____

_____

_____

_____

_____

_____

_____

_____

_____

_____

_____

_____

– 6 –

A Whole New World

It's not easy to be chronologically gifted in this time and place. It takes determination because American society continually erects new barriers to living a long, healthy, and satisfying life. I'm not just talking about the obvious either—like our gluttonous dietary habits, which lead to chronic obesity and other health maladies. I'm talking about the habits that are very good for society, but not necessarily good for longevity. For instance, our lives are more convenient now than ever before, but in the quest for convenience many of us have grown quite complacent.

An entire generation of young people—the Millennials—has grown up in an environment of instant gratification, making it difficult for them to plan for the future. At our fingertips, we have so many incredible technologies for staying in touch with loved ones. Yet in the world of smartphones and social media, ironically we're more isolated from one another—allowing digital screens and soundbite messages to substitute for face-to-face interactions and deeper relationships.

But what if we could live in a whole new world? What if we could restructure our lifestyles and home environments in such ways that the habits we've been talking about become continually reinforced by the circumstances in which we live, work, and play? If we could achieve that, perhaps we could reproduce in our own lives many of the conditions that help the world's centenarians outlive so many others. We could create our own personal Blue Zones—little "hot spots" of longevity, right in the middle of our otherwise comfortable American neighborhoods. This is where the goal of the chronologically gifted—to live a longer and better life— trumps popular preoccupations with privacy, convenience, and instant gratification.

Guess what? This is already happening, right now, in neighborhoods across the country. There are pockets of Blue Zone activity all around us—right here in our communities. Mark my words: if you know what to look for, you can see them popping up everywhere!

We've been making references throughout this book to Dan Buettner's groundbreaking work, uncovering and describing the world's longevity "hot spots"—what he calls Blue Zones. What began for him as a research project for a National Geographic feature has grown into a phenomenal self-help movement, and the chronologically gifted are indebted to him for thoroughly vetted methodologies and intensely practical insights. I highly recommend reading his book, *The Blue Zones: Lessons for Living Longer from the People Who've Lived the*

Longest[90], which is chock-full of interesting facts, fascinating anecdotes, and specific suggestions for incorporating these insights into your life.

I dare not attempt to reproduce here what Buettner has already done so well, but what I'd like to do in this chapter is apply the wisdom of the Blue Zones to how we structure our personal life environments. After all, according to Buettner, about eighty percent of the factors that determine how long we live are environmental. They are based on the circumstances in which we find ourselves (including the people we routinely encounter), coupled with the healthful ways we interact with our environments. The people who reside in the world's Blue Zones live in environments that are especially conducive to living long, high-quality lives. But the factors that make those environments so helpful can be reproduced elsewhere. At present, Loma Linda is the only recognized U.S. Blue Zone, but I have firsthand information that there are already plans in place to create further "hot spots" in America. Stay tuned!

What I'm suggesting is taking various steps—some simple, others more complex—to transform your home and social life into a private, longevity-promoting "hot spot" for yourself and others around you. You might want to think of this chapter as a master wrap-up exercise in applying all the principles of becoming chronologically gifted that we've examined. Here we'll talk about purging yourself of the people, places, and behaviors that obstruct your longevity goals and replace them with people, places, and behaviors that will reinforce your success. If we're on the same page, then I think you'll have some fun exploring this topic with me. Approached with thoughtfulness and determination, these concrete suggestions are an exciting way to fashion a whole new world for your chronologically gifted self.

Make your home a longevity sanctuary

Many people are shocked when they realize they spend about two-thirds of their time away from their homes and families. Don't believe me? Just do the math. There are 24 hours in the day. If you work full-time, you're going to spend at least eight of those hours at the office, leaving at best only 16 hours available for anything else. Subtract from that your commute and the eight hours of restful sleep that the chronologically gifted need and you're lucky if you have as many as six or seven hours in which to pursue anything else. And chances are good that only a portion of those hours are spent at home or with your family. In fact, the younger you are now, the more likely it is that many of those hours are being consumed by daily tasks and overtime at the office.

So, given the reality that you spend relatively little time at home, shouldn't your home be a place that uniquely reinforces your chronologically gifted lifestyle? Shouldn't your home be a launch pad for your day's adventures and the place to which you return eagerly at the end of a long workday? Shouldn't it be a place that energizes you when you get up in the morning even as it eases your concerns and helps you relax at the end of the day? Yes, it should be that kind of place. Your home ought to be a sanctuary from the assaults of the world and the endless barrage of stressors. Therefore, it ought to be optimized for *you* and *your* needs, arranged to accommodate *your* goals.

So, if your goal is to live a longer and more fulfilling life, then turn it into a "hot spot" like the world's Blue Zones. Make it a place where it would be easy to upgrade the quality of every day you have left to enjoy the world. There's no perfect formula for achieving this, but the tips we've talked about so far have given you a few ideas. Here are some more to help you get started:

1. *Choose your place of residence carefully to minimize the need to relocate.*

   As one who has lived in multiple countries and relocated many times, I want to caution you that moving—whether it's just a few miles away or to another continent—is a profoundly traumatic life event. And that's true even when the outcome of the move is otherwise positive. Chances are you're already familiar with the stress and chaos associated with moving, so you know that the process takes a lot out of you mentally, physically, and emotionally. Don't underestimate it. The fewer times you do it in your lifetime, the better.

   Now, don't misunderstand me. There are some very good reasons for relocating your home, including a few that can actually help you live longer. Great new job opportunities (or other chances for long-term adventures) sometimes beckon us out of our comfort zones, and we would be foolish not to pursue them! On the other hand, sometimes life changes force us to reexamine our resources. For example, if you've ever lived in an unnecessarily large house, then you know how the financial relief of downsizing can make a big difference in your emotional health.

Or perhaps you loathe city life and long to enjoy the serenity of a small town. If such a move could reinforce other longevity goals—like planting a garden or living closer to family—then it can be a positive decision. For that matter, you might dream of relocating to a specific part of the world someday. If the vision of growing old there spurs you to become more conscientious about how you approach life, you'll be in better shape to enjoy your dream destination. If that's the case, then by all means, go for it! Such change can be positively exciting!

Still, we do well to think of these moves for what they could be: intensely stressful experiences that undermine our longevity. Every move is a calculated risk. We're betting the longevity-promoting benefits of the new destination against the toll it will take on us. Some personalities weather the trauma of constantly being on the move better than others. A few even thrive on it. But for most of us, it's not a good idea to relocate our homes any more than we absolutely must. And for those who mistakenly believe that relocating is a good way to cope with stress, remember this: the chronologically gifted don't look for ways to get away so much as to get more deeply involved. That's why even though some may choose to relocate their homes later in life, most will simply look for ways to immerse themselves more fully in the communities they've come to love.

2. *To the extent that it's reasonably possible, live close to other family members.*

Many young people dream of getting out on their own, and for them that means moving as far from their childhood homes as possible. I certainly understand that impulse, and I think it's very good for young people to get out and see the world. It's part of growing up in a balanced way, where young adults deliberately expose themselves to other perspectives on life and other ways of living. But the research from the Blue Zones suggests that, when the time comes to get serious about the future, it's a good idea to settle relatively close to home. Proximity to family members pays statistical dividends in terms of longevity. "Studies have shown," Buettner says, "that elders who live with or close to their children are less susceptible to disease, eat healthier diets, have lower levels of stress, and have a much lower incidence of serious accidents."[91] The reason for this is very easy to understand, even though it might not seem apparent initially.

In areas of the world where the elderly are revered, older adults tend to be highly involved in the lives of younger family members. Grandparents have a primary role in participating with their grandchildren and passing on the wisdom of their generation. Their family roles are every bit as important as the ones they knew in their younger years when they were assisting in the care of their own parents and grandparents.

There is a demonstrated correlation between involvement in family members' lives and healthy longevity. The chronologically gifted don't have to be told this, of course. They naturally seek fulfillment in caring for their own aging parents and grandparents, recognizing that they're part of a tradition their own children and grandchildren will someday honor. By investing in their families, the chronologically gifted cultivate a healthy perspective on aging that relieves many of their fears about the changes they imagine senescence may someday bring upon them. And as people age, living in proximity to both family members and to places of primary care practitioners (doctors, hospitals, etc.) enables them to sustain their independence far longer than they could if they were living more remotely, away from a network of caregivers.

There is one caveat to this piece of advice—an unfortunate one, but important nevertheless. If (and only if) your family is a source of undue stress and emotional anguish, then living in close proximity to family members may actually contribute to a lower quality, shorter life. That's because instead of being more involved in the meaningful give-and-take of a well-functioning family, you'll be constantly stressed out by broken relationships. There are benefits to initiating meaningful reconciliation—including asking for forgiveness from those you've hurt and extending forgiveness to those who have hurt you. But sometimes, no matter how hard you try to reconcile, family members refuse to do their part. And if that's the case, it's not your fault. In fact, it might be a good idea to put some distance between you and the family members who are dragging you down. It may be wiser to settle in a more emotionally unencumbered living space, where you can seek out a new fellowship of people who share your life goals and who will serve as your surrogate family.

3. *Put food temptations out of sight.*

One of the surest ways to fall off the healthy eating track is to inundate your senses with temptations. You're going to encounter plenty of this every time you step out your door, so your home ought to be the one place where your commitment to properly fueling your body is consistently reinforced. Instead of having a candy bowl or cookie jar on the counter, place a colorful bowl of fresh fruit in plain sight. Put fresh vegetables in the most prominent places in your refrigerator, and keep healthy snacks like nuts and raisins near the front of your cabinets in easy reach. It's best if you don't even stock junk food items, but at least keep the ones you do have in higher cabinets. That way, they're out of sight and require a more concerted effort to access them. As much as possible, stock your pantry only enough to satisfy the current week's meals. This will help you resist unnecessary snacking and drive your appetite down to a healthy level.

Also, it's helpful to think about how you handle mealtime protocol. Typically, Americans serve themselves buffet style, where they load up their plates with as much as they want. Only after the meal is over do they put the leftovers away. This style encourages second helpings and overeating. (Indeed, the chef is often insulted when you don't go back for seconds!) Contrast this with the Okinawan custom of serving meals at the bar and then putting the rest of the food away before sitting down to eat. This practice communicates that the meal is over when you finish what's on your plate. Getting a second helping would be inconvenient, and it might prompt you to think a little harder about whether you're still hungry or just reluctant to stop eating.

If you know you're preparing a meal that you're prone to eat a lot of in one sitting, you can do yourself (and your guests) a favor by serving a reasonable portion and immediately putting the leftovers away. Not only will you eat less, but also you will have leftovers to enjoy the following day—and your kitchen will be easier to clean after mealtimes. If you're a guest at a meal and moderation prompts you to choose not to eat something, don't be afraid to use this as an opportunity for sharing your thinking and action with your friends and family—in the name of longevity! Don't preach, of course. But others can benefit from your perspective if you share it graciously.

4. *Use smaller plates.*

In Chapter Three, we talked about the importance of eating smaller portions to consume fewer of those unnecessary calories. The fact is that most dinner plates are far larger than they need to be to hold the food our bodies need for any given meal. When we use these larger dishes, unconsciously, we take more food than we require. Then our tendency is to finish everything on the plate—even when we're already full.

Do yourself a big favor by getting your favorite plates out of the cabinet and measuring them. If they're more than 10 inches in diameter, box them up and donate them to a local charity. Replace them with a set of smaller dishes so that when you prepare your meals, you can fill your plate guilt-free, knowing that your eyes and stomach will feel fuller on fewer calories as a result. If you find it's too difficult to part with your favorite dishes, a less radical alternative would be to store your larger dinner plates where they're less accessible, and use only the salad and dessert plates as your everyday serving-ware. You can reserve the larger plates for use with guests and on special occasions.

5. *Don't be ashamed to own (and get on) the scale.*

This one is simple, common sense, but you'd be surprised how rarely I see it practiced. We've talked about how maintaining a healthy weight is critical to high-performance longevity. The easiest way to stay on top of that goal is by checking your weight regularly. The chronologically gifted, unlike most American adults, have no fear of what their scales have to say, and they feel no shame taking an honest look at their bodies. They know that weight—like age—is just a number. If they're not happy with that number, they let it motivate and empower them to do something about it. They keep long-term goals in perspective, realizing that they can't manipulate their weight overnight. At the same time, they know that checking their weight keeps them on track and discourages them from sliding too easily into unhealthy eating.

Now, you may have heard some dieting experts say that it's not a good idea to get on the scale every day, especially when you're trying to lose weight. That is good advice if you're easily discouraged because normal weight fluctuates about two to five pounds on a daily basis. This is due to water retention and the digestive progress of your last meal. The best way to lose weight is slowly and steadily. That means even if you're actually headed in the right direction, there may be times when it seems like you've gained weight since the last time you got on the scale. If you take this in stride, you'll just make a mental note of it and check in again a few days later. But if you're like many people, that one- or two-pound gain may be so demoralizing that you'll be desperate to correct the number. You may succeed, initially, but you'll be even more demoralized a few weeks later when the number is going the wrong way again. Drastic weight-loss measures are usually unsustainable over the long-term.

If that scenario describes you, then you may need to weigh yourself less frequently, but it's no excuse for avoiding the scale entirely. Position yours where you will see it as you go about your daily routines. Let it encourage you to keep tabs on your health goals, and let it remind you that dieting and exercise instincts are often untrustworthy. In one study, participants who were given scales and advised to weigh themselves every day made substantially greater progress toward their weight loss goal over a period of one year than others who were not given scales. More importantly, those who made getting on the scale a habit during the year sustained their lower weight more consistently one year later than those who had not developed this habit. So treat your bathroom scale like a good friend who will tell you the truth—even when sometimes you'd prefer not to hear it.[92]

6. *Reclaim the original purpose for your kitchen and dining room tables and chairs.*

Far too many of us put our kitchen and dining room tables to the wrong use. They become display platforms for beloved place settings and centerpieces that are never intended for actual mealtime use (heaven forbid!). Or, worse, they become so cluttered with papers and other miscellaneous items anyone would be hard-pressed to find enough clear space on which to eat if they wanted. That's because, as a rule, very few of us routinely sit down at the table for meals anymore. Instead, we balance plates on our laps, eat at the kitchen counter, or take our meals-on-the-go in our vehicles. What that means is that we're eating mindlessly. That's a profoundly unhealthy habit and a hard one to break. We can give ourselves a little psychological leverage, however, by making it a point to keep our dining tables clean between meals and to resist using them for activities other than eating. By doing so, we make our tables inviting at mealtimes, increasing the likelihood that we'll actually use them.

7. *Cut down on the distractions.*

Most of us live in homes that are constantly noisy due to the TVs, smartphones, and other media devices in our everyday lives. I'm not opposed to them—even large ones with surround sound. Nor am I opposed to the integration of the internet and its dizzying array of media options for private consumption. Frankly, I think those devices are amazing and extremely helpful. What I am opposed to is the immoderate "always on" culture that so frequently accompanies this technology.

Especially within our homes, I think we need to exercise a fair amount of discipline to combat the cultural norm of turning on the TV for background noise while we go about other household activities. If we're not going to sit down to watch a program, it's just an unnecessary distraction from whatever else we were intending to do. If you're the type who enjoys listening to something while you go about your business, turn on the radio. Listen to upbeat music that makes you want to groove a little as you go about your work—something that boosts your mood and keeps you moving in rhythm. Resist the urge to keep your smartphones and tablets with you at all times, updating your Facebook accounts, texting friends, and playing online games while trying to do other activities that used to demand your undivided attention like cooking and communicating with others.

Many of my youngest readers may think I'm out of touch on this subject. Being constantly plugged-in we're told, is the only way to stay current and in the know. But let me tell you, for all its benefits, this kind of life is longevity-draining. The ability to multi-task is a myth. You can't do multiple things at once. You simply switch back and forth from competing mental activities very quickly. No matter how good you are at this juggling act, the fact remains that you're expending far more of your energy than you need to by forcing your brain to process multiple activities at once. Yes, in moderation, this promotes brain plasticity and keeps you functionally younger. But chronic multi-tasking saps longevity by forcing your brain to work on overdrive all the time.

One way the chronologically gifted honor the sacredness of the here and now is by making a concerted effort to quiet their homes. They watch TV—some more than others—but they do so *mindfully*, disengaging themselves from other activities. They set reasonable time limits on their consumption of media—both from the TV and the internet—and they turn off their devices or put them away while engaged in other activities like reading, cooking, relaxing, or socializing with friends. They also tend to own fewer media devices in the first place.

Many of us would benefit from periodically doing an inventory of our electronic media devices and pausing to ask with regard to each: "Do I really need this?" If you're not sure, consider taking a brief sabbatical (maybe a day or two) from that device. Try living without it and see what happens. You might be pleasantly surprised to find that you don't miss it as much as you expected—or you might discover that you're more addicted to it than you previously imagined. Either way, you can make a more informed decision about the role that device should play in your life.

I realize this advice might seem out of place in the 21st century. I'm not a naive technophobe. I have my own unhelpful habits in this realm, too. But you might be surprised how much you notice going on around you when you keep your phone in your pocket. The chronologically gifted aren't hopelessly addicted to a media-centered experience of their world. They're not hooked on their digital screens. They want the real thing. Being plugged-in can't compare to being fully engaged. If it's your goal to live a longer, more fulfilling life, then that will mean spending less time staring at electronic devices and more time face-to-face with friends and family who are eager to get out and actually be with you.

8. Add some green.

Research suggests that people who live in environments full of healthy plant life enjoy a higher perceived quality of life and exhibit a more positive outlook on life's circumstances. [93] It doesn't matter whether the plants are growing in the backyard or in a pot in the kitchen. There's just something about the greenery and vibrant colors of plant life that stimulates a part of our brains that wants to live and to live well. It has been shown that tasks performed in natural environments are executed with greater accuracy.

Additionally, bringing plants into the home helps increase memory retention and concentration. The aesthetic beauty of plant life seems to have a calming effect on stress hormones and makes people feel more vital and energetic as they go about their chores. Recovery times for hospital patients improve when plants are displayed in their rooms. People who routinely care for plants demonstrate more compassion and participate in deeper relationships with other people. Moreover, such pursuits tend to stimulate a healthy concern for the local environment. That decision leads to social bonding with like-minded people who enjoy working together for the greater good of their communities.

Perhaps you have plants in your home already. If so, find ways to showcase them where you and others who visit are sure to enjoy them. Think of them as silent companions on your journey toward a long, fulfilling life. And for those who don't keep plants in the house, consider visiting your local nursery for some advice on relatively low-maintenance indoor plants. Just don't go overboard. There's nothing more demoralizing than watching a bunch of plants wither under your amateur care. Like all hobbies, keeping plants requires learned skills. That means you can expect some trial and error before you get good at it. Some people have more of a green thumb than others, but anyone can do it. After you develop instincts for what works best in your home, you can begin experimenting with more and different kinds of plants.

9. *Create a space for entertaining others and use it.*

No matter how large or small your home is, make sure there is an area where guests feel welcome and can make themselves comfortable. We're social animals, yet so often in our preoccupation with our own comfort, we inadvertently structure our homes to accommodate us rather than our guests. By thoughtfully creating a space for entertaining guests, we may discover a new desire to invite company over more often. And when we know our guests are comfortable, we can linger over social activities a little longer than we otherwise might.

This doesn't need to be complicated. It could be as simple as having two comfortable chairs, inside or outside, that face each other and facilitate conversation. Or, it might mean a couple of bar stools at the kitchen counter for dialogue while preparing meals, or a little breakfast table for chatting over coffee. Most likely, such a space already exists in your home, but you've never given it very serious thought. Perhaps you could improve upon that space by removing clutter for maximum comfort.

But even if you make no outward changes to the space, just shifting the way you think about it is very important. That's because this space is a haven for the one activity that matters most in our lives: connecting with other people. Let this space be a constant reminder that social connections are the lifeblood of the world's

Blue Zones, and they ought to be an integral part of your daily life. If it's been too long since you've visited with someone in that space, then do something about it. Make a phone call. Invite someone over!

10. *Reclaim the original purpose for the bedroom.*

We talked about this already, but it bears repeating. There are only two activities that are supposed to take place in the bedroom, and both are great for longevity. Watching TV isn't one of them. Neither is catching up on Facebook posts or working out in your home gym. So it's time to banish everything from the bedroom that could distract you from enjoying sex and getting a truly restful sleep.

Many of us have a terrible habit of going to bed with electronic screens glowing in our faces. This has a well-documented adverse effect on the ease with which we fall asleep and on the quality of our rest after we do.[94] We also tend to clutter our bedrooms with objects that don't belong there, like exercise equipment and a home office. This may derive from an attempt to make the best use of limited floor space, but it sends confusing signals about the purpose of the bedroom to our brains. Are we there to work or to sleep?

Remember the importance of restful sleep for healthy longevity. Bodies with adequate rest are more energized for healthy activity while awake. The higher the quality of the rest, the longer you'll persist in your favorite activities before retiring. Invest in a high-quality mattress well suited to your body's contours. Use pillows liberally, and explore different sleep positions. Use soft, ambient lighting instead of harsh, bright lights. Also, install light-blocking drapes that will help you stay asleep. Train yourself to sleep in silence. Alternatively, if you find it hard to sleep in a quiet environment, get a white noise machine. Such devices, played at a low volume, help drown out distracting noises without overly stimulating the brain.

Once you've arranged your bedroom for sleep, embrace the sanctuary of that space. Avoid retreating to the bedroom until it's time for sleep or sex, and resist falling asleep anyplace other than the bedroom when you're tired. Get out of bed promptly after waking up, too. Such behaviors kinetically reinforce your body's association of sleep and the bedroom—giving it permission to power down when you retire for the night, helping you fall asleep more quickly and rest more soundly.

11. De-clutter your space.

Disorganized, cluttered spaces are a major source of stress.[95] Such environments overload your senses, confuse your focus, and impair your creativity. That's because all that stuff you might have accumulated just takes up space and is the equivalent of a dozen little voices yelling, "Pay attention to me!" Coming home day after day to a cluttered home is like creating a chronic stress bomb: one day it will explode. And it gets worse the older you get because you usually cling to objects that remind you of past experiences, previous accomplishments, and treasured relationships. The struggle is more profound as you age because after years of accumulating these mementos, you're more likely to attach deep and intense emotional significance to them. Parting with such objects lightens the pain centers in your brain.

Some of your clutter has irreplaceable sentimental value, and getting rid of it would be a mistake. Certain heart-felt mementos should occupy places of sacred importance in your home. They are conversation pieces that facilitate opportunities for you to bond with guests over what matters most. Nevertheless, you would do yourself and your family a tremendous favor by either getting rid of or putting into long-term storage those items that you neither need nor really want in your home. Inadvertently, too many people allow their homes to become live-in storage lockers full of junk, and they're literally burying themselves in a tomb of their own clutter.

The chronologically gifted surround themselves only with what will promote their goal of living longer, more fulfilling lives. They know that lasting memories don't depend on objects. Getting rid of a cherished memento doesn't have to diminish the memory. In fact, it can even be part of the ritual of savoring that memory or sharing it. Likewise, the chronologically gifted appreciate the way keeping these keepsakes in plain sight tends to draw their attention to the past. This is unhelpful because it invites them to fantasize unnecessarily about their younger days and tempts them to believe their past was more golden than their days are now. For someone who is determined to make the most of every "now" moment possible, reliving the past is distracting, and so the objects that promote it must go—out of sight, if not out of possession entirely.

More to the point, the aim of de-cluttering the house is to restore the space you call your home to a suitable condition for living. Your home should be a comfortable place to spend time—a space that invites relaxation and promotes your overall sense of well-being. What's more, this should be true of every room in your house. There should be no "junk" room into which you never venture. Wherever the clutter in your life tends to be hidden, that's where you need to attack it most fervently for what it actually is: psychological poison that inhibits your ability to live today the way the chronologically gifted do. If your home is to be a haven for longevity, it can't be a sanctuary for clutter.

12. Make your priorities known.

When someone first walks into your home, is what's most important to you immediately apparent to them? If not, then chances are it's not apparent to you, either, and your home may be subtly obstructing rather than reinforcing your life goals. If you think hard about this, you'll instantly know what I mean. You walk into certain homes and the way the furniture is arranged indicates thoughtfulness and purpose. You can instantly imagine life taking place within the rooms, and the decorative items on display invite others into the story of the family that lives within those walls. Each room has a purpose, and each seems optimally laid out for that purpose.

Conversely, you can probably think of times when you've walked into someone's home and thought, "Wow...who could live here?" This is true even of well-kept, immaculately clean living spaces, too. I've been in formal dining rooms that appeared perpetually set for a grand party that will never take place. I wonder why dishes that are on display never get used. I've been in living rooms with pianos that no one knew how to play—owned by people who had no plans to learn how, either. I ask myself: why show such pride in a musical instrument when music occupies only a small part of your life?

If living well is your priority, then your home should reflect what matters most to you. It should be a shrine for what inspires you to get up in the morning. Are there photos of your most recent family vacations on display? Are there pieces of your grandchildren's artwork on your refrigerator? Is there a guest bedroom that invites loved ones to stay when they visit?

Perhaps your faith is important to you, and religious icons and literature are exhibited. Or perhaps you love the adventure of traveling to faraway places, and paraphernalia from your trips fills the rooms— prompting interesting conversations with your guests and practically begging you to get started planning your next excursion. Or perhaps you're just the kind of people-person whose life revolves around entertaining others in your home. In that case, the most prominent feature of your house is its inviting sitting areas and comfortable chairs full of character from having been well-used over the years.

Remember, the chronologically gifted display the mementos that remind them why it's worth living audaciously, in the here and now, regardless of how many tomorrows might come. They take exceptional enjoyment in these expressions because they stimulate the *Ikigai* that compels them to keep doing what they're hardwired to do best.

13. Create a meditation space.

Does your home have a special area dedicated purely to your personal serenity? That is, do you have a place where you can go to escape all distractions, focus deeply on your inner self, and reconnect with your higher power? The chronologically gifted do. It's their favorite place because it's where they consistently retreat from the world and feel at peace. Spending time there represents spiritual fuel for the rest of their day. It recharges their batteries, enabling them to shed built-up stress and energize themselves for coping with new challenges. Some call it a "prayer closet." Others call it a meditation room. Still others simply consider it a personal space. The name isn't important. The intentionality is.

Our homes are rarely the sanctuaries we like to think they are. Many of the world's troubles follow us home at the end of the day, greeting us when we wake in the morning, and preoccupying us even as we go about our daily activities. At first, it may sound indulgent to create a personal space within our homes, but I would argue that it's nothing less than spiritual self-defense. It's one of the most proactive steps we can take to turn our homes into refuges for longevity. That's because taking valuable real estate and using it, not for storage or furnishings, but for something intimately spiritual is a choice we make.

Your primary purpose for this space is yours to decide. It might be a place where you literally come to pray to your higher power. It might be a place where you come to sit in silence and focus on your breathing as you clear your thoughts before bedtime. It might be a place to practice yoga or Tai-Chi, or to recite mantras of life purpose such as, "The self is made not given."(Barbara Myerhoff) It might be a place to listen attentively to classical music, purely for the enjoyment of it or to watch birds as they feast on a feeder you've thoughtfully placed outside a favorite window.

It might be a closet you've cleaned out and filled with your favorite memorabilia. Or it could be an entire spare bedroom you've converted into a quiet dojo. Perhaps it's a small garden alcove complete with a concrete bench and colorful annuals. Or maybe it's just your favorite bathroom, illuminated by the gentle glow of a single aromatic candle.

At any rate, I hope you're getting the picture. This space is 100% yours. The only constraint is that it should be as large or as small as you need for whatever activity or inactivity that helps you feel united with the cosmos. This is where you will sense your smallness in the universe as well as your importance as a human being. This sense of connection with something larger than yourself is an engine for longevity. Guard this space as one of your home's most prized possessions. Prevent other people and other distractions from intruding. Keep it clean and comfortable. Maintain it with the kind of love you'd show a dear friend because, in your time of need, you want it to be there to welcome you with loving arms.

Get out of your home more often.

Having spent so much time talking about how to invest in your home as a sanctuary of longevity, now I'd like to encourage you to take a different step by discovering reasons to get out of the house more often. If it seems like I'm contradicting myself, let me explain it this way. Sanctuaries become prisons when we fail to use them appropriately. Sanctuaries are places where we should escape for temporary reprieve. Also, they should empower us to venture out and enjoy life once more, feeling recharged and optimistic, confident that no matter what the world throws at us we can always return to our safe place when the day is over.

One of the stereotypes about older people is that as they age, they tend to become more eccentric and more reclusive. Unfortunately, there's a bit of truth to this perception because it's very tempting for older adults to spend an inordinate amount of time at home. Unless they deliberately seek out compelling reasons to get out and do something in their communities, many will find they have every excuse simply to stay home. They can do chores, watch TV, maybe connect with a few people via the internet, then go to bed early and do it all again the next day. What a tragic way to spend the last chapter of our lives! If we really want to live longer and better lives, then we ought to crave the stimulation that comes from getting out and engaging in our world. As Olga Kotelko's biographer explains:

> The trick of routines is that they take the vagaries of motivation off the table. ... But as important as routines are in getting things done, too much routine can be stultifying. Indeed, growth comes when we break routine, when we confuse our body and brains, jolting them out of the lazily efficient shortcuts they have developed, forcing them to adapt.[96]

By making our homes into sanctuaries of longevity, we're giving our bodies the permission to rest without becoming complacent. We're training ourselves to think of our homes as springboards rather than anchors—places that inspire new projects and new adventures while encouraging deeper involvement in our local communities. Here are a few suggestions for doing that:

1. *Get out in nature.*

    One of the more interesting habits that characterizes the Adventists who live in Loma Linda, California, is their appreciation for and deliberate enjoyment of the serene beauty of nature. (Remember, Loma Linda is the only American Blue Zone identified by Buettner's team.) The Adventists emphasize the importance of finding a "sanctuary in time" each week.

One of the principal means by which they do this is by observing the Sabbath. It's a tradition from my Jewish heritage in which family members spend the entire day—from sundown to sundown—performing as little work as possible. They stay home, but they do no chores. Instead, they commune with one another and frequently take nature walks to grow closer to their Creator. For those of us living in the 24/7, high-tech culture of American cities, such a deliberate effort to get out in nature once a week seems wasteful and foolish. But for the Adventists, it's a sacred rite, something they look forward to throughout the week.

No matter where you live, chances are good there's at least one park nearby with hiking and biking trails. Why not join or start a daily or weekly hiking group to explore them? Cognitive psychologist, David Strayer, believes that getting out in nature like this brings out the "natural wild" in us. It reconnects our brains to their primal "autopilot," allowing our prefrontal cortexes to relax and de-stress in a way that urban environments prohibit.[97] So far, the research supports his hypothesis. Even if it turns out to be purely anecdotal, the lesson is clear: getting out in nature is good for your emotions.

2. *Schedule walking or hiking dates.*

As we've discussed, the chronologically gifted enjoy the comprehensive benefits of walking as a routine exercise. It may be the easiest moderate-activity hobby that you can start doing tonight if you want. But most don't like the idea of going for a long walk alone, especially just for exercise. So don't. Invite a friend who shares your health goals to go walking or hiking with you a few times each week. Make it a date—an occasion for socializing as much as for exercise. When you walk with someone else, you're more likely to keep the commitment because it represents a social obligation. As humans we're hardwired to resist letting others down, even when we would let ourselves down time and time again. What's more, the social nature of the activity may cause you to look forward to your walks as bonding rituals rather than personal chores.

A simple walk around the block is better than nothing. If possible, however, try routing your walks in such a way that they introduce scenic variety into your life. Visual stimuli from different sources promote brain plasticity and keep you functionally younger than walking mile after mile on a treadmill. So make plans to meet in a different neighborhood or go hiking in a nearby state park once in a while.

Your walking partner doesn't have to be someone your own age. In fact, walking with someone younger than you are can be just the challenge you need to push yourself to keep up and avoid becoming complacent about your health. Or there may be others who will have a challenge keeping up with you. If you're feeling really adventurous, consider joining a local hiking group or learn more about walking tours where, in addition to getting some moderate exercise, you can learn more about the history or geography of unfamiliar locales. Your brain and body will thank you!

3. *Take up gardening.*

   At the risk of sounding cliché, I'd like to suggest that gardening may be the consummate hobby for any adult aiming to live a longer life. And I'm not just talking about those who happen to have green thumbs. There are many facets of gardening that make it an ideal Blue Zone activity. For one, it's a source of regular, low-intensity physical activity. This includes walking for endurance, standing and stooping for balance, and light to moderate lifting for strength. Secondly, gardening stimulates your brain with the sights and smells of the outdoors. It challenges you with the mundane but, nevertheless, complex tasks associated with cultivating a suitable environment for plants to grow. And, third, gardening provides ample opportunity for learning, for connecting socially with others, and for connecting spiritually with Mother Nature.

Many gardeners emphatically insist that pulling weeds is a profoundly spiritual activity—an opportunity for self-reflection and inner awakening. Plus, a home garden yields fresh herbs, fruits, and vegetables for your table—locally-sourced, organic ones, no less! And you're more likely to eat them simply because you put in the extra work to make them grow.

Gardens can be as simple as a planter box on your back porch or as complex as a cultivated field in your backyard. If you live in a city where gardening is difficult, you might consider joining a community garden club, where members share plots at a central location and learn from one another in the process. Don't be discouraged if your first attempts at gardening fail miserably. It takes time to get good at it. As you learn to take proper care of your plants, you'll also begin feeling more motivated to take similar care of your own body. You'll get a burst of optimism every time you see new flowers blossoming and colorful fruits and vegetables waiting to be enjoyed.

1. *Consider getting a dog.*

Owning any pet is a well-documented longevity-booster, but the benefits accrue especially well for dog owners. Why? Because dog owners are drawn organically into physical exercise and social interactions with other pet owners. Dogs require walking, and in most cases, that's going to give their owners a great excuse to get outdoors too. Dogs like to play, and they have an infectious way of garnering people's attention.

Moreover, dogs provide excellent companionship at home and invite conversations with strangers while their owners are out in public. As Alan Beck of Purdue University's Center for the Human-Animal Bond says, "If I saw you walking down the street, I couldn't comfortably start talking to you if I didn't know you, but

I could if you had a dog. It's an acceptable interaction that otherwise wouldn't be possible." Beck also observes that people in wheelchairs attract more eye contact from others when they're accompanied by a furry friend. There's just something about dogs that breaks down social barriers and encourages people to be more human. Isn't that ironic?

Also, pet ownership stimulates a sense of purpose and responsibility akin to parenthood. People take better care of themselves in order to make sure their pets have a good home too. In return, pets provide owners with a special kind of companionship that makes coming home a more joyful experience at the end of the day. Still, there are those for whom this added caretaker's role could become a source of stress or unwanted additional responsibility. If that describes you, that's perfectly fine, too.

2. *Enroll in something fun.*

There are myriad opportunities for those who are determined to do something fun. They seek out and enroll in regularly-scheduled community classes and activities. As I already mentioned, trying new activities is a perfect way to stretch your brain, inspire new interests, spark the spirit of volunteerism, and connect with something bigger than yourself. Many people I talk to say they'd love to get out and be more active, yet they lack the initiative. If that's you, talk to your friends or look for a community bulletin board at your local public library. Or opt for any of a number of other popular social gathering places, like coffee shops and recreation centers. Most public meeting places will have a central spot where people can post information about upcoming events, including concerts and sporting activities. It's also a great way to learn about the local services of low-cost providers for pursuits like music lessons and yoga classes. Also, local newspapers maintain online community calendars that feature links to activities of interest. You just have to start looking.

Regardless of how you learn, simply making the effort to step out of your comfort zone and go is the first and most important milestone on the journey. Once you get out and see that it is not scary, you'll relax a little and enjoy yourself. This will bolster your courage to get out and try something else in the future. Besides, there's no better way to connect with new people who share your passions and are just as dedicated to your hobbies as you are.

In addition to your job and other daily activities, one of the best ways to sustain your habit of getting out of the house is to connect with an organization—formal or informal—that explicitly promotes your interests, your passions, and your goals. These organizations provide structure for you in the here and now. They give you tangible resources for expanding your engagement in life's abundant opportunities for personal growth at any age. So go ahead and sign up for activities you otherwise might not—like a foreign language class, a book club, or volunteer positions. You don't have to do all the legwork to get new hobbies off the ground. Let others point the way forward. All you have to do is plug-in and grow.

Build your personal *moai.*

I want you to pay special attention to this section because, although it's a relatively small part of this book, this particular topic is one of the most powerful ones we'll cover together. In the Blue Zones, people tend to congregate in mutual support groups called moai *(MOE-eye)*—which is a Japanese term that roughly means "meeting for a common purpose." The *moai* represents a concept that is foreign to the American ideal of ultra-independence. In Okinawa, where they take this cooperative social model very seriously, children are placed into their *moai* on the basis of common interests or life circumstances as early as at age five. The members of the group stay together throughout their lives. That means that as Okinawans enter old age, many of the people they spend time with have already been with them for decades— through the good and the bad times, every step of the way since childhood. These people have expressed their dreams and fears to one another, shared their financial gains and accepted one another's financial burdens, participated in many joys and grieved many sorrows together. It was never an option not to. That's just the way of life in this culture. No one is an island. Life is meant for experiencing community.

The formal concept of *moai* derives from an ancient method of promoting financial security in uncertain times. That's why certain expressions of it are illegal in Japan now. The authorities consider it a variation of gambling. In an interview, one Okinawan woman describes it this way: Moai *works like this: a small group gets together and decides how much money they want to wager. ... Every time we meet—usually once a month—each person puts ten thousand yen into the pot. Then we decide among ourselves who's going to take the pot of cash that month. It usually goes to someone who's financially strapped, you know, a person who has a son or daughter getting married, or someone who needs a new refrigerator or something. If several people need the money, we draw straws to see who gets it. When we meet the following month, everyone puts ten thousand yen into the pot again. Only this time it gets complicated because we add interest. ... The people who pay interest are the ones who've already received the money ... The people who hold out until the end are the ones who make the most cash because they get all that interest along with it. No one really complains about having to pay the interest or anything, though. If we borrowed money from the bank, we'd have to pay interest anyhow, wouldn't we?*[98]

I quote this woman at length because I think it's important for us to appreciate the raw, practical origins of the concept of moai. It's about survival in a difficult environment. While the term has come to mean something considerably more benign in modern times, the principle is no less significant. We're still talking about life and death in a world that, if we let it, will tempt us to forego everything that would help us live longer, more fulfilling lives.

Those familiar with Buettner's discussion of *moai* will recognize that the term has become a trendy catch-all for any serious longevity-minded support group—and that's a term I loathe. "Support group" tends to conjure up the wrong impression. It makes us picture weight loss or addiction recovery or cancer survivor groups. It sounds like something we would join from a place of weakness rather than strength. That's why I prefer the phrase "extended family." A *moai* is comprised of the kind of people whom you would gladly trust with your most valued financial possessions. In the original sense of the word, a *moai* represents a risky venture in which participants may very well lose everything at the hands of a selfish member.

Over the course of many years of this shared financial venture, they grow intimately close and draw far more from their interactions than mere financial security. They learn to appreciate and support one another through their difficulties. When someone takes money, it's a collective decision. All members have heard the difficulties people in the group are facing, and all have agreed on how to prioritize their needs. Likewise, generosity is the privileged choice. When you have the means to do so, supporting others' financial needs pays bigger dividends. In this scenario, there is a genuine incentive to give more than you take, yet doing so means you actually receive more than what it costs you to participate in the first place.

Now that Okinawa has moved out of much of the poverty that stimulated the original practice of *moai*, the groups meet mostly for emotional and spiritual support. This is the model in which Buettner and others recognize their longevity-boosting potential. Yet even as the financial aspect of *moai* assumes a secondary purpose, the implicit trust and intimate fellowship remain paramount. Most of us have been brought up to live fiercely independent lives. Even if we're privileged enough to have an inner circle of friends we've known since childhood, we may have trouble appreciating what an organic American *moai* would look like.

Do you have a support network like a *moai*? Do you have a group of three or four people you meet with on a regular basis—not separately, but together—who know you so intimately that they can recognize instantly when something is out of the ordinary and coax you to share it with them? And once it's known, do they help bear the load with you (emotionally and otherwise)? Are these the kind of people you could instantly (and shamelessly) ask to loan you money, with the knowledge that you would repay it in full? Could others expect the same of you? Would you trust them to be your children's caregivers and your business partners in a risky financial pursuit? If you're like the majority of people, I expect your answer is, "No. Not really. But who does?" The chronologically gifted do.

This reality doesn't come about by accident. Remember, in Okinawa, these groups are formed in childhood as a matter of cultural expectation. In Loma Linda, they form organically out of the Adventists' religious emphasis on jointly sharing the intimacies of daily life as a way of connecting with God. In poorer nations, like Mexico, similar groups develop as a way of shielding one another from the sudden devastation of illnesses and other financial crises that are easier to bear as a group than individually.

But in the average American city, unless it relates to a profitable business venture, there aren't many compelling reasons why someone would deliberately bind themselves to a group of other people—emotionally, financially, or otherwise.

On the contrary, most people are taught to fend for themselves. They're trained to believe that it's shameful to depend so explicitly on others for their daily needs. This stems from believing that a well-adjusted, financially independent adult ought to be able to control his or her own destiny. In this context, if a support group is the answer, so be it. But we shouldn't need one in order to get by.

The chronologically gifted perspective is very different. "We evolved as social pack animals," claim aging experts Crowley & Lodge. "It's not a choice; our survival depends on being part of a group. ... There's no such thing as a solitary human in nature, because isolation is fatal. We were designed to be emotional creatures."[99] They go on to explain that the human limbic system—a function of the brain's complex architecture and the portion responsible for emotion, behavior, motivation, and long-term memory—leads people to crave companionship for its own sake. That is, it's a physiological reality that human beings, left to their own highly-refined natural instincts, "want to belong and to matter to those around [them]," or, put more simply, "to love, and to be loved in return."[100]

This is why Crowley & Lodge highly recommend that older adults who are losing their hearing get a hearing aid sooner rather than later. It helps avoid the inevitable, self-imposed social isolation that comes from being left out of the conversation for shame of asking people to speak louder and repeat themselves, and for inviting others' frustration over misunderstood words and phrases, etc.[101] The chronologically gifted, who value socialization late in life (even more than they did when they were younger) accept reality and use a listening device without shame, rather than be excluded from the conversation.

One of the ways we can honor the biology of aging is to pledge earlier in life, before we experience the signs of aging, to surround ourselves with an inner circle of people who will be our traveling companions into the uncertainties of getting older. But it's never too early nor too late in life to stop and take notice, making sure we engage in community. As mental health expert, Ruth Sutherland, keenly puts it, "We could have a perfect pension plan in place, we might be running marathons into our eighties—but if we have no one to share these things with, later life becomes lonely and unfulfilling."[102] Ideally, these people will be our best friends in the truest sense of the term. That means they may or may not be the people you already consider your friends. Even when you're close to certain people and enjoy their company, that doesn't necessarily mean they are good inner circle members for your personal *moai*.

Here are a few qualities to look for as you build your fellowship:

1. *Like-minded.*

   Like-mindedness is important, but that doesn't mean you should surround yourself with people who would otherwise look just like you. Diversity is stimulating for the chronologically gifted—particularly when it comes to intergenerational interactions within a closely-knit group. Young people can learn much in the company of their elders, and vice versa. It's a win-win! Be sure your *moai* includes members at both ends of the age spectrum.

Your closest friends ought to share your passions— the reasons you want to get up in the morning. They intuitively get what makes you tick because the same reasons make them tick, too. Such individuals are enjoyable to be around because they reinforce your lifestyle choices (and want to emulate them). They become life companions, providing a meaningful outlet for your joys, a sounding board for your sorrows, and a source of accountability for the shared values of your particular community.

This is one of the reasons why Adventists avoid socializing intimately with non-Adventists. Adventists recognize that outsiders consider some of their religious values eccentric, and they're okay with that. But they're also wary of the damage that misunderstandings and occasional outside hostility can do to the spiritual progress of their society. For them, purposeful relationships are simply a matter of self-defense. They keep those who don't share their values at arm's length because such people represent a potential threat to the lifestyle they love.

We could learn a lot from the Adventists in this regard. How often do we keep certain people in our lives simply because they're related to us or because we've known them for a very long time? Isn't it true that many of these same people neither understand nor support our most significant interests? Do they even make snide comments that lead us to avoid certain conversations with them? It's good to be able to socialize with people who don't share your values, of course. But keeping relationships on life support simply because we feel obligated to is hardly the way to promote longevity and a higher quality of life. It creates rather than relieves stress and it tempts us to abandon our goals rather than hold fast to them. We do well to gently but deliberately disengage ourselves from these relationships. We don't have to hurt others' feelings unnecessarily. At the same time, we ought to respect ourselves enough to assert our need for space when it feels like someone's attitude is intruding on our inner well-being.

There's a real danger in surrounding ourselves with people who lack the driving joy of life that fuels our chronologically gifted lifestyle. These are "go with the flow" people. They don't take the long view of their lives, aren't proactive about their health, and lead more sedentary lifestyles that fit the popular mold of the average American adult. In youth they may have seemed happy and healthy. Yet as they enter their senior years, they may be encumbered by a greater number of difficulties and are more likely to die at an earlier age than necessary. Such people may not actively criticize our longevity pursuits (and they may even encourage them), but they don't share our passion for living well into old age. As a result, they'll drag us down subtly even without trying.

Motivational speaker, Jim Rohn, is often quoted saying, "You are the average of the five people you spend the most time with, including yourself."[103] The logic of his statement is compelling. It is because we spend so much time with them that they have such a profound influence on the individuals we become. That's because we naturally emulate others especially when we associate them with pleasurable feelings of well-being. So if we associate with people who like to drink and smoke when they get together, we're more likely to engage in these activities as well and associate them with having a good time. According to a 2007 study[104], people whose closest friends are obese tend to become obese themselves. But the reverse is also true. People who spend time with others who seek to improve themselves usually feel inspired to make positive changes in their own lives too.

The next logical step in this progression is to surround ourselves with the type of people we would most like to become. If we want to combat procrastination, for instance, it would behoove us to spend more time in the company of productive people. If we want to feel inspired to serve others, we should spend more time with our servant-hearted acquaintances. And if we want to become chronologically gifted, we should surround ourselves with others who already understand the principles of living a longer and healthier life with more purpose and passion into their nineties and beyond. We need like-minded people in our lives so that we can stay strong when others around us succumb to messages of weakness and frailty as they age.

2. *A source of encouragement.*

Do you know people perpetually seem to have a black cloud hanging over their heads? Have you ever noticed the way they tend to bring that black cloud over your head when you spend too much time with them? It's true. Attitudes are contagious. Being in the company of others who are in a bad mood tends to put us in a bad mood right alongside them. Being around people with a more positive outlook on life tends to make us feel hopeful and invigorated instead.

Everyone has bad days, but some seem to have them more frequently than others. Look for friends who bounce back quickly from adversity, who focus on life's joys rather than life's sorrows, and who seem to come out on the other side of challenges better for having gone through them. Such people are a constant and much-needed source of encouragement. They will become more important than ever later in your life, when certain difficulties may multiply rather than diminish with age. Let them inspire you to seize joyfully the here and now of your day, leaving the regrets of your past and the vagaries of an uncertain future where they belong—in second place to the life-giving enjoyment of the present.

3. *Willing to listen.*

Good friends invest themselves in others by taking the time to listen—really listen—to what their friends have to say. They don't seem distracted while they're talking to them. Nor do they constantly seem to forget the little details of their friends' lives, forcing them to repeat the specifics. Recognizing that friendship is a bilateral relationship, they take genuine interest in a friend's thoughts and feelings and don't monopolize conversations. That's not to say that they're necessarily quiet people, of course. It's just that good listeners really take in what people tell them and process it before responding. What is shared makes a difference both ways. As a result, friends grow closer, regardless of who is doing the talking at the moment. In the end, there is mutual fulfillment for having shared the time together.

By contrast, avoid spending too much time with people who are self-involved, even if they appear otherwise. Such people may deserve your respect—perhaps even your admiration—but they're often poor listeners who take more from their friendships than they put back into them. Don't try to invest yourself in an effectively unilateral relationship, where conversations generally flow one way all of the time. It will drain your emotional reserves.

4. *Loyal to a fault.*

Members of your inner circle ought to have your back, no matter what. It's just that simple. You have to be able to trust them with your secrets, sincerely believe they have your best interests at heart, and count on them to defend you against others who are out to defeat your passions and deflate your dreams. Being chronologically gifted is difficult enough without the emotional setbacks that come from being betrayed by a close friend. You need teammates you can count on.

When I say "loyal to a fault," I don't mean these will be people who simply reflect back at you the person you want to see, regardless of whether it's true or not. Flattery results in a narcissistic preoccupation with ourselves that hides fatal flaws and minimizes the consequences of poor life choices. Real friends—truly loyal friends—don't let their companions persist in self-destructive behaviors without protest. They respect their friends' right to make decisions for themselves, but their loyalty prevents them from even tacitly supporting them in choosing an unhealthy, longevity-defeating lifestyle. Likewise, truly loyal friends entertain no illusions that their companions are always right. Nevertheless, they will err on the side of defending the dignity and honor of their loved ones in public and gently confront them in private.

There's a connection between loyalty and *moai* too. It is a kind of extended family. Typically, we think of the love of our family members as being unconditional, and we hope their support for us will be just as loyal. But not all of us will be so fortunate. A truly loyal member of your *moai* may occasionally have to do for you what your own blood family either can't or won't. This becomes especially important when you think of your inner circle following you into your later years in life. Loyalty during that time may mean prodding you to seek medical attention for a health condition your family isn't around to see. Or it might mean taking drastic steps to help you preserve your independence at home when your family is making overtures toward having you prematurely placed under others' care. It might even mean assuming a measure of financial responsibility for an unforeseen expense that your other loved ones simply don't have the resources to bear for you.

Although you may not be at that point in your life now, someday it will happen. So just take a moment to ask yourself, "If bad turns to worse, can I depend on my friends to do for me what I would be willing to do for them?" If the answer is no, then you need more loyal friends in your life.

5. *Authentic.*

This is a tough one because most of us aren't as comfortable in our own skin as we'd like to think. Some of us are better at living in a way that honors the reality of who we are, while others tend to make Herculean efforts to live as though they are someone else. The people who make good friends for our inner circles are the ones who are courageously authentic. That is, they've come to terms with everything they bring to the table—the good, the bad, and the ugly—and they love themselves enough to be honest about their flaws, while still taking pride in their strengths. They neither look to others to prop them up, nor do they tolerate people who tear them down. Instead, they surround themselves with people whose strengths complement their own, who help temper their own weaknesses even as they help others overcome theirs. Everyone's on the same team because that's how the give-and-take of authentic friendships work.

You may need to do a little work to be more authentic yourself (most of us do). But if you're reading this book, you're already on the right track. The chronologically gifted recognize that life is too short to spend their years perpetuating an inaccurate portrait of themselves or others. Reality is what matters. They want to be around people who can model what it looks like to love oneself truthfully—having the courage to let others challenge them in the process of their evolving to become the best they can be. People incapable of seeing and appreciating themselves realistically are unable to see and appreciate the best in others too.

6. *Available.*

Even the best longevity resource is useless unless it's there when you need it. The same is true of your friends. Whatever other qualities they may possess, your friends' availability is of paramount importance. If they're not there, they simply can't make much of a difference.

Do your friends expect you to accommodate their schedules all the time, or do they make efforts to spend time with you on your terms? If you commit to meet on a set schedule (like once weekly or once monthly), do they clear time and space for your conversations, or do they frequently make excuses and reschedule? When you're talking, do your friends seem to be "present" for the conversation, or do they often seem distracted, as though other, more important issues are on their mind? Can you be certain that, in a personal emergency, they would move mountains to be there for you when you really need them?

I don't ask these questions to impugn your friends' characters. I simply want you to think hard about how available they really are for you. The chronologically gifted are purposefully available to their inner circle. As they seize the day, they waste no time doing what's important while the opportunity is there. And because they prioritize their relationships with others, their schedules tend to revolve around not merely their own desires, but also around others' needs. They keep their appointments with friends, and they relish the times when an impromptu walking date turns into an unhurried coffee date afterwards. They would rather miss a favorite TV show or get to bed a little later than usual if it means an opportunity to bond a little more deeply with a close friend.

You should be able to expect the same from your moai. So when you're looking for traveling partners on this journey toward a longer, healthier life, be sure to pay attention to who shows up most consistently. Those are the people who are the real players in your life. The others are just spectators.

Now that you know what to look for in your life's companions, let's close with a consideration of what you can do to attract these people:

- *Cultivate empathy.*

  You may hear about empathy frequently, but a lot of people fail to appreciate what the word really means—confusing it with similar concepts like compassion and sympathy. True empathy is a practiced ability to feel what others feel—not merely to appreciate how they feel. In this way, the appropriate social behavior can be selected in response. It's not a strategy as much as it is a quality. Empathetic people behave more compassionately and more sympathetically, but not because that's what seems appropriate. It's because those behaviors are what come naturally for them in response to their shared experience of others' feelings. When people are happy, the entire group experiences joy as well. Similarly, when a group member goes through a tragedy, an empathetic person shares the sadness and the emotional burden.

  Of course, there are some disadvantages to being hyper-empathetic. You don't want your own emotional well-being to be subjected to the whims of others' emotional states. This can be detrimental if you want to participate in a group setting in a meaningful way. But most of us could use a little more empathy in our lives and would benefit from trying to understand all the angles of what different people are feeling. To develop empathy, place yourself in the same position as others in order to begin feeling what they're feeling. This can be a tremendous show of solidarity with friends who are suffering, especially when their experiences mirror those we have had. In that context of shared suffering, coping strategies that might have helped us move on in the past become available for helping our friends move forward in the present, too.

For some, what may be more difficult is expressing true empathy when others are happy, coveting their friends' happiness and the circumstances that have brought it on. We can smile and say the appropriate words, but to experience the true happiness our friends our feeling is considerably more difficult. This is an area where the chronologically gifted exhibit a fundamentally different response. It takes practice, but they discipline themselves to share others' joys in a meaningful way. In doing so, they diminish the effect of any pain and suffering they may be going through themselves.

They know there's a time for sharing grief and other unpleasant emotions with their friends, but they truly look forward to their friends' celebrations—because in a very real sense, they're celebrating, too. And this is a big part of why the chronologically gifted tend to be happier people. They experience joy in relationship with others, even when their own lives are temporarily beset with challenges.

- *Be likable.*

As a general rule, outgoing and sociable people do better in life than insular people. "Throughout history," Grierson writes, "extroverts got an evolutionary leg up. They were the ones with the energy and will to forge helpful alliances and make useful discoveries, out there in a world full of scary other people."[105] This perspective is just common sense. Extroversion is a personality trait, so it's not something that will come naturally to everyone. And introverts—those who are exhausted by social situations and prefer to be alone—play an important role in close-knit groups of friends, too.[106] So we have to be careful, lest we suggest that being chronologically gifted means trying to be the "life of the party" all the time. But no matter how you slice it, likable people are going to attract more friends, and likable people tend to have more extroverted qualities—even if they have to drum them up from time to time.

Extroverts enjoy themselves in large groups and are not easily intimidated by strangers. They have a certain amount of self-confidence that enables them to greet others without fear or hidden suspicions that others are judging them. They can graciously receive compliments without seeming arrogant. They have interesting ideas and stories to share and people want to hear from them. At the same time, they don't try to monopolize conversations because they're equally interested in hearing from others in the group.

You can't become an extrovert, or even behave like one consistently, through sheer force of will. Yet you might be surprised at what you can learn from one, even if you're the most quiet, introverted person on the planet. You can boost your likability factor and feel better in your own skin the way an extrovert does by avoiding gossip and making it a point to complain less. Instead, you can talk about what you're grateful for. You can resist calling out your own or others' faults habitually and look for the best in people, making it a point to compliment them. You can stay up-to-date on current issues so that you can talk intelligently about them in social situations. Most importantly, you can be the one at the table who looks for the silver lining in every tragedy, who prefers to be the voice of moderation when others are advocating extremes, and who chooses to bring up positive subjects instead of dwelling on life's challenges.

If you can behave that way in social situations, it doesn't matter whether it comes naturally to you or not. Either way, you'll attract more high-quality friends.

- *Know when and how to keep others' secrets.*

Trust is the bedrock of all meaningful relationships, and it's of paramount importance within the confines of your inner circle. The privilege of vulnerability with your friends entails the responsibility of holding their confidences in sacred trust and never divulging them.

There is one exception to this rule, and it ties back to what I said earlier about how friends are loyal to a fault. When a friend confesses something that leads you to believe he or she is caught in a pattern of self-destruction, it may be unloving for you to keep that secret from others who would try to help him or her. Such is the case in addictive cycles, where friends so easily become enablers of others' problems even though they earnestly want what's best for their friends. It's honorable for friends to refuse to be enablers but, before you divulge a secret, be sure to check your motives. Be absolutely certain that your reasons for breaking trust are pure and that anyone with whom you share a friend's secret is in a position to help them.

Before people are willing to share their big secrets with you, you'll have to demonstrate your ability to be trustworthy on a smaller scale. Enough said. If trust and secret-keeping are a problem area for you, then you're not ready for the emotional commitment and solidarity of a moai.

- *Go the extra mile.*

There's no room for selfishness in a moai-type relationship. That's because these types of friends are willing to go above and beyond social expectations to demonstrate their love for one another. In fact, an Oxford University study found that, given the opportunity, volunteers will endure greater pain for the benefit of their closest friends than they would for mere acquaintances, blood relatives, or even themselves.[107] This suggests that the bonds of close friendship exert a far more powerful altruistic force on us than we typically expect. And since altruism is a powerful source of life purpose, it's little wonder that the mutually supportive nature of a *moai* has such potency for longevity. Feeling strongly connected to others with a shared purpose draws out the best in us by focusing our attentions on the welfare of others—not just ourselves.

Members of a *moai* celebrate successes more fully than what others outside the circle might consider insignificant victories. For example, when a group member is trying to lose weight or eat better, all members hop on board and do it with them—whether they need to or not. They lend to those in need, and make every effort to show their friends that they understand and care about them. And yet they do this in a way that simultaneously reveals that they aren't looking for applause or a pat on the back.

In short, the people who make up a good *moai* are looking for others who will unconditionally drop their own priorities in a time of need and go to limitless lengths for love's sake. If that doesn't describe you—or if others can't figure out from the way you interact with them that it's true about you—you have some work to do. This attitude should be present before trying to build an inner circle that will support you unconditionally on your quest to become chronologically gifted.

Let's get to work!

More so than any previous chapter, this one contains many practical suggestions for making your home and private life into a personal longevity hot spot. Nevertheless, it's a lot of information to take in at once, and I highly recommend that you work on one section at a time. As you get started, here are specific suggestions for putting this chapter's ideas into concrete action right away:

Suggestion #1: Inventory your primary living spaces.
Have you ever had to do a home inventory for your homeowner's insurance policy? It's really tough. You're supposed to go room by room, listing all of the valuable items you own so that if—destiny has it—your home should be broken into, destroyed by fire, or otherwise come to ruin, your insurance company would have a concrete replacement value for your most precious belongings, enabling you to start over. But as you walk through the rooms of your house, immediately it becomes obvious that no check from your insurance company, no matter how large, could enable you to replace certain items—like childhood photos, children's artwork, the sofa you inherited from your grandmother, or the books you took with you to college. Such items are, in a very real sense, irreplaceable. They're laden with sentimental value, and their loss would be excruciating for you.

In this context, I'd like to suggest a similar activity, but one focused much less on the financial value of your possessions and more exclusively on their sentimental value. Go through your home, room by room, making a list of all the objects that are immediately visible as you enter. (Never mind what is out of sight for the sake of this activity.) Structure your list into three columns. In the first column, write what you see. In the second, write a concise statement of why you have that object. And in the third column, write what that object means to you today.

This list will take many days for you to develop, and that's part of the point. I want you to experience the time it takes to inventory the objects in your home that compete for your attention. Doing so you'll realize, even as you make this list, that realistically there's no way for you to give all of them the attention you think they deserve. Start by going through your primary bathroom (which should be the simplest). Then proceed to your bedroom, and finish with your main living area. (Save the other rooms of your house for later.) When you're finished compiling your lists, put them away for a week or two. Then take them out again for a review.

Now it's time to do some serious soul-searching. As you go through your lists, ask yourself this question about each item: "How does this object help me achieve my goal of living a longer, better life than the one I'm living now?" If you can immediately and clearly articulate a response to that question, mark the letters "CG" (for "chronologically gifted") next to those items. These will be the objects you will not only keep, but also showcase in your home more prominently (where appropriate).

Now go back through your list for a second time. Ask yourself this question: "Does this object in any way distract me from my goal of living a longer, better life?" That's a tough question because it requires some honesty—brutal honesty. Perhaps you know, for instance, that looking at the picture of your estranged daughter is a source of sadness for you. Why would you continue to display that picture in your hallway, where you have to see it every time you leave your bedroom? I want you to place an "X" next to the objects you think are distracting, committing yourself to either getting rid of them or to putting them out of sight.

As for the rest of the objects—the ones that are neither clearly promoting your goal nor obstructing it—the choice is yours. Decide what constitutes clutter and if it does, donate it to charity. If it's not, find a way to make better use of it.

Suggestion #2: Make a "get away from it all" plan, and be ready to use it.

We've talked about how important it is for our aging brains to experience periodic interruptions in our routines. Such interruptions are best when they come organically into our lives. That's because they require us to adapt in the moment and to grow more resilient in the face of circumstances we can't control. As a proactive measure for the growth of the inner limbic brain, plan a mini-vacation from "life as usual," and be prepared to activate that plan at the first sign of a stressful situation.

This should not be a complex or elaborate plan. In fact, the more flexible, the better. Once you've decided to activate it, having gaps in the procedural details will help stimulate the adaptive part of your brain to treat it as a mini-crisis that needs to be resolved. The result will be a memorable life event that will help shed the temporary stress that led you to activate the plan. From this experience, you'll gain the confidence to make another getaway plan when you need it next.

Pull out a world map. Look for places you've always wanted to visit but, for whatever reason, never have. In particular, look for sites of intellectual and spiritual stimulation. Tibet, anyone? This exercise will promote the kind of limbic growth that, even at a relatively young age, helps stave off dementia and other chronic maladies later in life. Once you've identified a few ideas, write them down and display them in a prominent place—such as on your refrigerator—where you'll be reminded about the getaways you are contemplating. And feel free to add to the list anytime new ideas occur to you!

The hope is that the more you see your list of ideas, the more appealing at least one of them will become until, one day, you'll just decide it's time to do it. Why wait any longer? Then, contact a couple of your closest friends and invite them to come along, forging a new shared memory in the process. When you come back, you'll all be saying, "We should do that again sometime."

And you will. Because that's what the chronologically gifted do. They see their world as a palette of limitless opportunities, if only they're willing to seize the day and step out of their comfort zones to try new ventures. By the way, if no one in your life is able or willing to join you—do it by yourself. You can do it!

Suggestion #3: Inventory your primary relationships.
Pull out an address book, open your list of email contacts, or get out your most recent photo albums. Spend some time going through these records, lingering over each one. As you do, picture the person's face. Think about your most recent encounter with that individual—whether it was positive or negative. Think about the shared stories that you have with that person. Try recalling how you met him or her as well as whether you've stayed involved with each other since then.

That sounds like a lot to think about, but for our purposes you are interested primarily in the memories that most vividly come to mind. After you've given some thought to each individual, go back through the list and ask yourself two questions. First, "How would I assess my current relationship with this individual: 'as good as it's ever been;'

'okay, but there's room for improvement;' or 'it was nice while it lasted'?" Then, "Does this relationship help or hurt my goal of living longer and better, and how?"

The answer to that second question ought to prompt action on the first. If it's a good relationship that you're convinced is helping you become chronologically gifted, then write a capital "M" next to that person's name and circle it—they're already a part of your *moai*. If you know someone is good for you in helping you achieve your goals, but you know your relationship could use some work, write an "m" next to that person's name and make a commitment to do your part to strengthen that bond. And if you find anyone on your list who obstructs your chronologically gifted values, place an "X" next to their name, noting that you should probably look for ways to keep a little psychological distance from their negative influence on your life. That doesn't mean cutting them out of your life altogether—especially if they're family. But it does mean giving yourself some objective permission to reduce their access to you. Also, it subtly reminds you of the importance of remaining open to new, potentially life-enriching relationships.

BE GIFTED–Do the hard thing: forgive someone.

There is one behavior the chronologically gifted refuse to engage in, and that's holding grudges. They recognize that resentments are like poison, slowly killing the enjoyment of their remaining years. All too often, we hold onto these grudges out of unresolved anger and bitterness, failing to see the damaging nature of what we're doing to ourselves in the process. The people against whom our contempt is directed, however, continue to go about their lives, unaffected by the negative feelings we're harboring toward them. And if someone actively tries to make amends for the past and attempts to reconcile a damaged relationship, our grudges only serve to make that process more difficult for them, perpetuating the very situation that forced us apart in the first place.

In other words, we're the ones who get hurt most by our grudges. They raise our stress level, foster a poor outlook on life, and corrode our ability to relate to others in a positive way. They short-circuit our attempts to live longer, better lives by introducing life-shortening and joy-killing preoccupations with what we can't control. This mindset keeps our attention miserably fixed in the past when it should be focused instead on our enjoyment of the present and our goals for the future.

Letting go of a grudge requires forgiveness, and this isn't easy. "Grudges come with an identity," writes social worker Nancy Colier. "As much as we don't like it, there also exists a kind of rightness and strength in this identity. ... To let go of our grudge, we have to be willing to let go of our identity as the 'wronged' one.... We have to be willing to drop the 'I' who was mistreated and step into a new version of ourselves, one we don't know yet, that allows the present moment to determine who we are, not past injustice."[108] Forgiveness is entirely dependent on our own determination to do it, not on the offender's apology, contrition, or overtures toward amends and reconciliation. And that means it's something we can do with or without the offender's remorse. We can forgive even when the offender isn't sorry. Or we can hold the grudge despite the offender's attempts to right the wrong.

I suggest we look at forgiveness as a way to love ourselves even more than it's a way to love others. No matter how sorry an offender might be, we don't forgive because that person deserves it. We do it because we deserve to be free of the anger, resentment, and poisonous influence of being wronged in the past. We deserve to be able to live more mindfully in the present and to do so without the encumbrances of stress, negative attitudes, and physiological symptoms that come from harboring unresolved grudges. Those grudges sap our longevity, which is precisely why the chronologically gifted embrace forgiveness: it simply helps us to live longer, better lives, beginning right here and right now.[109]

Be sure you don't confuse forgiveness with terms like "pardon" or "reconciliation." When we pardon people, basically we tell them that what they did wasn't that bad. When we pursue reconciliation, we're trying to restore relationships to the place they were before the offense. Forgiveness doesn't require either of these conditions. You can forgive someone without dismissing or minimizing the hurt that person has caused, and you can do so without necessarily feeling any desire to have a restored relationship with that individual.

Forgiveness is choosing not to hold the offense against the offender. That means choosing not to think negatively about the person every time you hear his or her name. It means deciding not to bring up the offense time and time again to hurt the person and defame them in others' presence. It means opting not to think about the offense and giving up on your expectations of being treated differently as a result of being a victim. In a nutshell, it means being the bigger person—being the one who chooses to thrive in the aftermath of hurt and to grow as a result. It's either that or doing the easy thing by wallowing in self-pity and waiting for the offender to make things right.

Forgiveness is transformative. Often, expressing forgiveness to offenders stimulates their desire for reform. Suddenly and earnestly, they want to make amends for the hurt they caused others, seeking reconciliation with people they have been estranged from through past behavior. It's powerful when that happens, but always remember that forgiveness takes place first. You can forgive someone without necessarily deciding to express that forgiveness to the person who wronged you. But if you choose to express it, be prepared for different possibilities. The truly impenitent offender may say something like, "I don't need your forgiveness. I never did anything wrong." The remorseful offender, on the other hand, may misinterpret your forgiveness as a sign that you're okay with going back to the way things were before the offense.

Forgiveness is hard work. The chronologically gifted choose to forgive immediately. They don't wait for the offender to show remorse or apologize because life's too short for that. They release themselves from the pain and suffering of past hurts by releasing those who have wronged them from con-demnation for what they have done. They hope for recon-ciliation and may even take the initiative in restoring broken relationships. They do this even when they're not at fault and are fully aware that reconciliation may never occur. They're okay with that outcome because they know that either way, they'll live a happier, longer life because they chose to forgive.

In all probability, there is at least one person that imme-diately comes to mind when I talk about harboring grudges. My challenge to you is to think hard about what it would take for you to forgive that person—whether or not you choose to express that forgiveness to him or her. It might help to seek the perspective of a trusted friend or a professional counselor in this endeavor. But don't think of it as a request to help the person who offended you. Instead, think of it as an invitation to finally rid yourself of an emotional weight that is dragging you down and preventing you from living today as though your best years are still ahead of you.

Let go and move on. YOU CAN DO IT!

The bottom line

We may not live in one of the world's Blue Zones, but that doesn't mean we can't pattern our lifestyles after the people who do. We can't control the cultural and physical environments that surround us on a daily basis, but we can control how we interact with them. Blue Zones offer some potent lessons.

If we choose, we can turn our private lives—our homes and our relationships—into longevity hot spots that reinforce our chronologically gifted values. If you're serious about making the most out of the years you have left, then it pays to live in a whole new world of your own making. Don't settle for the mundane, lowest-common-denominator standard of American retirement culture. Make your living environment a place where life matters—for as long as you still have breath.

I'm doing it. So can you!

Personal Journal Pages

Personal Blue Zone—Envision It. My ideas for making it happen:

_____

_____

_____

_____

_____

_____

_____

_____

_____

_____

_____

_____

_____

_____

_____

_____

_____

– 7 –
You Can Do It!

We're nearing the end of our time together, but we're not done just yet. As a motivational speaker, I address audiences of all kinds—young and old alike—who have one belief in common: they're weary of the business of living. For many, life is hard. Our culture is full of quick fixes that don't work and easy coping mechanisms that compound rather than solve our biggest problems.

It's my mission to reinvigorate people's confidence and remind them that they truly can lead much happier and more fulfilling lives. Now, they just have to resolve to do what they know they have the power within them to do. There's no magic in that statement. It's just simple, profound truth. It's the truth that so many of us forget in our quest for self-fulfillment, and it's the truth I want to emphasize in this final chapter. I want readers to remember one concept as we end our time together. There's nothing—literally nothing—that we've talked about that is beyond your grasp. If you want it badly enough, you can be chronologically gifted. It's a choice, not a birthright.

There's nothing that I've suggested in these pages that I haven't tried myself. All the content in this book arises from what I've known to work for others as well. I don't pretend to have any big, esoteric secrets about the art and science of living longer. I do, however, believe in the power of the chronologically gifted lifestyle to add more years to your sojourn on this planet. More importantly, I believe in the power of the chronologically gifted perspective to lend meaning and purpose, not only to your "here and now," but also to the "there and then" of your remaining years. I am convinced that if more of us lived the way the chronologically gifted do, we could make this world a much better place, one where society would consider it a privilege—yes, a privilege—to get older.

Many of us read a self-help book like this, and we turn each page voraciously, nodding vigorously as each suggestion hits home. We resolve to put the insights into action immediately. But then we close the book and feel only vaguely better off than when we started reading. That's because we realize that no book can infuse us with the author's personal experiences and the knowledge of how to use the information presented. Too often what happens is that we read a book like this, feel a temporary burst of hope and motivation, perhaps start working on a few action items, and then realize how naive we were to think it could be so easy. In this demoralized state, we forget what we've learned, give up on the habits we thought we could acquire, and start looking for another solution to our problems. And the cycle begins all over again.

That's why I'm writing this chapter. I believe in the power of what we've been talking about, and I'm not willing to let you accept a less than a chronologically gifted way of life. I'm not writing it for the person you are now, but more the person you can become. In other words, I'm writing it for the future you—the one who will not be tempted to give up just when you're on the cusp of a major breakthrough. No one wants to re-read an entire book, but I hope you'll come back time and time again to this chapter—as often as necessary—and let it rekindle your purpose and passion to live a longer, more fulfilling life. Let it inspire you to go back to the other chapters if you're struggling in a particular area. What I've included in this book is life-elongating wisdom, culled from experience and deep personal research on the subject.

So here's my main message for you in this chapter:

You can do it!

Yes...you CAN do it!

YOU (and no one but YOU) can do it!

I wouldn't write this book or share the information with my audiences unless I believed that truth from the bottom of my heart. There are no prerequisites to becoming chronologically gifted other than the deep-seated conviction that you are worthy and capable of living out your years joyfully regret-free. Age doesn't have to determine our future. "It's a *choice*," write Crowley & Lodge, "not a sentence from on high. You can make up your mind—and tell your body—to live as if you were fifty, maybe even younger, for most of the rest of your life."[110]

Let's remind ourselves why we undertook this journey in the first place, and let's remember where we're headed—together.

We've covered a lot of ground.

I want to do you a huge favor. I can condense everything we've talked about in this book to ten simple principles. They encapsulate the key takeaways from each of the previous chapters, and they are suitable for posting on your refrigerator. Write these principles down in your own handwriting. Memorize them. List each one on an index card or Post-it™ note and put them all around your home. They will be reminders of the thought-habits that will (and do) define your determination to live the longest, best life possible.

Are you ready? Here we go with the 10 principles of the chronologically gifted.

1. *Get rid of the phrase, "I'm too old for that."*

   Eliminate it from your vocabulary and from your thinking. Instead of approaching old age as an imposition of new limitations, focus on opportunities to overcome challenges and acquire new skills. Be determined to embrace aging as part of the cycle of life—and really live each day for all it's worth. Start when you're 20, and it will be a habit that sticks with you until you're 100+.

2. *Find a reason for getting up in the morning.*

   Figure out what makes you tick when others just want to give up. Write it down. Make it your life mantra.

Anytime the difficulties of life threaten to overwhelm you, let your inner sense of purpose pull you up by your bootstraps and remind you that your life matters now as it will until the end of your days.

3. *Connect with something bigger than yourself.*

   In addition to your daily pursuits and occasional travel, volunteer your time for a worthy cause. Plug in to a spiritual community. Meditate. Pray. Read thought-provoking books that force you to contend with the big questions in life. If you can, get in touch with a higher power that simultaneously helps you feel your smallness and your importance in this crazy universe, where nothing is ever lost and no energy is ever wasted.

4. *Look on the bright side. Embrace a positive explanatory style.*

   Hardship is temporary. Victory is just around the corner. Find little reasons every day to be grateful for your life—even in the face of negativity. Resolve to live mindfully with purpose and passion so that you savor the best gifts that life has to offer. Focus on solutions, not problems.

5. *Get moving.*

   Pick a physical activity you truly enjoy—something you're really passionate about—and do it regularly. Take lots of walks. Use the stairs. Bike to the store instead of driving. Plant and tend to a garden. Find ways to incorporate low-intensity exercise of all kinds (strength, balance, and aerobic) into your everyday life to ward off the potentially debilitating effects of aging on your body.

6. *Stay fueled.*

Eat more fruits and vegetables and fewer simple carbohydrates. Drink lots of water and an occasional glass of red wine. Snack on nuts and berries. Serve yourself smaller portions, and put the rest of the food away before sitting down to eat. Pause to savor your favorite flavors. Don't eat on the go. Eat smaller meals more frequently, and put the unhealthy foods out of sight and out of reach to purge temptations.

7. *Create your own personal Blue Zone.*

Structure your home to encourage good sleep, healthy eating habits, and spiritual well-being. Get rid of excess technological noise, and create a space for meditation. Shed the clutter and add some greenery. Invest in comfortable pillows and light-blocking drapes for the bedroom. Display pictures of family and friends and souvenirs of treasured life experiences.

8. *Don't do it alone.*

Connect with like-minded, loyal, authentic people who will help you reach your goals. Spend time with them weekly. Share their burdens, and let them share yours. Rejoice with them in their victories, and let them rejoice with you in yours. Learn to forgive, and reach out to your estranged family members before it's too late to reconcile. Life is too short for grudges.

9. *Believe in yourself.*

Give yourself some credit. Right now, be determined to become the person you want to be and resolve to make it happen. Remember that obstacles are only temporary setbacks. You're stronger than any of them.

10. *Seize the day.*

Above all else, live today as though it really matters. Don't do anything you'll regret, but don't let fear prevent you from experiencing the fullness of life right here and now. Live today so that you could die tomorrow without regrets.

Now, even though we've reduced much of our discussion to these ten essential points, approach each one at your own pace. Don't try doing them all at once. Start gradually with the small steps that are easiest to implement in the short term, while working on one bigger area at a time. Especially in the wake of a major life event, like an illness or the loss of a loved one, it's instinctive to rush into gaining control over our lives. With our seemingly superhuman strength, we attempt to tackle everything on our master to-do list at once. That's good for getting started, but sustaining such a massive effort over the long run can be overwhelming. When that happens, we're more likely to give up on all of it than to break it down into achievable milestones. It's always better to start small and to build on past victories because lifestyle changes that happen at a slower pace are more likely to be permanent.

Live today a little more like the tomorrow you envision. And live tomorrow a little more like you envision the next day.

Don't let setbacks derail you. Give yourself permission to take a breath. Then get right back up and continue moving in the direction you were headed. Focus on the stretch right in front of you, and one day you'll look up and realize how far you've already come—and you'll stop caring so much about how far you still have to go.

The power of a good habit

There's no question that much of what we've talked about in this book is going to mean changing some hard and fast routines in your life. Most of us—let's face it—don't fit the chronologically gifted mold by default. We fit into society's self-destructive matrix, going along with unhelpful messaging about what the "good life" looks and feels like. We worship a concept of youth that is fixated on immediate gratification, outward appearances, and easy solutions. But the chronologically gifted perspective on life isn't guided by those values. It seeks long-term happiness by re-framing our understanding of what it means to be happy in the first place. It engenders meaningful change through sustained (and sustainable) lifestyle habits that are conducive to longevity, beginning now and continuing indefinitely. The chronologically gifted keep their eyes on the prize of living well, and they're willing to take concrete steps to reach that goal. Because today is a gift. And tomorrow—if granted to us—will be a gift, too.

Many of us talk about getting rid of our bad habits, which makes us feel like we're already on the losing side of the equation. We have to clean out the garbage of our life—a project that sounds like a lot of work that will involve pain and confusion. We don't even know how to start. "We tend to be comfortable with our behaviors and habits, even when they're not always beneficial—they're familiar," Dr. Creagan observes. "They give order and stability to our lives." No one likes change.

Okay, so that's the bad news. Strictly speaking, we need to get rid of certain unproductive (or counter-productive) habits if we want to live longer, more fulfilling lives. Changing those habits won't be easy or fun. But many of us would benefit from a more positive way of considering the matter. "Most people underestimate their ability to change," Creagan says. "And changing behaviors in small ways can add up to a big difference."[111] Instead of thinking in terms of getting rid of bad habits, we should think more affirmatively in terms of acquiring new, chronologically gifted ones. These hold the promise of a richer life now and tomorrow. They are the habits that define the kind of person we've already decided we want to become.

To make space to practice those new habits, we're going to have to do a little housecleaning along the way. But I never advise people to focus on the bad. For example, don't pay attention to your junk food habits, telling yourself, "I've got to start eating better." Instead, become seduced by the endeavor of exploring healthy new foods you've never tried before. Then set a goal of eating more of them. Instead of thinking about how lazy you feel when you just sit at home on a Sunday afternoon, make a plan to visit a friend you haven't connected with in a while. Let your goal of improving your relationship with that person displace your sense of guilt over being sedentary.

While we're on the topic, there's also some good news about what it takes to form new habits. Research suggests that new habits can become ingrained in as little as two months of consistent practice. The actual length of time varies with the complexity or difficulty of the task, the frequency of its performance, and the individual's determination and discipline. Researchers have also charted a correlation between early success and automaticity. That is, the more consistently a new behavior is successfully practiced during the first several weeks, the more likely it is to become automatic or habitual. So while occasional breaks from a good habit are to be expected, someone who is trying to acquire a good habit would do well to avoid taking those breaks until after the first two months.[112]

Business writer, Charles Duhigg, describes how neuro-scientists have traced habit-making behaviors to a part of the brain called the basal ganglia. This section of our brain is responsible, among other tasks, for our emotional development, memories, and our ability to recognize patterns. It's not the usual decision-making part of our brain, which is the prefrontal cortex. What scientists have discovered is that habitual behaviors aren't really conscious decisions made by our prefrontal cortex, but automatic behaviors that are regulated by the part of our brain that remembers patterns. Duhigg summarizes what researchers have come to describe in terms of a "habit loop:"

> First, there is a cue, a trigger that tells your brain to go into automatic mode and which habit to use. Then there is the routine, which can be physical or mental

or emotional. Finally, there is a reward, which helps your brain figure out if this particular loop is worth remembering for the future. Overtime, this loop ... becomes more and more automatic. The cue and reward become intertwined until a powerful sense of anticipation and craving emerges.[113]

In other words, when we apply this insight to the chronologically gifted lifestyle, we can say that our brains are wired to look for and take advantage of shortcuts that make us literally crave a longer, better life for ourselves. We simply have to show it the way to get from here to there—something this book has armed you to do more successfully than most others.

Habits offer an evolutionary advantage because they allow our brains to delegate certain routines to our inner autopilot. In this way, the decision-making part of our brains can focus on other, more pressing behaviors. It's a way of allowing us to do more with fewer resources. Overtime, our routines become so automatic that we don't have to think much about them, which is good news when the routine promotes longevity and bad news when it doesn't. Fortunately, the habit loop helps us understand how we can train our brains to adopt new routines and make them automatic. Also, it teaches us how to discontinue old routines that we no longer want.

The secret lies in the brain's pairing of a particular cue with a reward that reinforces your chronologically gifted lifestyle. Scientists have found that cues can be almost anything, from seeing a specific item on TV to being in a particular place at a given time. Or, it could even be any emotion or sequence of thoughts. And rewards are equally diverse. They could be physical sensations—like the pleasure of tasting favorite foods or the rush of endorphins that comes after vigorous physical exercise. Or they could be purely emotional reactions, such as a swell of pride or happiness in response to self-congratulation or a friend's affirmation.

When we want to form good habits, we need to look for the intrinsic rewards from these behaviors. Exercise, for instance, can leave us feeling sexier and more energetic. Yet, if the activity is itself a source of pride—like running or rowing—then it can also help grow our self-esteem and sense of achievement. Instead of focusing on the challenge of the activity, we celebrate the joy and pleasure of the finish. We savor it and amplify it in our minds so that our brains say, "Hey, this is pretty good. I really like the way I feel when we do this every day. Let's put that routine on autopilot to keep us going." When we allow these rewards to motivate our training and then actually get up and jog each morning, our basal ganglia begin associating the early morning with the routine exercise that brings the reward of an elevated mood. Also, this habit brings a healthy appetite for a good breakfast when we return. Increasingly, that early morning light makes us crave a good jog before breakfast, until even the act of sitting down to eat breakfast feels empty without being preceded by our routine exercise.

That's the power of a good habit. Properly channeled, our brain's addictive power can make the chronologically gifted perspective a self-fulfilling prophecy. As Dr. Amen explains, "... the way to make a "once-and-for-all decision" is to feed your brain new experiences and new learning until your neurons 'fire and wire together' to become new neuron nets, or new automatic thoughts and actions."[114] When you're working to form new habits, this automatic response can also help reduce the impact of temptation.

There's something profoundly beautiful about the way nature created us for this kind of efficiency. If we would cooperate with our bodies, we would find that they are perfectly engineered to carry us well into our 80s and 90s+ with limited disability. That's because the lifestyles that characterize those in the world's Blue Zones can be programmed into our brains to the point where we self-engineer ourselves to be longevity machines, while hardly noticing the difference. Especially given the continuing advances in medical care and technology, we ought to be living longer and healthier lives already. And I'm convinced that we would be, except for the popular shortcuts that encourage us to acquire unhealthy, life-shortening habits. These notions cause us to adopt a detrimental view of aging that leads us to fear and fight it rather than embrace it with dignity and grace.

Don't sell yourself short. No matter how entrenched your habits might be, no matter how scary it might seem to think about making serious lifestyle adjustments, the science proves beyond the shadow of a doubt that you can do it. Becoming chronologically gifted isn't a birth right. It's a matter of choice. You can tell your body to do what it was made to do best: to live, really live, and to keep on living. Like me, I hope you strive to live to the ripe old age of 123!

A parting word...

There is one point I'd like to make sure you don't misunderstand as a result of the pep talk in this chapter. Not every piece of advice in this book will work for every reader. And not every reader will share my vision of what constitutes a long and healthy life. That's okay with me, and it should be okay with you, too. One of the beautiful realities about the chronologically gifted perspective on aging with vitality, passion and purpose is that it's fully customizable. It's not a one-size-fits-all approach to life. The most important idea to remember is eloquently summarized by Crowley & Lodge: "As with any meandering road, it is less a matter of getting someplace and more a matter of enjoying the ride."[115]

I'm a firm believer in the idea that one's later years are no time for self-imposed misery. Everything I've written so far is conditioned upon one crucial principle: *you should feel good about the decisions you've made.* The chronologically gifted are determined to live without regrets, regardless of where they are on the age spectrum. They don't succumb to the fallacy that suggests that they've waited too long to pursue a chronologically gifted lifestyle. But also, they don't change their lives purely for the sake of changing them, taking a scattershot approach to their happiness in the hopes that something will work.

So here's an important rule of thumb I'd like you to apply as you begin exploring the ideas we've talked about. It's possible that a new practice or lifestyle adjustment will entail some transitional discomfort. At the same time it's entirely reasonable that within a few weeks of trying something new (and certainly after no more than a month or two), you should see some results. They can show up in your physical appearance or energy level or simply within your thoughts and emotional well-being. While you're exploring the chronologically gifted life, it's critical to pause periodically and ask yourself whether a particular lifestyle adjustment is right for you or seems to work. Because if it's not right, then continuing to pursue it will only add to your discomfort and produce new sources of chronic stress into your life. Worse, it could become a form of self-punishment, and that negativity would cancel out any potential benefits.

If the lifestyle of the chronologically gifted described in this book isn't quite where you see yourself going, that's okay. There's no shame in living life your way, even if it doesn't align with the information we've provided. What's important is that you are the one in charge, and that you are the one whose vote counts more than anyone else's. If you're like me, you don't want to enter your later years someday believing—as social pressures would dictate—that your best times are behind you. You want to own the truth that you're the one, the only one, who gets to decide the quality of the time you have left, whether it's ten years or fifty.

There's an unhelpful stereotype about grumpy old men. It suggests that as we age, our personalities degenerate and we become less pleasant to be around and more cynical about the world around us. Whatever positive qualities we used to have tended to fade into the background as our negative personality characteristics become more pronounced. But none of that is true. Quite the opposite, in fact. Ravenna Helson is a principal investigator in the Mills Longitudinal Study at the University of California at Berkeley. This 50-year investigation of adult development has been following a group of 120 women who graduated from Mills College in 1958 and 1960. Now in their mid to late 70s, these women yield some remarkable insights into the personality traits that help people thrive as they enter later life. One of those traits is the ability to reinvent oneself. "We have to modify our identities as we go through life," Helson says, "Even at 60, people can resolve to make themselves more the people they would like to become. In the Mills Study, about a dozen women showed substantial positive personality change from ages 60 to 70."[116]

I have no doubt that as these women begin approaching 80 and 90, we're going to see even more data to support the idea that the ones who live the longest are the ones who are perpetually looking to a future they're convinced lies just around the corner. These are the ones who are determined to be more like the people they want to be, regardless of how many years they have left to achieve it.

So this leg of your journey is up to you. Regardless of how your life has gone so far or whether you're still in the opening chapters or well past the midpoint, you're the lead character in your life's story, and the conclusion hasn't been written yet. Don't fill those remaining pages with the negativity that comes from our cultural influence. Take charge! Be the one who adds new characters, new plot twists, and an inspired happy ending to the story. It's in your power. When you use your power, you'll discover there are many more blank pages at the end of your book than you ever imagined. And that means there's still plenty of room to turn your story into a riveting bestseller.

Let's get to work!

One of the key points I hope you'll take away from this book is the message that it's never too early and it's never too late to make changes and enrich your life. In my speaking engagements, I address people in their 20s as frequently as I address people in their 40s and 50s and beyond. During those sessions, I tell people to live today as though they're going to live forever. And I mean it. As Dr. Weil wisely reminds us, "The earlier in life you start to think about how you want to age and start doing something about it, the better."[117]

So no matter how old you are now, you owe it to your future self to live today. I firmly believe that there is an energy that survives life. Nothing is lost in this universe, and everything we do matters. Of course, I also encourage people to keep their perspectives realistic. The past is gone, so why dwell on it? And the future may never be because tomorrow isn't promised to us. So today is what really matters. It's not a license to do something stupid, but let's have a little fun before this ride is over!

I've already provided a lot of information for improving your chances of living a longer, richer life. So in this final send-off section, I'd like to suggest a few big picture exercises that can help you keep your eye on the prize, which is what really matters. It makes everything we've talked about, like nutrition, exercise, and discovering your *ikigai* worth the trouble.

Suggestion #1: Revisit the "I'm too old for that" list.

Remember the exercise we did back at the start of our time together? The one where I asked you to make a list of activities that you thought you were too old to do or might someday be too old to do? Pull out that list, and look it over again.

In particular, check to see whether there's even one item on that list that you find yourself feeling differently about now. It might be a physical activity you used to enjoy, or a social group you used to hang out with, or an educational goal you had given up on. If today you're feeling just a little bit more optimistic about your ability to meaningfully participate in that activity, that's awesome! You're well on your way to being chronologically gifted. Let that confidence compel action. Make a plan to do something concrete to realize that goal. As you do, you're reclaiming a small portion of the functional youth you previously thought you'd lost or imagined you might lose someday.

Meanwhile, pay attention to what hasn't changed on your list. Perhaps you're realizing that certain activities are off-limits now, and that's okay. But what I'd like you to do is leverage the new coping skills you've learned during our time together and use them to foster appreciation for what the activities meant to you in the past. Then let them go. Be determined to focus less on what you can no longer or might not be able to do and more on the new possibilities that are yet to come. For each item that you've decided to let go of, write in the margin at least one replacement opportunity that you intend to explore instead. For instance, if you need to let go of your high impact workouts because of mobility impairment, check out less strenuous alternatives, like a low-impact aerobic dance class. Meanwhile, start building your competence in something equally rewarding. Why not try learning the basics of a foreign language, just for the fun of it?

Suggestion #2: Inventory your less-than-helpful personal habits.

Most of us don't have to think too hard to come up with half a dozen unproductive habits that we wish we could get rid of overnight, yet can't seem to shake. These are attitudes and behaviors that obstruct our happiness. So here's an exercise to help you change how you approach those habits. It will help you shed the guilt as well as focus on your inner power to reinvent yourself.

Take a piece of paper and draw four columns. In the first column, list three bad habits that come to mind. In the second column, list the rewards you get from engaging in those habits. Remember, rewards can be physical sensations or emotional responses. In the third column, list an alternative habit you would like to see replace bad habits. And in the final column, write down what you think the reward would be of adopting each replacement habit.

Try focusing on what makes the reward of your bad habits so compelling. Then see if you can find alternative ways to get the same reward. Meanwhile, let the potential rewards of your desired habits compel you to try adopting new routines for three to five weeks. Remember to be consistent in how you perform these new routines. They are what help your brain recognize the cues necessary to make them automatic. Brain plasticity is your ally! Resist the temptation to stay stuck! Move forward with newfound determination. You can do it!

Suggestion #3: Look in the mirror.

In Chapter One, I invited you to look in the mirror and fall in love with yourself. Here, I'd like you to do that again. Only this time, as you look in the mirror, say to yourself, "You're gifted. You can do this." Say it often to yourself. Do it when you wake up in the morning. Do it when you get bad news from a friend. Do it whenever you're tempted to throw in the towel. Do it to celebrate every small victory. Over time, the lure of that truth will be so irresistible that you'll have to believe it. *YOU CAN DO IT!*

BE GIFTED – Write your story.

Life is a gift and a journey, something to be cherished and shared. Your story is unique and worth telling, even if you think you've lived a relatively quiet or uninteresting life so far. In my experience, it's often those who think they have little to share who possess some of the most fascinating personal anecdotes. In this exercise, I want to encourage you to capture the ups and downs, the most memorable moments, and the most newsworthy or personally significant aspects of your life in a tangible form that you can pass on to others who will come after you.

This project could take a variety of forms: a scrapbook, a memoir, a collection of mementos from different time periods, a photo album, original artwork, etc. Of course, trying to capture a whole life story can be a daunting task for those who aren't accustomed to it. If you have trouble getting started, consider some of the questions your children or grandchildren have asked or might ask you someday. Think about the stories you wanted to know about your parents' and grandparents' lives—especially those you never had a chance to learn about. Other helpful ways to frame your approach might include a chronology of your childhood, teenage years, young adulthood, etc. Another approach is to think back over your various jobs, major travel excursions or family vacations.

The method you select isn't as important as the story you will craft. And the goal of doing this isn't to present the adult equivalent of a school history project. It's to boost your appreciation for the tapestry of life you've woven so far. It is intended to inspire you to discover the complex and unexpected patterns that have shaped your story and to invite others to see where your story has intersected with theirs. It's an activity that will invite many fond memories but will trigger some painful ones as well. Embrace it all. Laugh and cry as you build your story. Enjoy the process.

When you're done, share your work with a member of the younger generation—perhaps someone who isn't a member of your family. In doing so, you provide enrichment for others.

The bottom line

"Too many people resist the transitions that come with age and never allow themselves to enjoy who they are," writes AARP CEO Jo Ann Jenkins. "I urge you to embrace it and be fearless. Once you do, you will be liberated to bring all of your prior experience and wisdom to design the life you want to live."[118] That's really great advice, but it doesn't apply only to senior citizens. The predominately negative view of aging we've been taught for so long is a self-fulfilling prophecy, one that begins with how we choose to live our lives while we're still quite young. If we listen to what the rest of the world tells us about getting older, we'll engage in precisely those behaviors that actually create the future we dread. Now is the time to combat these self-destructive tendencies and tell the world, "No! I don't buy it! I'm going to live to 100 and beyond!"

If we focus on the process of continual growth and opportunity that aging brings for the chronologically gifted— that is, if we discipline ourselves to view our futures with optimism while discovering rich new reasons to be thankful for today—then we're more likely to live longer and better lives that prove the naysayers wrong. We have the power to form new habits that offer a surprisingly bright and hopeful way forward for those riding the "silver tsunami." Because for those determined to make every day count, beginning right now, the possibilities are limited only by our imagination.

I hope you'll join me on this journey of self-discovery. At the time of this writing, the oldest man in the world is 112 and the oldest woman in the world is 117. The longest confirmed human lifespan is still 122 years.

I'm shooting for 123. And I intend to be just as happy at 123 as I am today.

Don't tell me I can't do it.

Personal Journal Pages

My ideas for getting rid of the phrase "I am too old for...":

_____

_____

_____

_____

_____

_____

_____

_____

_____

_____

_____

_____

_____

_____

_____

_____

YOU CAN DO IT!

_____

_____

_____

_____

_____

_____

_____

_____

_____

_____

_____

_____

_____

_____

_____

_____

_____

_____

References

Chapter 1

1   Andrew Weil, M.D., *Healthy Aging* (New York: Anchor Books, 2007), 109.

2   See Anne Tergeson, "To Age Well, Change How You Feel About Aging," *Wall Street Journal*, October 19, 2015. [http://www.wsj.com/articles/to-age-well-change-how-you-feel-about-aging-1445220002]. Accessed September 19, 2016.

3   Weil, 127.

4   NPR staff, "'Silver Tsunami' and Other Terms that Can Irk the Over-65 Set" (19 May 2014) [http://www.npr.org/2014/05/19/313133555/silver-tsunami-and-other-terms-that-can-irk-the-over-65-set].

5   See Edward T. Creagan, M.D., FAAHPM, Medical Editor, *Mayo Clinic on Healthy Aging* (Rochester, MN: Mayo Clinic, 2013), 64-65.

6   See Avi Roy, "Lust for life: breaking the 120-year barrier in human ageing." *The Conversation* 3 June 2013 [http://theconversation.com/lust-for-life-breaking-the-120-year-barrier-in-human-ageing-14911]. For a more extended and highly accessible discussion of this topic, see Weil 2007, 13-17.

7   Research oncologist Goberdhan P. Dimri describes the implications of this observation for modern cancer therapy in "What has senescence got to do with cancer?" *Cancer Cell* Vol. 7 (June 2005), 505-512.

[8] For a good overview, see "Evolutionary Theories of Aging" at the *Journal of Evolutionary Philosophy* [http://www.evolutionary-philosophy.net/aging.html].

[9] According to published census data, there were 53,364 centenarians living in the US in 2010, a rather significant increase from 32,194 centenarians in 1980.

[10] "The way research is going," says Matt Kaeberlein, biogerontologist at the University of Washington, "I see maybe 20 to 50 percent increases in healthy longevity as plausible in the next 40 to 50 years" (quoted in Bill Gifford, "Living to 120," *Scientific American*, Vol 315 No 3 [September 2016], page 64).

[11] Currently, the official list of Blue Zones identified by researcher Dan Buettner include Sardinia, Italy; Loma Linda, California, USA; Okinawa, Japan; Nicoya, Costa Rica; and Ikaria, Greece.

[12] Gifford, 67.

[13] As a side note, philosophers have wrestled with the ethical challenges of immortality for centuries. Many argue that the fleeting nature of our lives is what makes us vulnerable, interdependent creatures. It's a huge part of what gives our lives meaning. As commentator Hillary Rosner observes, "Once we transcend it [death], I'm not convinced our humanity remains. Death itself doesn't define us, of course—all living things die—but our awareness and understanding of death, and our quest to make meaning of life in the interim, are surely part of the human spirit" (from "All Too Human" in *Scientific American*, Vol 315 No 3 [September 2016], 75).

[14] Paraphrased from Gifford, 67-68.

[15] According to its website [www.agingcure.com], the stated mission of Age Reversal Therapeutics, Inc., is "to identify, develop, and make available validated therapies that can induce measurable, systemic and meaningful reversals of degenerative aging processes in humans, while extending healthy lifespans." It is backed by the Life Extension Foundation.

[16] See Sherrie Oppenheimer, "Natural Compounds that Remove Aging Cells," *Life Extension*, October 2016, 50. The author recommends supplementing one's diet with 150 mg of quercetin daily, coupled with 100 mg of tocotrienols from a palm oil derived source.

[17] Michael Specter, "DNA Revolution," *National Geographic*, August 2016, 44.

18   Weil, 6.

19   Chris Crowley & Henry S. Lodge, M.D., *Younger Next Year: Live Strong, Fit and Sexy—Until You're 80 and Beyond* (New York: Workman Publishing, 2005), 33.

Chapter 2

20   Robert Kane, quoted in Dan Buettner, The Blue Zones: Lessons for Living Longer from the People Who've Lived the Longest (Washington, D.C.: National Geographic, 2008), 18-20.

21   Terman played a key role in the development of modern IQ testing, which aims to identify children in need of special education—either because they are "behind" or "ahead" of their peers. It is interesting to note that a person's IQ score is arrived at by comparing the mental age their test scores demonstrate to their biological age. A brain that performs "older" than its biological age is considered "gifted." A brain that performs the way you would expect a younger one to perform is considered impaired or delayed.

22   Interestingly enough, researchers at the Oregon State University recently demonstrated a link between longevity and remaining in the workforce past age 65. Though the exact mechanisms of the advantage aren't yet clear, it's believed that there's a positive correlation between working longer and longevity-promoting factors like social engagement with one's coworkers, a sense of meaning and purpose from the work itself, and greater physical activity leading to overall better health. See "Working longer may lead to a longer life," News and Research Communications, Oregon State University, 04/27/2016 [http://oregonstate.edu/ua/ncs/archives/2016/apr/working-longer-may-lead-longer-life-new-osu-research-shows]. Accessed October 11, 2016.

23   For a helpful summary of these findings and some practical suggestions for how to improve your level of conscientiousness, see Daniel G. Amen, M.D., Use Your Brain to Change Your Age: Secrets to Look, Feel, and Think Younger Every Day (New York: Three Rivers Press, 2012), 154-168.

24   Glenn Geher, Ph.D., "5 Psychological Lessons from Marathon Running," Psychology Today online, posted October 18, 2015. [https://www.psychologytoday.com/blog/darwins-subterranean-world/201510/5-psychological-lessons-marathon-running]. Accessed May 30, 2016.

25 Excerpted from Dr. Howard Friedman and Dr. Leslie Martin, The
    Longevity Project (2011: Hudson Street Press). [http://www.
    thedoctorwillseeyounow.com/content/healthcare/art3432.html].
    Accessed April 9, 2016.

26 Buettner, 52.

27 Some anthropologists believe that this sort of behavior may help
    explain why humans have generally longer lifespans than their primate
    cousins, in fact. The idea is that by helping raise their grandchildren,
    grandparents increase the chances of these young children surviving,
    and young mothers who are more supported in their childrearing duties
    tend to live longer as well. Over time, these longevity-promoting genes
    are passed on to subsequent generations as a form of evolutionary
    advantage. It's a controversial theory, but fascinating nevertheless. For
    a summary of its current treatment in the research, see Roni Jacobson,
    "Revisiting the Grandmother Hypothesis," ScienceLine, posted February
    20, 2013. [http://scienceline.org/2013/02/revisiting-the-grandmother-
    hypothesis/]. Accessed May 30, 2016.

28 Suzuki, quoted in Buettner, 18-20.

29 Quoted from Pete Williams, "The Longevity Prescription: An Interview
    with Dr. Robert Butler," EXOS blog, posted July 6, 2010. [http://www.
    coreperformance.com/daily/live-better/the-longevity-prescription-an-
    interview-with-dr-robert-butler.html]. Accessed May 30, 2016.

30 Toshimase Sone et al, "Sense of Life Worth Living (Ikigai) and Mortality
    in Japan: Ohsaki Study" (Psychosomatic Medicine 70:709-715 [2008]).

31 Quoted from the book of Ecclesiastes (3:22) in the Hebrew Bible. Many
    think King Solomon wrote these words as he was nearing the end of
    his life and reflecting back upon the ways he had vainly attempted to
    discover happiness, both through wealth and extravagant living and
    through hard work and great achievements. In the end, he concluded,
    death has a way of making us all equals, and so the best thing we can
    do in this life is to find enjoyment in the things God sees fit for us to
    have—especially the work of our hands.

32 Quoted in Rebecca Webber, "Reinvent Yourself," Psychology Today, June
    2014, 56b, 58a.

33 See Buettner, 246.

34 Two simple-to-use variants are available at http://www.humanmetrics.
    com/cgi-win/jtypes1.htm and https://www.16personalities.com/. It's
    a good idea to try both and compare the results. But remember: these
    inventories are not an exact science, so if the results don't seem to

describe you perfectly, it may just mean that you exhibit characteristics of more than one type. Few people are "textbook" examples of any one type in particular.

35 A free version of this assessment can be accessed here: http://www.truity.com/test/big-five-personality-test.

36 Life Coach Spotter (http://www.lifecoachspotter.com/how-to-find-life-coach-guide/) has a very helpful white page on the topic that can help you better understand what to expect from life coaching sessions, along with an excellent review of the kinds of things to watch for in selecting a life coach.

37 Chris Crowley & Henry S. Lodge, M.D., Younger Next Year: Live Strong, Fit and Sexy—Until You're 80 and Beyond (New York: Workman Publishing, 2005), 264.

Chapter 3

38 Edward T. Creagan, M.D., FAAHPM, Mayo Clinic on Healthy Aging (Rochester, MN: Mayo Clinic, 2013), 63b.

39 Dan Buettner, The Blue Zones: Lessons for Living Longer from the People Who've Lived the Longest (Washington, D.C.: National Geographic, 2008), 59-60.

40 Chris Crowley & Henry S. Lodge, M.D., Younger Next Year: Live Strong, Fit and Sexy—Until You're 80 and Beyond (New York: Workman Publishing, 2005), 110.

41 Bruce Grierson, What Makes Olga Run?: The Mystery of the 90-Something Track Star and What She Can Teach Us About Living Longer, Happier Lives (New York: Henry Holt, 2014), 61-62, 64, 65.

42 Crowley & Lodge, 50.

43 Daniel G. Amen, Use Your Brain to Change Your Age: Secrets to Look, Feel, and Think Younger Every Day (New York: Three Rivers Press, 2012), 131.

44 Wansink, in Buettner, 235.

45 Creagan, 236.

46 Creagan, 218.

47 Incidentally, exciting new research demonstrates how calorie-restricted diets stimulate longevity-promoting enzymes called sirtuins. The natural reduction of these enzymes as we age has been affirmatively linked to

neurodegeneration in the brain, vascular inflammation, increased fat storage and production, insulin resistance, fatigue, and loss of muscle strength. So quite apart from promoting good health, consuming fewer calories can help us live longer by awakening cellular-level longevity constructs already latent in our anatomy! (See Chancellor Faloon, "Understanding the Genetics of Centenarians" in *Life Extension*, October 2016, page 80.)

48 Amen, 78.

49 Grierson, 130.

50 Creagan, 201

51 Find an online version and a free tool you can use to customize a dietary plan based on your weight-control goals at www.mayoclinic.org.

52 Amen, 87-88.

53 Results of Euromonitor research summarized in Roberto A. Ferdman, "Where people around the world eat the most sugar and fat," The Washington Post [https://www.washingtonpost.com/news/wonk/wp/2015/02/05/where-people-around-the-world-eat-the-most-sugar-and-fat/]. Accessed February 26, 2016.

54 The Mayo Clinic publishes a very helpful online resource for understanding the different kinds of alternative sweeteners and other sugar substitutes" [http://www.mayoclinic.org/healthy-lifestyle/nutrition-and-healthy-eating/in-depth/artificial-sweeteners/art-20046936]. Accessed February 26, 2006.

55 Oscar Wilde (1854-1900)

56 Robert Kane, in Buettner, 15.

57 Amen, 97.

58 Amen, 78.

59 Mayo Clinic staff, "Nuts and your heart: Eating nuts for heart health," [www.mayoclinic.org/diseases-conditions/heart-disease/in-depth/nuts/art-20046635?pg=1]. Accessed February 15, 2016.

60 Andrew Weil, M.D. "Berries for the Brain," [http://www.drweil.com/drw/u/WBL02297/Berries-for-the-Brain.html], accessed February 15, 2016.

61 Creagan, 204.

62 Ansel Oliver, "Major Study Affirms Adventists' Vegetarian Diet," Adventist News, 6/6/2013 [http://archives.adventistreview.org/article/6357/archives/issue-2013-1515/15-cn-major-study-affirms-adventist-s-vegetarian-diet]. Accessed February 18, 2016.

63 Amen, 38-39.

64 Andrew Weil, M.D., *Healthy Aging: A Lifelong Guide to Your Well-Being* (New York: Anchor Books, 2007), 249.

65 Crowley & Lodge, 29.

Chapter 4

66 Andrew Weil, M.D., *Healthy Aging: A Lifelong Guide to Your Well-Being* (New York: Anchor Books, 2007), 141.

67 Adapted from insights gleaned from Jonathan Haidt, *The Happiness Hypothesis: Finding Modern Truth in Ancient Wisdom* (New York: Basic Books, 2006), 138-140.

68 Daniel G. Amen, M.D., *Use Your Brain to Change Your Age: Secrets to Look, Feel, and Think Younger Every Day* (New York: Three Rivers Press, 2012), 234-235.

69 Amen, 22.

70 The "evidence" for this claim is mostly anecdotal and will, of course, vary from one place to another. But generally speaking, the lower atmospheric humidity of winter means less haze to obstruct the direct sunlight reaching our eyes. This effect is amplified by the presence of snow, of course.

71 Bruce Grierson, *What Makes Olga Run?: The Mystery of the 90-Something Track Star and What She Can Teach Us About Living Longer, Happier Lives* (New York: Henry Holt, 2014), 153.

72 Researchers performed a fascinating study on this topic several years ago. They found, among other things, that depressed older adults have something in common with young people: both dwell a lot on missed opportunities and tend to engage in risky behaviors to try balancing that feeling. But whereas young adults have opportunities to make and bounce back from new mistakes, older adults who engage in these kinds of behaviors may only exacerbate their problems, having little opportunity to course-correct late in life. See Ferris Jabr, "The Rue Age: Older Adults Disengage from Regrets, Young People Fixate on Them," in *Scientific American* online [http://www.scientificamerican.com/article/old-people-manage-regret/]. Accessed August 13, 2016.

73 Mayo Clinic's March 2015 Health Letter details some important health benefits of gratitude, too: lower risk of mental health disorders, greater

happiness, an increased sense of personal fulfillment as a result of self-acceptance and independence from peer pressure, positive relationships, and better sleep as a result of less anxiety and fewer negative thoughts before falling asleep.

74 University of Maryland Medical Center, "Laughter Is the Best Medicine for your Heart" (July 14, 2009). [http://umm.edu/news-and-events/news-releases/2009/laughter-is-the-best-medicine-for-your-heart]. Accessed July 23, 2016.

75 Sarah Stevenson, "There's Magic in Your Smile," Psychology Today guest blog. [https://www.psychologytoday.com/blog/cutting-edge-leadership/201206/there-s-magic-in-your-smile]. Accessed July 23, 2016.

Chapter 5

76 Based on the findings of a 1999 study by Rogers et al (referenced in University of Colorado at Boulder, "Research Shows Religion Plays a Major Role in Health, Longevity," *ScienceDaily*, May 17, 1999 [www.sciencedaily.com/releases/1999/05/990517064323.htm]). Accessed November 30, 2016. See also Dan Buettner, *The Blue Zones: Lessons for Living Longer from the People Who've Lived the Longest* (Washington, D.C.: National Geographic, 2008), 251-252. Buettner here references a study appearing in the *Journal of Health and Social Behavior* that found that people attending religious services at least once monthly reduced their risk of death by a third.

77 See, for instance, Nigel Barber, "Do Religious People Really Live Longer?" *Psychology Today*, February 27, 2013 [www.psychologytoday.com/blog/the-human-beast/201302/do-religious-people-really-live-longer].

78 Edward T. Creagan, M.D., FAAHPM, *Mayo Clinic on Healthy Aging* (Rochester, MN: Mayo Clinic, 2013), 124.

79 Andrew Weil, M.D, *Healthy Aging: A Lifelong Guide to Your Well-Being* (New York: Anchor Books, 2007), 285-286.

80 Finding such a group may be difficult in some less populous areas. Online Web and social media searches are probably your most fruitful avenue for discovering them.

81 As a side note, many who find atheism attractive are not themselves atheists. They're probably better described as agnostics—people who

believe you can't know the answers to religious questions with absolute certainty. They don't reject the existence of a god or gods outright, and many believe in life after death. But they tend to be skeptical of overtly religious claims, believing instead that all religions ultimately point toward the same god-principle latent in humanity. They would like to tap into spiritual insights from multiple religious perspectives. If you find yourself in that group—somewhere between an atheist and theist—there are communities that share your thinking, too. One of the largest such organizations is the Unitarian Universalist Association (uua.org). Check to see whether there's a congregation already meeting near you.

82 Because Hinduism is a minority religion in America, finding a Hindu community to connect with can be difficult. It may help to start by browsing a list of the Hindu temples in the United States, to see where relatively concentrated "pockets" of Hindus are likely to congregate in your area. Wikipedia offers a list here: https://en.wikipedia.org/wiki/List_of_Hindu_temples_in_the_United_States.

83 Jacobs, T. L., et al. (referenced in University of California – Davis, "Positive well-being to higher telomerase: Psychological changes from meditation training linked to cellular health," *ScienceDaily*, November 4, 2010 [https://www.sciencedaily.com/releases/2010/11/101103171642.htm]). Accessed November 30, 2016.

84 See Ben Griffin-Smith, "Mind over matter: how to think yourself healthy," *Journal of Young Investigators* online, February 2007 [http://www.jyi.org/issue/mind-over-matter-how-to-think-yourself-healthy/]. Accessed August 20, 2016.

85 Finding a Buddhist community in your area may be a little challenging, but certainly not impossible. I recommend browsing the online directory maintained by the Buddha Dharma Education Association here: http://www.buddhanet.info/wbd/country.php?country_id=2.

86 If you're not sure where the nearest synagogue is in your community, this search tool can help you locate one: http://www.myjewishlearning.com/article/find-a-synagogue/.

87 Summarized by Allison Gaudet Yarrow, "May You Live Until 120: DNA Uncovers Secrets to Jewish Longevity," Forward, August 3, 2011 [http://forward.com/culture/140894/may-you-live-until-120-dna-uncovers-secrets-to-je/]. Accessed August 20, 2016.

88 Buettner, 111.

89   Bruce Grierson, *What Makes Olga Run?: The Mystery of the 90-Something Track Star and What She Can Teach Us About Living Longer, Happier Lives* (New York: Henry Holt, 2014), 171.

Chapter 6

90   The most current edition is Dan Buettner, *The Blue Zones: 9 Lessons for Living Longer from the People Who've Lived the Longest,* second edition (National Geographic, 2012). Buettner also makes a very interesting free online assessment tool available online at https://apps.bluezones.com/vitality/. Called the Vitality Compass, this application asks a series of questions to help you understand to what degree your lifestyle already incorporates the lessons of the Blue Zones, with suggestions for how to improve.

91   Dan Buettner, *The Blue Zones: Lessons for Living Longer from the People Who've Lived the Longest* (Washington, D.C.: National Geographic, 2008), 255.

92   Findings paraphrased in Agata Blaszczak-Boxe, "Stepping on a Scale Daily May Help You Lose Weight," posted June 25, 2015, on Live Science [http://www.livescience.com/51332-weighing-daily-helps-lose-weight.html]. Accessed August 16, 2016.

93   Paraphrased from "Health and well-being benefits of plants," feature for the Ellison Chair in International Floriculture, Texas A&M University Agriculture & Life Sciences [https://ellisonchair.tamu.edu/health-and-well-being-benefits-of-plants/#.V7Swoq2jCJI]. Accessed August 17, 2016. See also Chelsea Harvey, "Why living around nature could make you live longer," in The Washington Post online [https://www.washingtonpost.com/news/energy-environment/wp/2016/04/19/why-living-around-nature-could-make-you-live-longer/?utm_term=.1bd1ca6e6deb]. Accessed August 17, 2016.

94   Heather Hatfield, "Power Down for Better Sleep," *WebMD* [http://www.webmd.com/sleep-disorders/features/power-down-better-sleep#1]. Accessed August 15, 2016.

95   For a helpful summary, see Mikael Cho, "How Clutter Affects Your Brain (and What You Can Do About It)," posted July 5, 2013, at *LifeHacker* [http://lifehacker.com/how-clutter-affects-your-brain-and-what-you-can-do-abo-662647035]. Accessed August 15, 2016.

96   Bruce Grierson, *What Makes Olga Run?: The Mystery of the 90-Something Track Star and What She Can Teach Us About Living Longer, Happier Lives* (New York: Henry Holt, 2014), 135-136.

97   See Florence Williams, "This Is Your Brain on Nature," *National Geographic*, January 2016.

98   Quoted in Ruth Ann Keyso, *Women of Okinawa: Nine Voices from a Garrison Island* (Ithaca, NY: Cornell University Press, 2000), 29-30.

99   Chris Crowley & Henry S. Lodge, M.D., *Younger Next Year: Live Strong, Fit and Sexy—Until You're 80 and Beyond* (New York: Workman Publishing, 2005), 245.

100   Crowley & Lodge, 251.

101   See Crowley & Lodge, 190.

102   Ruth Sutherland, "Relationships in Later Life and Why They Matter," *Huffington Post*, June 6, 2013 [http://www.huffingtonpost.co.uk/ruth-sutherland/relationships-in-later-life_b_3508699.html]. Accessed September 25, 2016.

103   Life coach Celestine Chua has a great introduction to this concept at her website, *Personal Excellence,* here: http://personalexcellence.co/blog/average-of-5-people/.

104   Cited in Gina Kolata, "Obesity spreads to friends, study concludes," *New York Times* July 25, 2007 [http://www.nytimes.com/2007/07/25/health/25iht-fat.4.6830240.html?_r=0]. Accessed August 18, 2016.

105   Grierson, 144.

106   For those who are insatiably curious about where they fall on the spectrum, author (and proud introvert) Susan Cain offers a very helpful 10-question survey to help you get a basic feel for yourself on her website at http://www.quietrev.com/the-introvert-test/. More helpful, perhaps, than the test itself is the explanation of the results that comes at the end.

107   See "Paying the painful price for friendship," posted April 1, 2011, at *PhysOrg.com* [http://phys.org/news/2011-04-painful-price-friendship.html]. Accessed August 18, 2016.

108   Nancy Colier, "Why We Hold Grudges, and How to Let Them Go," posted March 4, 2015, at Psychology Today [https://www.psychologytoday.com/blog/inviting-monkey-tea/201503/why-we-hold-grudges-and-how-let-them-go]. Accessed August 19, 2016.

109 The rsearch on the health benefits of forgiveness is astounding. Sammy Nickalls helpfully summarizes this material in her online article "Let It Go...For Your Own Sake: 5 Health Benefits of Forgiveness" [http://inspiyr.com/health-benefits-of-forgiveness/]. Accessed August 19, 2016. Among the statistics she cites: the proclivity to forgive rather than harbor a grudge lowers cortisol, blood pressure and heart rate, while raising one's pain threshold and extending longevity.

Chapter 7

110 Chris Crowley & Henry S. Lodge, M.D., *Younger Next Year: Live Strong, Fit and Sexy—Until You're 80 and Beyond* (New York: Workman Publishing, 2005), 6.

111 Edward T. Creagan, M.D., FAAHPM, Medical Editor, *Mayo Clinic on Healthy Aging* (Rochester, MN: Mayo Clinic, 2013), 233.

112 Paraphrased from Emily vanSonnenberg, "This Is Your Brain on Habits," *Positive Psychology News*, February 1, 2011 [http://positivepsychologynews.com/news/emily-vansonnenberg/2011020116315]. Accessed September 22, 2016.

113 From Chapter One of Charles Duhigg, *The Power of Habit: Why We Do What We Do in Life and Business* (New York: Random House, 2012). Available in preview edition at https://books.google.com/books?id=xQ1_z5_kj6sC&printsec=frontcover&source=gbs_ge_summary_r&cad=0#v=onepage&q&f=false. Accessed September 24, 2016.

114 Daniel G. Amen, M.D., *Use Your Brain to Change Your Age: Secrets to Look, Feel, and Think Younger Every Day* (New York: Three Rivers Press, 2012), 136.

115 Crowley & Lodge, 297.

116 Quoted in Rebecca Webber, "Reinvent Yourself," *Psychology Today*, May 6, 2014, 56.

117 Andrew Weil, M.D., *Healthy Aging: A Lifelong Guide to Your Well-Being* (New York: Anchor Books, 2007), 169.

118 Quoted in *AARP Magazine* (June 2016), 42

About the Author

Dr. Erica Miller, a Holocaust survivor, holds a Ph.D. in clinical psychology. She owned and operated a chain of mental health clinics and is currently the CEO of Miller Properties in Austin, Texas.

Throughout her career, Dr. Miller has spoken and written extensively about topics related to positive psychology. In addition to "Chronologically Gifted – Aging with Gusto", she is the author of "The Dr. Erica Miller Story: From Trauma to Triumph" and "Don't Tell Me I Can't Do It: Living Audaciously in the Here and Now." (Available on Amazon.com)

Appealing to audiences of all types and ages, Dr. Miller's presentations offer a unique perspective and keen insights on building an empowered life, passion and perseverance, communications, adapting for business success, living fearlessly and, of course, aging with gusto. When she shares her stories and wisdom with her audiences, people can't help but listen intently and take them to heart. A five-foot tall dynamo with an effervescent spirit, she has overcome challenges throughout her life that are diffi cult to fathom.

For speaking engagements, please contact Gerri Knilans (gerri@tradepressservices.com) or Debbie Moss (debbie@ tradepressservices.com) at Trade Press Services at 805 496-8850.

For more information about Dr. Miller, visit www. drericamiller.com, facebook.com/erica.miller, @ericamillerPhD. Author photography: Gary Moss

For more information about Dr. Miller,
please visit www.drericamiller.com.

10514419R00191

Made in the USA
San Bernardino, CA
29 November 2018